Elgin's Love-gift
Civil War in Scotland and the Depositions of 1646

A portion of the roll of The Elgin Depositions of 1646, commencing with the deposition of Grissell Lermonth (claim 53) and ending with the deposition of George Readhead (claim 61).

Elgin's Love-gift
Civil War in Scotland and the Depositions of 1646

John Barrett
and
Alastair Mitchell

Phillimore

2007

Published by
PHILLIMORE & CO. LTD
Chichester, West Sussex, England
www.phillimore.co.uk

© John Barrett and Alastair Mitchell, 2007

ISBN 978-1-86077-474-4

Printed and bound in Great Britain

Dedication

This book is dedicated, with heartfelt thanks and deep respect,

to

Dr David Iredale

who, as Moray District Archivist, permitted publication of The Elgin Depositions and whose generous encouragement and wise insights have been invaluable – in this and much else besides.

Contents

Preface	ix
Elginum; Elgin	x
Chapter 1: In Montrose Tyme	1
Chapter 2: The Said Toune of Elgin	17
Chapter 3: Waisted and Plundered All Within	33
Chapter 4: Tryell and Probatioun	47
The Elgin Depositions: Document A: Individual Claims	63
The Elgin Depositions: Document B: The Town's Losses	111
Appendix 1: The Elgin Burgh Stent Roll of 1646	115
Appendix 2: The Forres Commission	118
Appendix 3: Biographical Notes	120
Appendix 4: Glossary	123
Notes to Chapters 1-4	127
Select Bibliography	129
Index	132

Preface

In 1645 and 1646 Elgin townsfolk found themselves in the front line of the Civil War which wracked the three kingdoms of King Charles's realm.

Military forces (both friends and foes) ravaged the town. Houses were burnt, homes were looted; the people were terrorised, the royal burgh's pride affronted and its kirk despoiled. The new word, 'plunder', was added to popular vocabulary.

Elgin's sufferings during this *annus horribilis* are graphically documented in a unique roll of honour, now published, by kind permission of Dr David Iredale, Moray District Archivist, as The Elgin Depositions. This astonishing record was compiled as a testimony – to the Scottish nation and to posterity – of the community's steadfast commitment to the cause of the Covenant.

The story, untold until now, is narrated in the partial accounts of contemporary observers, in unpublished local archives and in unregarded national sources. At the heart of this history, The Elgin Depositions offer unrivalled insights into just one of the many little local triumphs and disasters that compose, indeed epitomise, the national history. The Elgin Depositions speak in the authentic voices of ordinary Scottish folk – the merchants, craftsmen, men and women who, though they never went to war, were nonetheless true and faithful warriors of the Covenant.

Elginum

Laudibus Elgini cedunt Peneïa Tempe,
　　Et Baiæ veteres, Hespendumque nemus.
Hinc maris, inde vides prædivitis æquora campi.
　　Frugibus hæc populum, piscibus illa beant
Huc sua Phæces miseruut poma, Damasci
　　Pruna nec hîc desunt, vel corasuntis opes.
Attica mellifici liquistis tecta volucres,
　　Et juvat hic pressis cogere mella favis.
Æmulus argento fæcundos Loxa per agros
　　Errat & obliquis in mare serpit aquis.
Arcibus Herôum nitidis urbs cingitur, intus
　　Phebeii radiant, nobiliumque lares.
Omnia delectant, veteris sed rudera templi
　　Dum spectas, lachrymis, Scotia, tinge genas.

The author of 'Elginum', Arthur Johnstoun (1587-1641), was a leading Latin poet of his day and composer of a metrical psalter in flowing elegaic verse. Johnstoun's epigrams on Scottish royal burghs were published in *Poemata Omnia* (Middelburg, Zeeland, 1642)

Elgin

TO ELGIN'S *Praise* the *Ancient* BAJÆ yeelds
HESPERIAN-*Gardens*, and *brave* TEMPE'S-*Fields*:
Both *Sea* and *Land* doth still *Thy* needs supplie,
　　That *Fishes*, This *Cornes* doth afford to *Thee*.
CORCYRA, *Aples* unto *Thee* hath sent,
DAMASCUS, *Pruns*, CERASUS, *Cherries* lent.
The *Bees* seem to have left *their* ATTICK-*hyve*,
And come to *Thee*, their *Honey-trade* to dryve.
The *Silver Streams* of LOSSIE *here* doth glyde,
By *crooked paths* unto the *Sea they* slyde.
With *Stately-Castles Thou'rt* environed,
Within with *pleasant Buildings* garnished.
All *Here* is *lovely* and *delights* the *Eye*,
But the *torne-Walls* and *Rubbish* when you *see*
Of that *Great* TEMPLE, which *e're* yet appears,
Bid SCOTLAND now bedew *Her* Cheeks with tears.

Translation of Arthur Johnstoun's poem by John Barclay, Minister of Cruden; published in Alexander Skene's *Memorialls for the Government of the Royall-Burghs in Scotland*, printed by John Forbes, printer to the city and university of Aberdeen, 1685

Chapter 1

In Montrose Tyme

The Irishes are coming! The Highlanders are on the march! The Gordons are at the gate!

These were alarums to chill the blood of honest Elgin folk. A spasm of frenetic activity convulsed the royal burgh. Canny merchants hurried to hide their gold and silver, coin and plate, beneath the hearthstone or behind the wainscot panelling of the hall. Careful craftsmen buried precious tools and wares under the middens of their roods. Carters whipped up their horses and the lumbering wagons creaked away, piled high with the townsfolk's best clothing and household plenishing. The wealthiest burgesses meanwhile, bustled their wives and daughters out of town to the safety of country cousins' castles. Amid the general panic, some few of Elgin's terrified townsfolk perhaps paused to consider how and why their peaceable royal burgh had been thrust into the front line of the civil war.

The roots of the conflict lie in the reign of James VI, in whom the crowns of England and Scotland were united following the death of Elizabeth I in 1603. James's doctrine of divine right was embraced by his son, Charles I, who pursued his father's episcopalian religious policies with an arrogant insouciance that dismayed subjects throughout his kingdoms. Charles's high-church Anglicanism outraged English puritans and offended many, even in the Church of England. Progressive religious reforms imposed in Scotland undermined the Calvinist foundations of the national kirk. The introduction of a new service book to replace John Knox's *Book of Common Order* was a step too far; a step, it seemed, along the road to popery and perdition – and more than presbyterians could thole.

Presbyterian ministers warned their congregations against the King's new liturgy. Samuel Rutherford, writing from Aberdeen, exhorted his flock at Anworth in Galloway:

> to beware of the new and strange leaven of men's invention ... of the superstition and idolatry of kneeling in the instant of receiving the Lord's Supper and of crossing in baptism ... Countenance not the surplice, the attire of the mass priest, the garment of Baal's priests. The abominable bowing to alters of tree is coming upon you. Hate, and keep yourselves from idols. Forbear in any case to hear the new Service Book[1]

Vigorous seeds of dissent, nurtured by incendiary preaching, came to fruition in Edinburgh's St Giles Cathedral on 23 July 1637. As Dean John Hanna nervously began to read the stately opening words of King Charles's new liturgy for the first time, a storm of clapping and catcalls drowned out the solemn intonation. Cries of 'False Christian', 'Wolf', 'Beastly Belly-god' (and worse) rose in a crescendo. The congregation's angry shouts were accompanied by a clattering hail of missiles – including bibles and Jenny Geddes's righteous stool – hurled in outrage at the hapless dean. At last (and too late) the town guard arrived. The demonstrators allowed the soldiers to shepherd them out of the kirk and onto the cobbled causeway of the high street. Here they waited with patient fury to pelt the bishop, dean and other dignitaries when, having finished the service, they left the building.

Similar orchestrated demonstrations disrupted attempts to introduce the new liturgy elsewhere in Scotland. At Aberdeen, however, under the influence of the powerful Gordons and the academic episcopalianism of the university, opposition was muted. At Brechin, Bishop Whitford ensured a quiet reception for the new service book: he entered his cathedral church with the service book in one hand and a pistol in the other, and a gang of armed retainers at his back.

In response to disaffection at all levels of society, the King clung even closer to his conviction of his divine right. Incapable of understanding the deep resentment of his presbyterian subjects, Charles was unable either to retreat or compromise.

Presbyterianism's formal response to the King's intransigence was a wordy legal document, conceived as a covenant, binding the signatories in a solemn pact sanctioned by biblical precedent. The basis of this National Covenant was an earlier declaration, known as the negative confession, subscribed by the young King James VI during an episode of anti-catholic hysteria in 1581. The new National Covenant opened with a long paragraph listing and denouncing papist idolatry, superstition and error. Then followed a citation of several dozen relevant Acts of the Scottish parliament. The kernel of the Covenant was a solemn agreement 'to adhere unto and defend the foresaid true religion' and to forebear 'the practice of all innovations'.

On Wednesday 28 February 1638, presbyterian nobles and barons crowded into the Greyfriars' church at Edinburgh to sign the Covenant. Next day some 300 presbyterian ministers subscribed the document. Edinburgh burgesses and townsfolk added their names on 2 March. Copies of the Covenant were then despatched throughout the kingdom.

The Covenant was rapturously received in the provinces. Fiery sermons and extravagant extempore prayer fanned the fires of a religious hysteria. Some, it was said, signed the Covenant in their own blood. James Gordon of Rothiemay (himself no friend of presbyterian extremism) described the fervid atmosphere:

> And such was the zeale of many subscribents, that for a whyle, many subscrybed with teares on their cheekes ... Such ministers as spocke most for it wer heard so passionately and with such frequencye, that churches could not containe ther hearers in cittyes; some of the devouter sexe (as if they had keeped vigils) keeping ther seates from Friday to Sunday, to gett communione givne them sitting; some sitting allway let befor such sermones in the churches, for feare of lossing a row or place of hearing; or at least, some of ther handmaids sitting constantly ther all night till ther mistresses came to tack upp ther places and to releeve them; so that severall (as I heard from a very sober and credible man) under that relligiouse confynment, wer forced to give waye to ther naturall necessityes, which they could no longer containe, bedewng the pavements of churches with other moysture than teares[2]

To defend the Covenant, a Scottish army was quickly recruited and marched into England. The invasion forced the King to call – then to dismiss and then recall – his English parliament. Once recalled, the fractious English MPs passed Acts to prevent another dissolution. Charles found himself trapped between a rebellious parliament at Westminster and a covenanter army in the north.

Meanwhile, in Scotland, the leading actors in the unfolding drama emerged – either for or against the Covenant. James Graham, Earl of Montrose, thrust forward as a prominent covenanting lord and military commander. Courting popular approval following the service book riot of 1637, he harangued the citizens of Edinburgh from an ominously precarious perch upon the burgh scaffold. He personally led the covenanter army into England, ostentatiously wading the River Tweed to demonstrate to his cautious soldiers that the ford was safe. He subdued the Gordons in the north east: defeating Viscount Aboyne (James Gordon, 2nd son of the Marquis of Huntly) at Brig o' Dee to drag the reluctant burgh of Aberdeen into the covenanting fold; capturing Huntly himself in a disgraceful episode that the Marquis would never forgive or forget. Then, as the rift between the King and his English parliament became unbridgeable and civil war inevitable, Montrose declared for Charles against the Covenant – and was made a marquis.

Other mighty subjects chose sides under the compulsion of sincere religious conviction and honourable political loyalty. Whether for or against the Covenant, all came to the fight under the banner of God, king and country. The growing political crisis also opened opportunities for the pursuit of personal ambitions and the settlement of ancient grievances.

Archibald Campbell (*MacCailen Mór* – son of Great Colin) Earl (later Marquis) of Argyll, signed the Covenant in April 1639, bringing the huge military potential of Clan Campbell to the cause. Fearing a military expedition from Ulster, promoted by the catholic Randal McDonnell, Earl of Antrim, Argyll took precautionary action. He strengthened his hold on the west (and enlarged the Campbell domain) by seizing Colonsay, the last possession of Clan Iain Mór. Campbell soldiers took captive the chief, Col MacGillespick MacDonald (known as *Col Ciotach* – left-handed Col). However, Alasdair MacDonald, son of *Col Ciotach*, escaped to Ireland vowing bloody vengeance on the Campbells and their presbyterian chief.

In the north east, George Gordon, Marquis of Huntly, followed family tradition by supporting the crown in a crisis. Huntly's personal instincts were royalist and episcopalian – and unswayed (indeed arguably reinforced) by the determined presbyterianism of his covenanting brother-in-law, the Earl of Argyll. In practice, the Gordons' military potential was never fully realised. Huntly was a timid and ineffectual general preferring bombastic gestures to determined action. He was reluctant to commit soldiers to campaigns beyond the Gordon sphere of interest in the north east, instead favouring concentration on soft targets and personal territorial ambitions.

Less august but more effective military leaders emerged from among the Scottish gentry. These included experienced professional soldiers who had learned their trade in European wars. For example, Alexander Leslie fought in the Netherlands and later under the protestant King Gustavus Adolphus of Sweden. William Baillie and David Leslie also went to war in the Swedish army. John Hurry acquired military experience in Germany, and John Middleton in France.

Elgin caught the general mood and began to adopt a military posture. On 18 February 1639 the town council minutes recorded: 'John Fraser in Elgin wnder tuik to be dreill master within the burghe of Elgin to tryne vp the persones in dreilling with thair wapones'. By 1640 the town had a squad of 12 soldiers under arms. The trained band comprised eight 'Muscattis' armed with matchlock firearms, and four 'Pickmen' armed with pikes. The usual equipment for a pikeman consisted of an iron morion helmet, a cuirass with tassets to protect the thighs and groin, and a sword, in addition to an 18ft pike. There was, however, no mention of body armour for Elgin's soldiers. A musketeer was not usually armoured. He was encumbered with a heavy matchlock with a forked rest (staff) to support the long smooth-bored barrel; a bandolier with 12 charges of powder; a powder flask; a bag of bullets (purs); a strike-a-light with lengths of spare slow-match. Musketeers typically affected flamboyant hats with broad brims that they pulled down as protection from the flash of powder in the matchlock pan; thus, intriguingly, almost every musket shot of the civil war was fired blind.

An Elgin town council minute dated 18 May 1640 gives the names of the burgh's defenders and also a description of the mismatched, incomplete and borrowed weaponry with which they were equipped. Most of the recruits possessed a sword – a fashion essential for every man worthy of the name – though only one volunteer, James Chalmer younger, was able to provide a full set of equipment for himself. However, there were arms aplenty in the town, and several burgesses had weapons to spare for loan to the burgh's soldiers:

> Names of theis that wndertakis to be souldieris for the burgh of Elgin
> are as followis viz.
> muscattis
> Iames chalmer younger toddies furnissit be himself In armour
> Alexander alves receavit Iames keyis muscatt with bandileir conteining
> 10 measuris & ane purs hes a suord of his avin
> Androw forbes receavit Ionet guidis muscatt with bandileir with 12 measuris purs and staff hes a suord of his awin receavit ane new belt
> Ion Robertsone receavit alexander Tarres muscatt with full bandileir & staff receavit ane new belt with ane suord cost fra Iasper haye
> Walter grigor receavit Iames douglas his muscatt with full bandileir & purs with suord cost fra Ion chalmer merchant at 8 merkis
> Iames adie receavit the provest mr Ion haye his muscatt with full bandileir
> hes ane suord of his awin
> Robert grigor hes receavit ane muscatt quhilk perteinit to Ion myln with ane bandileir conteining xj measuris ane purs & receavit ane suord fra andro
> annand receavit ane new belt
> Thomas Dunbar receavit ane muscatt quhilk perteinit to thomas Murdoch
> with ane suord fra Iohn mylne receavit ane new belt with ane staff & full
> Bandileir fra the said Thomas Murdoch
>
> Pickmen
> Thomas Tuloch j pick ane suord of his awin receavit ane belt
> Alexander zoung j pick ane suord of his awin
> Iames mcraye j pick tayn fra andro annand ane belt & receavit ane suord perteining to Iames findlay
> Iames findlay receavit ane pick hes ane suord of his awin[3]

A footnote to the list suggests that the final volunteer, James Findlay, got cold feet and resigned. Findlay's place was taken (together with his pike and sword) by 'Ion dow'. No further information is given regarding this transfer. John Dow is not a usual Elgin name. The name may be an unusual spelling variant of Duff (for Gaelic *Dubh* 'black'). On the other hand, John Doe was the name normally given to the fictitious protagonist in a collusive action at law: it was the name of a man who did not exist, though pikeman Dow's wages continued to be paid.

The burgh supplied sword belts to several of the soldiers. It is pleasant to visualise these shiny new leather belts as a kind of uniform, proudly worn across each man's breast

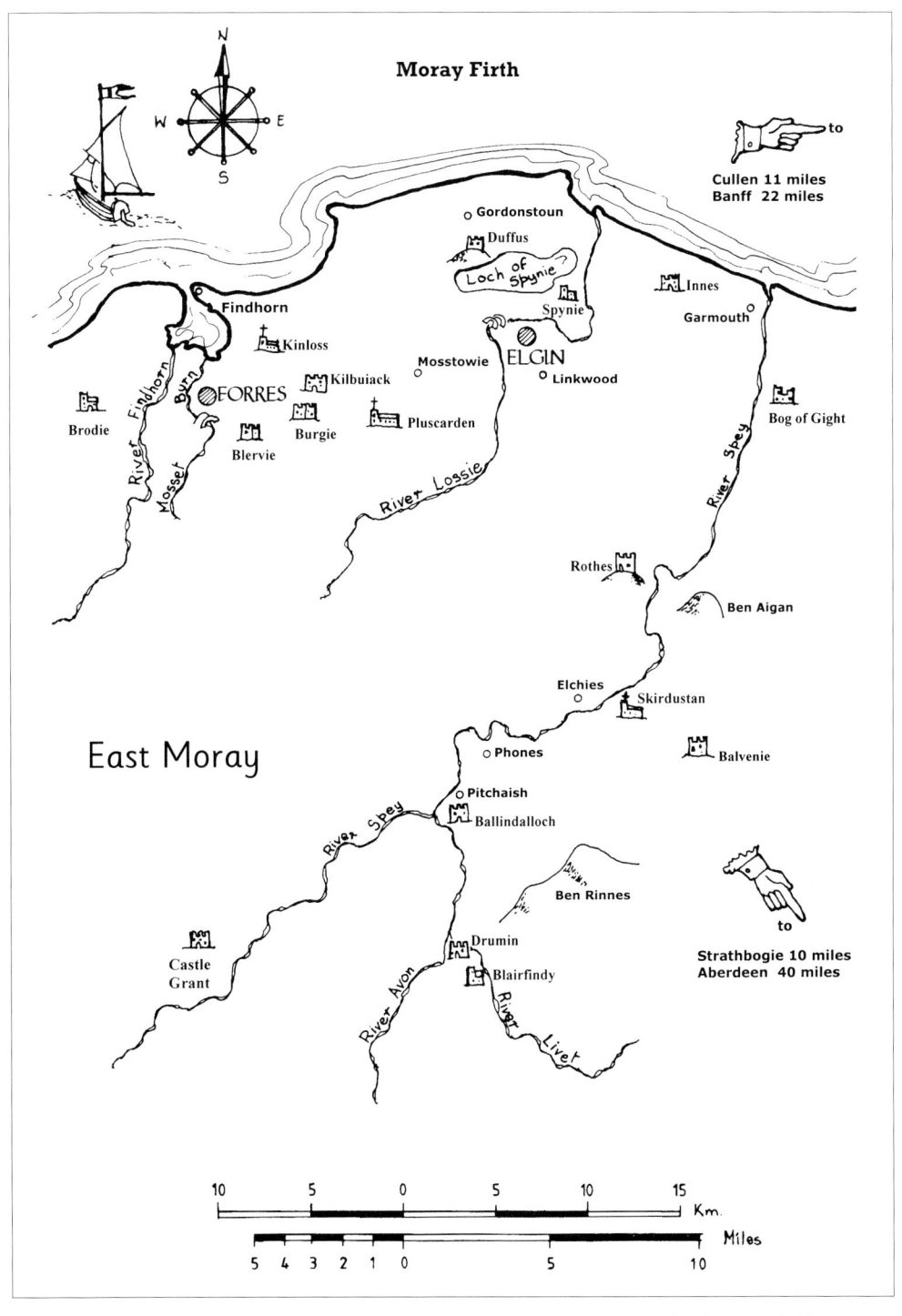

1. Eastern Moray showing principal places mentioned in the text. (Drawn by Christine Clerk)

and embellished with a shiny bracteate or tooled device representing the burgh arms. The cost of the belts (10s. each) was deducted from the men's wages of 42s. per week:

> nota Andrew Annand on ye 29 Iunij 1640 being Mon Daye gaiff to the tuelff souldieris thair weikis vaigis & he tuik allowance of sex of thame for 3 lib' for sex suord beltis[4]

The haste with which the 12 soldiers were recruited and equipped soon gave rise to problems. Generous burgesses who supplied arms for the defence of the community began to fear that their loan was being regarded as a gift, or perhaps that the soldiers' weapons were finding their way into other hands. John Hay, a cautious notary, ensured that his ownership of certain military equipment was formally documented in the town council minutes for 1 June 1640:

> it is condiscendit that the Muscatt & bandiler & pick & staff quhilk Mr Iohn Haye Lent to Iames aidie sojor salbe restorit to him again or iff the said Iames aidie happines to put aveay the said Muscatt & bandiler In that case the said Ion hayeto haue fra the thesaurer of the burgh In nam of the counsell as guid as hisawin Or els such pryce therfor as he gaiff for the samyn[5]

The new militia probably paraded for the first time in June 1640 when:

> The counsel appoyntis the 15 instant to ane wapenschawing and all men to be in thair best array in armour and that on thursdaye the 4 instant the samyn to be proclamit by touk of drum[6]

There was, of course, nothing new in the drilling of this local defence force. Wappenschawing was an ancient obligation revived in Scotland in 1625.[7]

Meanwhile, in an emphatic show of strength, Major-General Robert Munro marched a covenanter army into Moray. Huntly castle, caput of the Gordons, was sacked. In July 1640, Munro invested the episcopal palace of Spynie with 800 men and six artillery pieces. On 16 July Bishop John Guthrie surrendered. For a few weeks the bishop was allowed to remain in his castle, supervised by a covenanter garrison consisting of a captain, a lieutenant, a sergeant, a corporal and 23 men. On 4 September 1640 Guthrie was arrested, accused of simony, dancing and various other irregularities, and imprisoned. In 1641 the King granted the vacant castle of Spynie to James, Earl of Moray. Immediately a dispute arose between the Earl and his nephew John Innes of Leuchars (near relative and nearer neighbour of Innes of that ilk). The castle was placed in the keeping of Provost John Hay while the rival claims were considered. The difficulty was resolved when Moray was confirmed as constable. Leuchars, however, was paid 2000 merks compensation by the Earl and installed in the castle with his wife and family, as Moray's castellan.

In October 1641 King Charles's brimming cup of troubles overflowed as Ireland flared into rebellion. Native catholics rose up against the protestant settlers who had been planted in ever-increasing numbers, particularly in the north of the island, since the accession of James VI to the English throne. The atrocities inflicted by the catholic rebels were described in gruesome detail in depositions sworn by protestant witnesses. Some 30 volumes of these depositions (now in Trinity College Library, Dublin) enshrine a testimony to the hideous cruelty of catholics and the patient suffering of godly protestants – including many Scottish presbyterians.

Popular and sensational news-sheets published grizzly reports of Irish atrocities. These newsbooks (the ancestors of modern newspapers) broadcast news from Ireland, battlefield despatches, and other topical stories to a mass audience. Lurid accounts of the sufferings of protestants at the hands of blood-crazed Irish catholics were staple copy for the editors of the earliest newsbooks:

> Some Ministers in Ireland, as hath been lately massacred by the Papists, as namely Mr German, Minister of Brides, his body mangled, and his members cut off; and one Fullerton Minister of Langhall; and one hastings his eares cut off; and one Blandry, his flesh pulled off his bones in the presence of his wife[8]

Protestant ministers were obvious targets for catholic rebels. A typical example described a massacre in Armagh in language, which, even at the time, must have appeared clichéd. The rebels, it was alleged, had murdered protestant settlers:

> in a most cruell and bloudy manner, with their wives and children: first deflowering many of the women, then cruelly murdering them, and pulling them about the street by the haire of the head, and dashing their children's brains out against the posts and stones of the street, and tossing their children upon their pikes, and so running with them from place to place, saying that those were the pigs of the English sowes.[9]

Recent historical opinion treats the Irish depositions and newsbook reports with proper caution, suggesting that the statements contain a good deal of exaggeration. Thus estimates of the death-toll have been progressively down-graded from William Petty's contemporary figure of '37,000 … massacred in the first year of the tumults'[10] to the modest 1999 guestimate of historian Robin Clifton: 'perhaps as many as two thousand settlers were directly killed in the first three months of the rebellion and another four thousand died from exposure, and other causes, after being expelled from their homes'.[11]

The truth can never be known. Indeed, truth was an early casualty of the mounting political crisis that was engulfing Britain and Ireland. In the highly-charged religious climate of the 1640s, protestants in general and Scottish presbyterians in particular were predisposed – even eager – to believe the worst calumnies against the papist rebels. No one was likely to offer a countervailing view of the Irish uprising: as a crusade by a long-suffering remnant of the true holy catholic church against the persecuting hordes of alien invaders and protestant heretics. Subsequently, atrocity stories were accepted uncritically and believed implicitly amongst Scottish presbyterians because such stories were consistent with deep-rooted popular religious hatred.

Prejudice was reinforced by scripture. The Bible affirmed that injustice and suffering might be a proof of godliness and a confirmation of grace. The assault upon protestant settlers in Ireland was seen by Scottish presbyterians as the opening of a new front in the unrelenting war between the forces of Christ and Antichrist. After all, Jesus himself had declared, 'blessed are they which are persecuted for righteousness' sake' (Matthew 5:10); and the apostle Paul had written, 'unto us it is given, not only to believe in his name, but also to suffer for his sake' (Phillippians 1:29). The Moray presbyterian, James Fraser of Brea, further articulated the sentiment for his local congregation:

> Sufferings … are not only our duty but our privilege; to suffer for Christ is one of Christ's love-gifts[12]

As Elgin learned of the Irish rebellion, kirk session minutes recorded a 'contribution for the distressed that cam out of Irland was intimat to be gathered'. Over the following two years a stream of protestant refugees appeared in person before the session. A record of their sufferings was solemnly inscribed in the session minutes and also, presumably, broadcast from the pulpit. These testimonies naturally reinforced Elgin's presbyterian prejudices against the Irish in particular, and catholics in general.

Many of the refugees who petitioned the kirk session for assistance bore typical Elgin surnames: for example, 'ane ministers daughter cald Marjorie Hay, who had hir father killed in Irland be the Rebells'. Kirk session minutes for 18 March 1643 recorded the case of:

> ane distressed Irisch woman cald Anna Griffith, sometime spous to mr William Murray, ane minister in Irland, whom the rebels there, as hir testimonial declared, crucified

On 9 February 1644, session minutes recorded 'twa dollars' paid out of the Irish contribution 'to foure distrest people that came out of Irland who hade their testimonials: their names were James Hay, Francis Hay, Margaret Hay, Jean Hay'. The outgoing provost of Elgin in 1643 was John Hay, and a further five Hays are named in the Depositions. It is tempting to presume that the Irish Hays came to Elgin because they had relatives in the burgh. A minute of 2 April 1644 described, perhaps, another crucifixion victim in: 'ane poore woman who was creple of both hands be the rebels in Ireland, she being called Margaret Duncan'. As each new batch of refugees passed through the town, rumour and speculation fuelled a steady crescendo of outrage and anti-catholic prejudice.[13]

Scotland was an active participant in the momentous events of the early 1640s, A Scottish covenanting army was sent to Ireland to defend fellow presbyterians, and as English political divisions polarised into civil war between king and parliament, Scotland was drawn into the conflict on the parliamentary side. The alliance was cemented by a new covenant. Under this Solemn League and Covenant a Scottish army was despatched to fight against the king in England; in return the Scots were allowed to believe that England would embrace a presbyterian religious establishment on the Scottish model. Under this delusion, Scotland became a part of the general civil war in which Scottish recruits on both sides fought and died for the same god, king and country

Elgin folk were expected to play their part in the war. The Scottish parliament required levies of men for military service from shires and burghs throughout the kingdom. To meet its obligations, Elgin town council ordered, on 25 March 1644:

> the drum to goe through the toune with the proclamation for desyring of sojoris to goe for the toun to the airmie in england quha sall haue of levie money tua dollaris four tailit quoats [tailored coats] and ane pair of newe schone[14]

It is not recorded whether any Elgin folk took up the offer. By this time, however, George Smythe, son of Walter, the kirk session moderator, was captain of the town's trained band, receiving on 20 April 1644, the generous sum of 'ten dolloris … for his paynes takin on the touns sojors'.[15]

As the war swung in parliament's favour, King Charles commissioned the sometime covenanter James Graham, now Marquis of Montrose, to open a second front and pursue a campaign of disruption in Scotland. The objective was to relieve pressure on royalist forces in England and Ireland, and ultimately to force the Scottish armies to return home. Montrose, meanwhile, convinced the King that the appearance of a royalist army on Scottish soil would inspire loyal Scots to abandon the covenants and rally to his cause. The core of Montrose's expeditionary force was three regiments, comprising some 1600 experienced Irish catholic soldiers, provided by the Earl of Antrim and commanded by

Lieutenant-General Alasdair MacDonald – *Alasdar Mac-Cholla Ciotaich Mhic-Gilleasbuig Mhic Alasdair Mhic Iain Chathanaich* (variously referred to as Alasdair MacColla, Col or *Col Ciotaich*/Colkito) – 3rd son of Col MacGillespick MacDonald (the original *Col Ciotach*) chief of Clan Iain Mór.

Through 1644, Elgin folk listened anxiously to reports of Montrose's lightning campaign. At any time, it seemed, one of the Marquis's astonishing forced marches might bring his Irish cut-throats to the gates of Elgin. On 4 March 1644 the town council instructed:

> That the haill toune be advertised to haiue ther Muscattis and gunnis in readiness with ball conforme & pulder … wnder the payne of fyve Pundis money[16]

On at least four occasions the burgh was occupied, although in the event, the troublesome troops were friendly forces demanding food and quarters. Burgh officials naively expected that the cost of this quartering would be readily reimbursed by the Scottish parliament. Twice the burgh was host to Argyll's crack cavalry, and once at least to the Marquis himself:

> my Lord marqueis of argyll came to Elgin One Satyrday nicht the nynteint day of maij [1644] whois trayne consisted of ane hundreth men and hors

> My lord argyll his lyff gaird … consisting of fyiftie hors & abowe … in the moneth of November [1644] for Sevin Dayes & four seuerall Dayes theiraftir[17]

Troops from Sir Frederick Hamilton's regiment of horse and infantry belonging to Sir George Buchanan's foot, demanded quarters in Elgin. The principal role of these regiments was the defence of Inverness. In Autumn 1644, however, their activities included wasting the Grant estate of Elchies on Speyside and visiting Elgin to arrest the malignant Thomas Mackenzie of Pluscarden. Documentary evidence for these visitations is contained in The Elgin Depositions which, however, were concerned primarily with the financial cost incurred by the burgh as a result of these quarterings:

> Sir Patricke McGie [Mackie of Larg] … wpon Tuysday the aucht day of October [1644] accumpanied with fyve Troupes

> Capitaine williame and Capitaine Harie Bruces … with Tuo hundreth & Tuentie foot Sojoris wpon the Tuentie aucht day of October [1644][18]

On 1 September 1644 Montrose and MacColla defeated a covenanter army at Tippermuir and marched triumphantly into Perth. Thence Montrose advanced into the north east. The army crossed the Dee to confront covenanter forces defending Aberdeen at Justice Mills. A parley was convened but the truce was broken by a shot from a covenanter gunman, which killed a drummer in the royalist parley party. In the battle that followed, covenanter infantrymen were cut down without mercy. The city fell, and for three days Montrose's Irish took terrible revenge for the murder of their drummer:

> killing, robbing and plundering of this toune at thair pleasour. And nothing hard bot pitiful houling, crying, weiping, murning, throw all the strettis … sum wemen thay pressit to defloir, and other sum thay took peforce to serve thame in the camp … The men that thay killit thay wold not suffer to be bureit, bottirrit thame of thair clothis, syne left thair naikit bodies lying above the ground[19]

When the blood-letting finally ended, at least 118 Aberdonians lay dead. The killing affected all classes; the dead included advocates, burgesses, merchants, maltmen, fishermen, tailors, wrights, millers, websters, a piper, a cooper, a cook, a student, and a gardener. The sufferings of Aberdeen at this time are recorded in the report of a commission appointed by parliament 'for trying the Losses of Aberdein':

> upon the 13th September 1644 the Irisches under the conduct of James Graham eftir ane bloodie fecht enterit the towne in ane hostile way quhair, by the loss of 160 men, they did suffer in thair goodis by plundering and destroying particular menes houses quhilk in the haill will extend to 135,004 lib. 7sh. 4d.[20]

Montrose then moved through Aberdeenshire, gathering Gordon recruits as far west as Huntly's stronghold at Bog of Gight (Gordon Castle) on the Spey, but he did not cross the river into the covenanter province of Moray. In December Montrose was in Athol. Thence the war moved westwards. Inverary in the Argyll heartland was plundered and burnt, and some 900 Campbell men of military age massacred as MacColla's highlanders, took routine revenge upon their traditional enemy.

Pestilence followed war with apocalyptic inevitability; marching through Scotland with the armies and travelling from town to town with refugees. Epidemics described as plague flared with terrible ferocity, killing covenanters and royalists without distinction. Urban communities bore the brunt of the plague. Elgin was miraculously spared, though some 1,600 men, women and children (one-fifth of the burgh population) died in Aberdeen. The disease (probably not bubonic plague, possibly typhus or paratyphoid) killed more ordinary burgh folk of all classes – burgesses, craftsmen and labouring folk – than any soldiers, either of the King or the Covenant.[21]

The campaigning continued regardless of the suffering in its wake. On 2 February 1645 Montrose's royalist army defeated a much larger Scottish parliamentary force at Inverlochy in the shadow of Ben Nevis. Following the rout of this covenanter army commanded by the Earl of Argyll, Montrose led his victorious Irish regiments and highland clansmen to Kilcumin at the head of Loch Ness. Here he drew up the 'Kilcumin bond' – an oath of loyalty to God, king and country, contrived to suit both protestants and catholics. Then, 'having allowed his men some days to refresh themselves, after the immense fatigue they had undergone', Montrose led his army along the east side of the Great Glen; thence 'passing through Strath-erri-gig, Strathnairn, and Stratherin'.[22] The army followed the usual travellers' route, climbing from the Great Glen to march through the populous landscape of Stratherrick; descending along the Nairn valley to cross the river, probably by the ford of Kilravock; bypassing the garrisoned burgh of Inverness to sack the defenceless burgh of Nairn before entering the shire of Elgin and Forres.

Montrose came to Moray determined to reach the Gordon territory beyond the River Spey. His strategic objective was to recruit the Marquis of Huntly to active military participation in the King's cause. In the words of the royalist historian, Patrick Gordon (curiously borrowing a phrase from John Knox's *History of the Reformation in Scotland*) Montrose was 'hoping by the wneited forces of that family [the Gordons], to resist, and by God's grace, to team or danton ther [the covenanters'] greatest furrie'.[23] However, an opportunity to punish supporters of the Covenant along the way, must also have been a strong consideration as 'most of the inhabitants of the shire of Murray were extremely addicted to the covenanters'.[24] In addition, the royalist army was wearied by its winter campaign and in need of rest and resupply. What better than to quarter on and plunder a hostile population and, in the process of resupplying, danton the rebellious province while depriving parliament of vital resources?

Montrose swept through the province 'with fire and sword', though the documentary evidence suggests little if any use of the sword. The houses of covenanting lairds were targeted: 'the place of Grangehill, pertaining to Ninian Dunbar; the place of Brodie pertaining to the laird of Brodie; the place of Cowbin [Culbin] pertaining to _____ Kinnaird; the place of Innes pertaining to the laird of Innes; and Redhall [were] burnt and plundered'.[25]

News of Argyll's defeat at Inverlochy must have reached Elgin within a day or two. As Montrose drew nearer, the anxious burgesses received reports of the burning and plundering of the lands and biggings of covenanter lairds: the Irish horde's 'approach was heralded by the smoke of their burning homesteads'.[26] Men such as Alexander Brodie of Brodie, safe in a 15th-century towerhouse, behind a high bawn wall, might indulge in a little bravado and 'disclaim any safety he might get', resting confident 'that all his safety may be from, in and to the Lord'.[27] But as Montrose approached, Elgin folk remembered the fate of their Aberdeen brethren. The covenanting ardour of many townsfolk cooled. They did not stay to embrace the privilege of suffering; those who could, fled:

> with their wives, bairns, and best goods which they could get carried here and there, but chiefly to Spynie, and few bade within the town for plain fear, which incensed the soldiers worse against the town than if they had bidden and kept their houses[28]

The community that remained within the town was bereft of leadership 'fewe of the magistrates and counsell being at home'.[29]

The burgh's squad of soldiers also made a tactical retreat to prepared positions in the great tower of Spynie. On 17 February 1645 the local committee of war, which had convened in Elgin, dissolved before the advancing royalists. Sir Robert Innes of Innes, 'who for witte and policie, was esteemed as ane oracle throw all that countray … retyred himselfe, with Ballandalloch Grant, to the strong castell of Spynie, belonging formerly to the bischope of Murray'.[30] While the leaders of the community defied the malignant army from the battlements of Bishop Davey's tower, humbler folk shifted for themselves. Where they went, or how they prepared for the enemy's arrival, is not recorded; but Alexander Andersone, mason in Elgin, claimed for the 'great loissis sustenit be him be the Enemie in flying the countrie to eschewe the taking of elgin' (claim 183).

In some other burghs ,flight from the enemy was regarded as a defection from the covenants. In Dundee, for example, 'Ane missive letter was ordained to be written to the town of St Andrews, for Robert Lundie that he may be returned to abide his censure for removing himself when Montrose and his adherents came against the burgh': the unfortunate Lundie was penalised in the substantial sum of 300 merks 'for his deserting the town, contrair his ayth and covenant'. Two other Dundonians, George and James Wighton, were each 'unlawed in the soum of one hundred merks' for similar desertion. Alexander Bowar of Bomerichtie, who had been reckoned a 'discreet burgess', suffered the exemplary penalty of 400 merks 'for his deserting the town [of Dundee] when Montrose and the Irish rebels came against the same'.[31]

In Elgin, a significant section of the war committee simply capitulated unconditionally. George Mackenzie, Earl of Seaforth (who had been meeting with the war committee though not a member), and his brothers, the lairds of Pluscarden and Lochslin, with Sir Robert Gordon of Gordonstoun and Grant of Grant, supinely (or wisely) went over to Montrose and, in due course, signed the Kilcumin bond. Allegiances, however, were notably fluid in

Scotland's civil war and Seaforth later reneged upon his Kilcumin oath. He subsequently returned to the covenants, apologising by letter to the committee of estates in Aberdeen and claiming 'that he yeilded only through fear, and that he avowed to bide by the good cause to his death'.[32] (Though by the end of 1645 Seaforth had again joined Montrose.)

The most committed of Elgin's presbyterians may, perversely, have welcomed the approach of Montrose's army, believing that their covenanted community was long overdue for the 'love-gift' of persecution. After all, Aberdeen, where support for the Covenant was at first lukewarm, had suffered aplenty. Elgin, whose covenanting credentials were unequivocal, had, unaccountably, been overlooked. Each of Elgin's faithful presbyterians, confident that 'outward trouble from the hands of persecutors maybe ... a testimony for Christ and his truth',[33] was equally confident in the promise that God 'would not lay more upon me then he gave me strength to bear'.[34] Thus Brodie of Brodie soothed his cousin, the Laird of Lethen, during the burning of his Nairnshire estate with the comforting declaration: 'My heart is calm, and I do rejoice in God and bless his name ... To us it is a token, not of wrath, but of salvation to us of God, and to our adversaries of perdition'.[35] Lethen's response is not recorded.

On 19 February 1645, Montrose with his lieutenant-general Alasdair MacColla led King Charles's army into the royal burgh of Elgin. Without a garrison or a circuit of defensive walls, the town could offer no resistance, and remembering the price paid by Aberdeen for defying Montrose (as both covenanter and royalist), none of Elgin's covenanters was inclined to fight. Perhaps, indeed, the ports were thrown open to the 'comonn enemie' by the burgh's royalists. Certainly, The Elgin Depositions preserve no record of the burgh gates being forced or damaged by Montrose's men; nor of any brave apprentice boys slamming shut the ports in the faces of MacColla's Irish.

The kirk session minutes noted, with blandly bureaucratic understatement, 'the Irisches with Montrois and Col cam into Elgin and spoyled it and stayed till Sunday 2 of March 1645'.[36] While the army was at Elgin, Lord George Gordon, Huntly's eldest son, who until then (hedging the Gordon bets) had sided with the covenanters, changed allegiances. Despite his father's implacable personal resentment of Montrose, Lord George joined the royalist army, bringing with him his younger brother Lewis (Ludovick) and a troop of 200 Gordon horse. The Gordons joined with the Irish regiments and MacColla's highland levies in plundering the defenceless town.

A detachment of royalists was sent, perhaps at the instigation of the Gordons, to ravage the Speyside estates of John Grant of Ballindalloch. The castle of Ballindalloch stood near the marches of the Gordon lands, and there had been a long tradition of animosity, feuding and marriage between the two families. Now Ballindalloch's 'three houses, bigging, and corn-yards of his haill grounds, and his haill lands, [were] plundered of horse, nolt, sheep and other goods'[37] by his familiar enemy.

The presbyterian Laird of Innes was similarly punished and his property 'burnt and plundered'. The town of Garmouth, belonging to Innes, was also ravaged.[38] This settlement at the mouth of the Spey had been Elgin's port since at least 1393. Presumably the plundering involved the looting of Elgin merchants' dwellings in the town and warehouses on the waterfront.

When Montrose's army marched away on 2 March, not even the burgh's royalists were sorry to see the soldiers leave.

Montrose advanced to the Spey, then took gate towards the coast. The burgh of Cullen was left a smoking ruin. Banff was plundered. The army then turned south to continue the campaign of disruption. On 8 May 1645 Montrose re-crossed the Spey. He entered Moray this time in pursuit of Major-General Sir John Hurry's covenanter army. Hurry had himself crossed the river only five days before. He was meeting with the local war committee at Elgin when he received word that Montrose had forded the river and was assembling his forces on the Moray side. The enemy was thus barely two hour's march away. Hurry began a rapid tactical retreat westwards, his rearguard conducting occasional skirmishes with Montrose's van. During one of these fights, a royalist laird, James Gordon of Rhynie, was wounded. He was left behind with an attendant 'in a labourer's house' as Montrose's army pursued Hurry. Rhynie's whereabouts could scarcely remain a secret among the covenanters of the Moray countryside, and news concerning the unfortunate Gordon soon reached the covenanter stronghold of Spynie. A party from the castle garrison, led by Captain George Smith, son of Walter Smith, merchant burgess of Elgin, sought out the injured malignant and 'cruellie murthered that wounded gentleman in his bed'.[39] On 9 May 1645 the armies of Hurry and Montrose met in pitched battle at Auldearn. As the fight began, Montrose gave the order 'no quarter', and as the battle ended, the royalists cut down Hurry's defeated covenanters and despatched the wounded: taking unrestrained and bloody revenge for the murder of Rhynie – and for the earlier killing, in a squalid skirmish in the streets of Aberdeen, of the popular royalist captain, Donald Farquharson, 'the pride o' Braemar':

> For that which made the slaughter mor cruell and merciles, was the murthering of Donald Farquharson in Aberdein, and James Gordoune of Rhynie, in Murray, which had incensed them to a reuenge … [and] this was the only cause of the great slaighter[40]

The order 'no quarter' and the consequent massacre of defeated covenanters, perhaps seemed less shocking to contemporary observers than it does to modern commentators. In practical terms, the mobile tactics that the royalist army adopted offered little scope for keeping prisoners, furthermore, it was a 17th-century commonplace that massacre followed military victory:

> Even as a conqueror first casts all his enemies down: the most part are wholly slain; others are but half dead but never noticed till they begin to peep up with their head & make some stir – & then they are killed outright[41]

On 11 May 1645 Montrose and his victorious army returned to Elgin, plundering the lands of Lethen, and of the Earl of Moray enroute. In Elgin, it was supposed, Montrose's 'wounded men were better accommodated with surgeons and medicines'.[42] However, The Elgin Depositions record the losses of only one surgeon, Alexander Urquhart. No other claims were made by fellow surgeons or by physicians and apothecaries, thus suggesting that 'alexander wrquhart Chirurgiane burges of elgin' (claim 13) may have been the burgh's only medical practitioner. Plundered from him were:

> Insicht plenissing cloithes abuilziementis Ornamentis wynes drogges cornes wictuall Armor household provisione and wtheris of that kind with ane hors – 50 lib' money … Extending … his loissis To the Soume of ane thowsand thrie hundreth fourtie four punds Sex shillingis aucht penneyes money

During the three days of occupation in May 1645, amid the usual plundering, the properties of those suspected of killing James Gordon were especially targeted. The murderers' houses were burnt and inevitably, there was some collateral damage:

> Isobell forbes ... Deponit that ther was [plunderit] from hir be the commone Enemie ... of insicht plenissing money cloithes wictual household provisione & loissis be the burning of Robert gibsones hous (claim 185)

Montrose's summer campaign was conducted southwards: victories at Alford (where the Lord George Gordon was killed), and at Kilsyth; thence to Philliphaugh near 'Selcriche ... wher they had ane rancounter to the uter routing of Montros all his foote and hors being cut of not ane man escaped of the Irishes'.[43]

Huntly, meanwhile, returned to Strathbogie, and busied his forces during the winter of 1645-6 where the danger was least and his own advantage greatest. His sons and followers besieged the castles of Moray covenanters. Lethen especially suffered as his estate was stripped of grain and livestock. Huntly also invested the stronghold of Spynie (now commanded by John Grant of Ballindalloch), conscripting local peasants to construct his siege works. Amongst this forced-labour squad were tenants of the late Earl of Rothes, punished for the sins of their laird who had been a leading light among Moray covenanters. Meanwhile, the Gordon soldiers used Elgin as a comfortable base for rest and recreation from their labours – 'Living at Randome' and 'waisting at thair pleasor'.[44]

The comings and goings of Huntly's troops, detailed in The Elgin Depositions, are confirmed in general terms by Provost John Hay's petition to parliament, which insisted that the Gordons occupied Elgin for some four months:

> in December ... 1645 and Januarij februarij mairch and apryll 1646 ... The late lord aboyne and Lewes gordoun did constantlie reside ... in Elgin ... with [Ane] hundreth foot and about four scoir horse[45]

The Elgin Depositions record that:

> Efter the marquis [of Huntly] reteered haime he left behind him his tuo sones & with them four troupes of hors wherof tua remained still at Elgin with fourtie foot the wther tuo with ... the Strathboigye Regiment consisting of Tuo hundreth & abowe with thair officiaris was Imployed about the blocking wp of the hous of Spynie Theise Tuo troupes consisting of a hundreth hors strong with Fourtie foot Remained at Elgin Thrie weiks Living at Randome[46]

Elgin kirk session recorded on Tuesday 16 December 1645: 'The Marquess of Huntlie cam to Elgin with ane armie'. From that day and throughout the occupation during January, February, March and April 1646 there was 'no preaching bot prayers'. Preaching in St Giles kirk in Elgin high street, recommenced on 17 May 1646. The sermon-starved town was treated to a double helping, as 'mr Murdoche Mackenzie preached befornoone and Mr Thomas Law efternoone'.[47]

During February 1646, John Middleton's covenanter army recaptured Aberdeen and reduced various royalist strongholds in the north east. In the spring Montrose was again in Moray; and from 19 April 1646 his forces besieged Inverness. Surprised by the rapid advance of Middleton's army from Aberdeen, Montrose fled across the Ness. Middleton's troops, going to and from Inverness, quartered in Elgin. When news arrived that the opportunist Gordons had retaken Aberdeen, the covenanting army hurriedly departed. In their haste to respond to the new emergency, Middleton's officers neglected to provide 'tickettis' – documentation that would allow the burgh to reclaim the cost of entertaining the troops.[48]

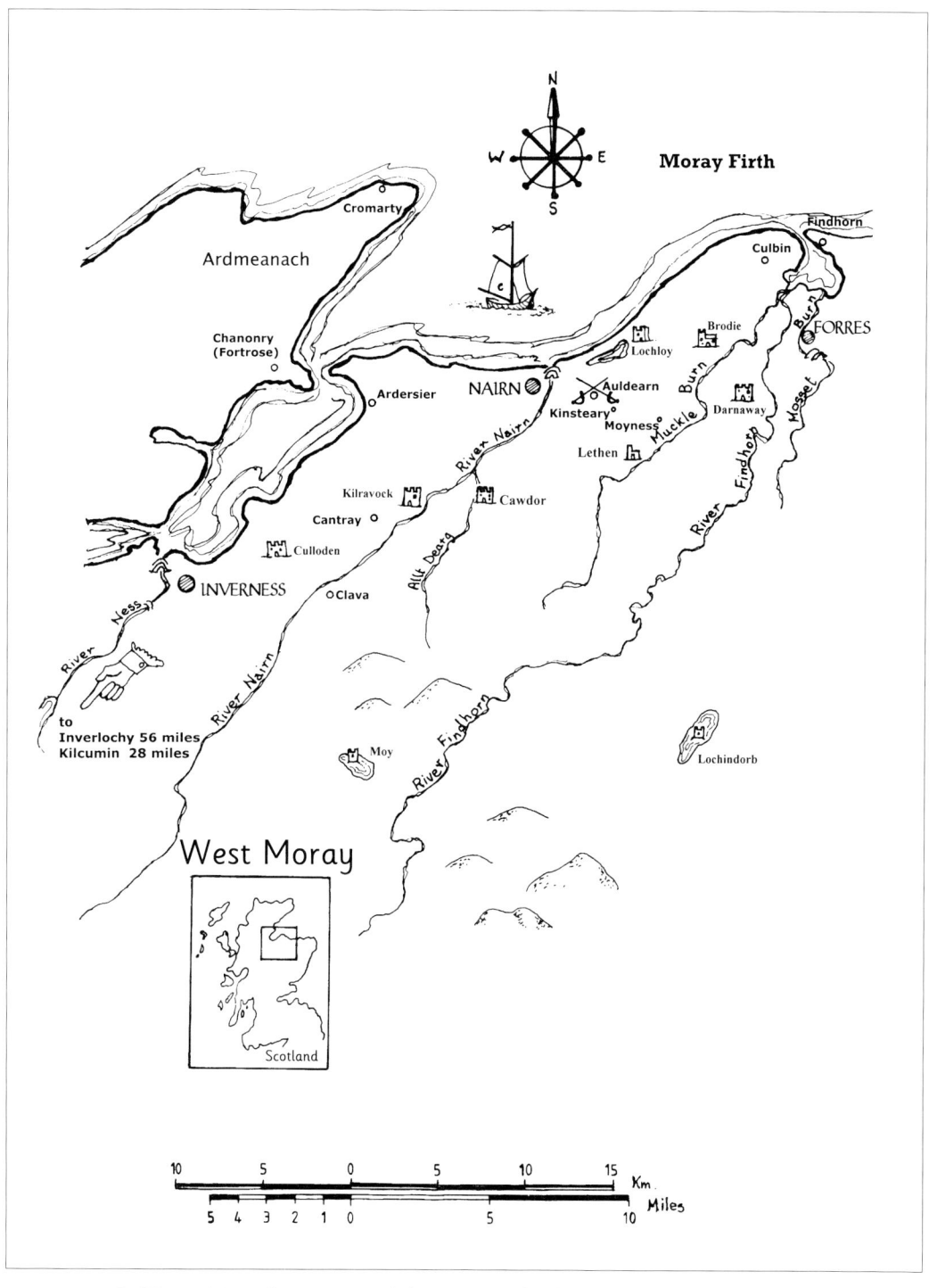

2. Western Moray showing principal places mentioned in the text. (Drawn by Christine Clerk)

But perhaps that was a small price to pay for the removal of the royalist threat; Montrose's military glamour was eclipsed. He would return, allied with John Hurry, in Charles II's cause in 1650, but he would not again alarm the covenanted burgh of Elgin. Montrose's paltry second army was routed at Carbisdale on the distant northern border of the Province of Moray. Montrose died, ingloriously, where he had begun, on the Edinburgh scaffold. Few in Elgin had reason to mourn his passing but none would soon forget what had been suffered at his hands; some may well have made the pilgrimage to Aberdeen, there to view with grim and godly satisfaction, a pickled limb of the defeated common enemy.

Chapter 2

The Said Toune of Elgin

The province of Moray was a discrete lowland enclave tucked between the mountains and the sea in the north east of Scotland. The province extended from the River Spey to the Dornoch Firth encompassing the counties of Moray, Nairn and Cromarty with parts of Inverness-shire and Easter Ross. The province was recognised as a distinct territory in the cartographic work of Timothy Pont at the close of the 16th century. The published version of Pont's map (by Robert Gordon of Straloch in Jan Blaeu's *Atlas Novus*) continued to recognise the geographical identity of Moray in 1654.

Moray was fertile and prosperous. The province had been a place of Pictish power and continued to enjoy a political status disproportionate to its size even after Pictish culture was overwhelmed by immigrant Gaels from the west. During the early Middle Ages, the men of Moray were independent-minded and potentially rebellious.

From the reign of David I (1124-53) onwards – and even arguably from the time of King Macbeth (1040-57) – modernising kings of Scotland planted their realm with incomers from the Anglo-Norman world. The land of Moray was also granted, over the heads of native Gaelic chieftains, to an alien governing class. These new lords enjoyed their estates, manors, titles and privileges as feudal vassals owing military and other services within a hierarchy of lordship under the monarch. The rural peasantry of Moray clustered in townships (identified by the Gaelic *baile* or English *tun*). Township land was allocated in strips among the peasantry and cultivated according to communal customs regulated by a feudal lord (laird). Peasants enjoyed their strips in the arable fields, and also rights on common grazings and peat cuttings, in return for labour service and other dues, paid in money and in kind, to the laird.

Kings of Scotland sponsored innovative urban settlements throughout the kingdom. These new towns were planned on the English model and described by the English word *burh* (burgh), which indicated a fortified settlement serving as a local seat of power. A chain of royal burghs was strung across the coastal plain of Moray. These included Elgin, Forres, Auldearn, Nairn, Inverness, Dingwall, Fortrose, Dornoch and Tain – with Cullen and Banff on the coast to the east. The role of the royal burghs was to control, civilise and Normanise the Gaelic populations of their hinterlands. In practical terms, the burghs served as centres of royal authority (justice, administration, taxation) and wealth-creation (trade and industry).

Medieval Scottish monarchs followed English models when establishing their royal new towns. The burghs of Moray were spaced according to the pattern expounded in the 13th century by Henry de Bracton: each serving a hinterland extending the radius of one third of a day's journey or 'six miles and a half and the third part of a half'.[1] In Moray this meant that burghs could be sited strategically at river crossings, which also provided links by water to the sea: Elgin on the Lossie, Forres on the Mosset, Nairn on the River Nairn. Auldearn, which breaks the pattern, was a short-lived creation which had lost its burghal status long before 1645 and shrivelled to a village sitting forlornly within its medieval burgh boundaries, overshadowed by its royal castle motte.

The royal burghs were planted initially with immigrants from England, Wales, Brittany, Normandy, Picardy and Flanders – the commercial go-getters of the Anglo-Norman world. The language of the burghs was English, which in due course (and certainly before the 17th century) became the vernacular tongue of lowland Moray.

The pioneering settlers who took up feus in the new royal burghs were known as burgesses. The community of burgesses was independent of feudal magnates and self-governing, owing fealty directly to the crown. The burgesses were entitled to elect town councils, levy petty customs and make (and enforce) laws regulating commercial life, community relations and building works. The burgesses enjoyed monopolies on trade within a defined territory. Burgh courts acted as sheriff, dispensing the king's justice within the liberties. Initially, the burgesses supplemented income from commerce and industry with subsistence agriculture. For this, the community enjoyed extensive arable lands with common grazings and peat cuttings. These common good lands were granted to the burghs by the king and were divided, allocated and managed in the usual medieval communal manner. The lands and privileges enjoyed by royal burghs were guaranteed in charters issued and reiterated by successive monarchs.

A common seal, symbolising the corporate identity of the royal burgh, was used to authenticate official documents. The seal of Elgin was, in the usual way, emblazoned with the burgh's arms. This heraldic device depicted the burgh's tutelary saint, Aegidius (Giles), a French hermit, patron of cripples and the indigent. St Giles was notably popular among medieval merchant communities; in Elgin, Giles displaced native saints with real connections to Moray, such as the Gaelic missionaries Maelrubha and Moluag.

The Elgin Depositions assert that during the occupation by Montrose's forces from 19 February 1645 'Thair Comone seale aboue Four hundredth zeir auld Miscarried'.[2] The theft or destruction of the burgh seal struck at the heart of the town's corporate identity. Indeed, the matrix 'Miscarried' in February 1645 may have been the first and only seal the burgh had ever possessed. At over 400 years old, the seal antedates the earliest surviving burgh charter (granted by Alexander III in 1268), and appears to belong to the time of the creation of the Moray burghs in the late 12th century.

By destroying the common seal of Elgin, the royalists hoped to hamper public business and local administration. Without a common seal, difficulties would arise in authenticating official legal documents. Property transactions, theoretically, could not be completed without a seal to fix to title deeds, feu charters and other writs. Burgesses could not be created without a seal to append to their burgess tickets. Further problems would arise in respect of commercial dealings and the management of burgh finances, but somehow burgh officials muddled through. How they managed without an official seal is not recorded, but public business did not cease in its absence. Indeed, Elgin seems to have coped without a seal for almost a generation – until 1678 when a new seal was authorised by the Lord Lyon. The practical difficulties arising from the disappearance of the seal, and the cost of commissioning a replacement, paled to insignificance in the glare of the symbolic meaning of its loss; destruction of the seal struck at the heart of burghal pride – as a collective injury and insult, that would take more than cash compensation to heal, and which would not soon be forgiven or forgot.

From the very beginnings of the royal burgh's life, landward magnates sought to exercise influence within the community. The magnificent Trinity Church, cathedral of the bishops of Moray, outside the eastern boundary of Elgin, cast a long shadow over the town. In Elgin's sister burgh of Forres, episcopal influence was assured in the person of the archdeacon who enjoyed the parish church of St Lawrence. Lay magnates, meanwhile, might purchase burgh properties and acquire burgess status in order to engage in trade and burgh politics. Indeed, local lairds were frequently prominent in burgh society. Brodie was a notable presence in Forres; and Innes was, from the 16th century, oppressively influential in Elgin. The earls of Huntly acquired a property at the east port of the burgh. The lairds of Pluscarden and Duffus were leading property owners in the Elgin stent roll for 1646, both attracting the hefty assessment of 36s.[3]

Norman kings of Scotland divided the province into shires. In each shire a sheriff exercised royal authority and dispensed royal justice, ostensibly from a base in a royal castle, typically located just beyond the boundary of the leading royal burgh. The king's castle motte with defended bailey enclosures, was an integral element in the planning of Moray's royal burghs. The burghs of Elgin and Forres were often treated as equals within the sheriffdom of eastern Moray, which was known as the shire of Elgin & Forres. By the 17th century, however, Elgin had emerged as the senior partner: the more prosperous commercial centre, the more populous town, the seat of county justice, and second only to Inverness in the province of Moray.

In 1645 Elgin was a typical small Scottish royal burgh. The population of the town at this time is not recorded. Seventeenth-century bureaucrats did not require population statistics to facilitate local administration. Indeed, presbyterian fundamentalists might find a biblical injunction against such demographic enterprises in 2 Samuel 24:10:

> And David's heart smote him after that he had numbered the people. And David said unto the Lord, I have sinned greatly in that I have done.

The earliest population figure available is found in Alexander Webster's statistical survey, compiled (on the eve of clearance) in 1755. Webster estimated the population of the parish of Elgin at a dubiously precise figure of 6,305. The burgh's share of this (including men, women, children and servants) might have been around five thousand. A century earlier, Elgin may have been somewhat smaller with perhaps fewer than 4,000 souls.

National taxation records give a clue to the rank order (and so also relative population and prosperity) of Scottish burghs. A taxt roll for July 1649 was headed, of course, by Edinburgh with a tax liability assessed at £6,480. The capital was followed at a respectful distance by Aberdeen (£1,200), Glasgow (£1,170), Perth (£720) and St Andrews (£600). Among medium-sized burghs, Inverness (with a population of perhaps around 5000 souls) was assessed at £450, followed by Kirkcaldy (£432), Montrose (£360) and Dysart (£252). Small burghs included Dunbar (£198), Irvine (£180), with Anstruther and Kirkudbright (£144). The Moray burghs are among the smallest communities of the taxt roll. Elgin, with Tain and Peebles, was assessed at just (£90). Banff (£60) was more prosperous than Forres (£54), whilst Nairn (£36) joined Forfar, Whithorn and North Berwick at the foot of the list. Of course it is likely that the Moray burghs were somewhat undertaxed as a concession to communities that had been impoverished by acts of war. Cullen was not included on the 1649 taxt roll: presumably the burgh had not yet recovered from Montrose's visit and was incapable of paying anything.[4]

Elgin declared enthusiastically for the Covenant in 1638. The economic prominence of the town meant that the burgh became a focus in Moray for resistance to Montrose's

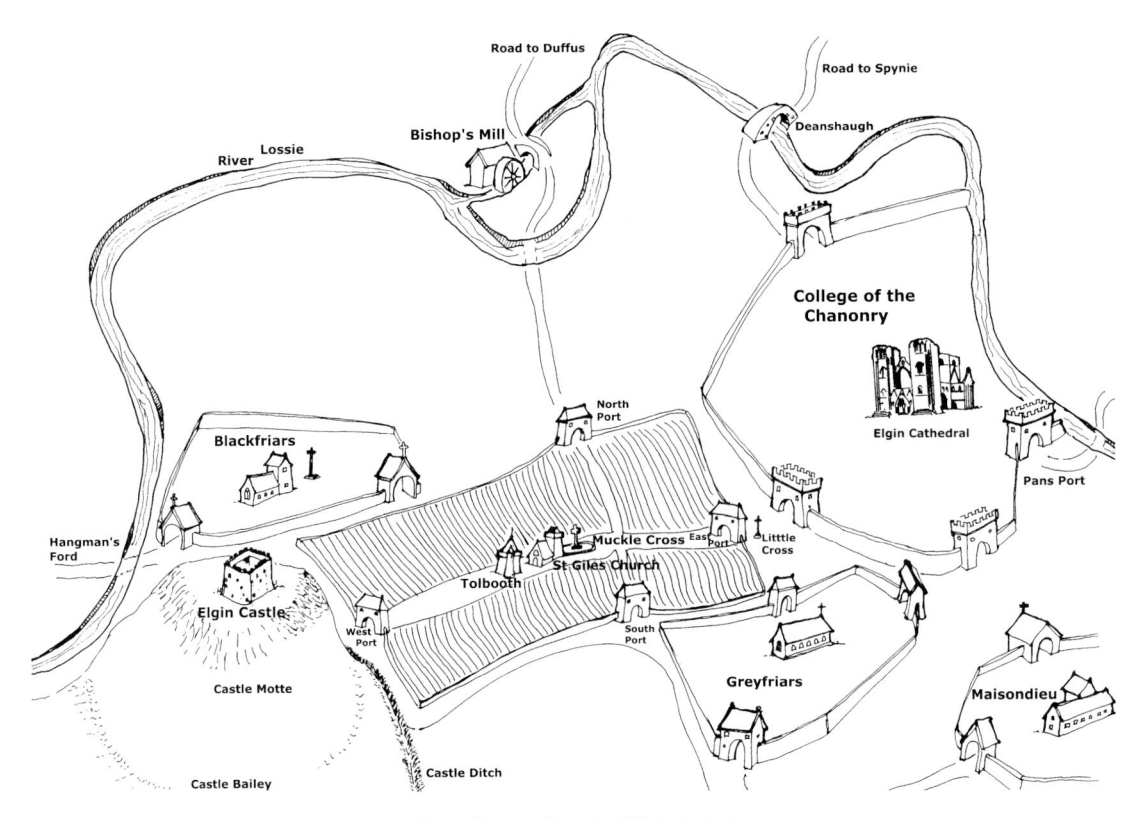

3. Plan of the royal burgh of Elgin in 1646

royalist campaign. The local war committee convened in Elgin, perhaps meeting in the council chamber of the burgh tolbooth – if not more comfortably accommodated in the fair lodging of a leading burgess. These committees of war were established throughout the provinces as the Scottish parliament recognised:

> the danger imminent to the true protestant religioune his majestie's persoune and … peace of his Kingdomes by the multitude of papistes prelates and ther adherents now in airmes in Ingland and Ireland[5]

In the frontier province of Moray (threatened by Gordons in the east and highlanders to the north and west), the war committee, appointed from among the covenanted gentry, encompassed 'the shereffdome of Elgine Nairne and a pairt of the shereffdome of Inuernes with the toun thairoff and Strathspey'.[6] The integrity of the province was thus recognised by parliament for military and political purposes even in the 17th century.

In the eventful year 1645, the town of Elgin appeared to its royalist occupiers as an unremarkable Scottish burgh. The medieval plan of the town was familiar to Montrose's soldiers – and indeed also to MacColla's Irish – as a commonplace pattern, known throughout the Anglo-Norman world (including Ireland). The Norman plan is clearly visible even today at the heart of the town, though the burgh broke its medieval bounds during the mid-19th century to spread streets down the curving strips of the burgh's arable acres, and across broad expanses of common grazings.

Medievally – and in the 17th century – the wide market place of the high street was the communal and commercial heart of the town. On specified market days, people from the rural hinterland came to Elgin to sell surplus produce; burgh merchants and craftsmen set up stalls and opened forebooths before their houses to trade in imported wares and local manufactures.

Only a few public buildings were permitted in the cobbled causeway of the high street. The parish church stood at the heart of the market street. The walled burial ground to the east, its turf surface raised several feet above street level by four centuries of burials, was used for communal and commercial purposes on market days. The space was largely uncluttered by gravestones which had not yet become a fashionable, widespread (or affordable) essential of the Scottish funerary cult.

The mercat cross (with joggs attached for the punishment of petty criminals) stood in the high street as a symbol of burghal and royal authority. The mercat cross also stood as a reminder of Christian values for traders on market days; though presumably, by 1645, Christian images had been removed to leave a plain pillar, perhaps topped with a heraldic device or a useful sundial. In addition to the cross, a trone (public weighing machine) was erected in the high street. Here, for a fee, traders could check the weight of goods offered for sale, and burgh officials could enforce statutory national standards. Occasionally a pickpocket or unfree trader was nailed by the ear to the wooden shaft of the trone.

West of the church stood the tolbooth. This substantial public building contained the burgh's courthouse and jail. A public clock was installed in the tolbooth tower whose architectural pretension – like a lairdly towerhouse – reflected the pride of the community and its prosperous independence. Store rooms in the tolbooth were stocked with arms to equip the town's soldiers. Strongrooms housed the town's little treasury of coin, plate and regalia, and also the administrative archives of the royal burgh with the cadjet (strongbox) holding 'manie guid wreittis & evidentis' – including the burgh's precious royal charters.[7]

Montrose specifically targeted the archives in the tolbooth. During 'the space of Ellewin Dayes' of occupation from 19 February 1645, 'the public registeres & evidentis of the said burgh war Pittifullie spoyled and Scattered'.[8] However, this claim does not entirely accord with calendars of Elgin archives prepared by record office archivists at the end of the 20th century. It seems that the hyperbole of 'Pittifullie' exaggerates the damage actually done. For example, medieval charters survived and today show no more damage than might be expected from the normal use and abuse of several centuries. Similarly, town council minutes, accounts and burgh court books from the 16th century all escaped the vandalism of Montrose's men. The pages of these volumes are intact; the bindings are tight; the covers (made from recycled medieval illuminated parchments) are scarcely scuffed. Indeed, the volumes show no more wear than might be expected from occasional consultation during four centuries of sometimes careless storage.

On the other hand, town council minutes are amissing for the Civil War period. Leaves are missing from the minute book following the record dated 22 July 1644. An otherwise commonplace minute survives for business conducted on 23 November 1646. This minute lists 'Cordinaris wnlawit for break of Statutis'. The offending cordwainers (with their fines) were: William Petrie (fined £4), Iames Gordoun (£6 13s. 4d.), Patrick Gregor in Dollas (40s.), Andro Laying (53s. 4d. – one dollar), Alexander Forsythe in Monachtie (40s.), George Malice in Quhitefield (40s.), Ion Hervie (£4), Patrick Winchester (£4), William Donaldsone (53s. 4d.), Alexander Hervie (40s.), Iames Pedder (£20), Alexander Innes (£4), George Hendrie (40s.), Alexander Duff (£4), William Wilsone (£4), and Andro Kay (£5 6s. 8d. – two dollars). Similar prosecutions had been mounted in previous years and it may be that the fines were regarded more as a periodic tax than a judicial penalty. Clearly some of these craftsmen were substantial businessmen: for example Iames Pedder who could afford a hefty fine and who also stood as cautioner for two fellow cordwainers.[9]

The town's carters followed the cordwainers: 'fynit for transporting guidis in cairtis alongis the brig of lossie'. Presumably the carters were bypassing the burgh's elegant new bridge (the Bow Brig), perhaps fording the river to avoid tolls. The offenders comprised: Thomas Schipheard, Thomas Gray, Iames Tulloche, Iames Glas, Iames Walker, Iames Suthtoune, Robert Mcgill, Richard Walker and William Sutherland. Each was fined 13s. 4d. (one merk) and 'actit heirefter not to doe the lyke wnder the payne of confiscatione of their horssis & punishment of their persones'.[10]

On the same leaf, immediately following the cordwainers and carters, is the minute of a meeting held on 23 April 1647. The record thereafter is continuous. Town council minutes are, therefore, lost for a period much longer than the occupations of Elgin by Montrose in February and May 1645, and indeed longer than the subsequent Gordon occupations from December 1645 until April 1646. The gap in the record is, thus, not wholly explained by the alleged scattering and spoiling of 'public registeres and evidentis' by the royalists. In seeking an explanation for the absence of records an intriguing possibility suggests itself. Were minutes of decisions taken during this traumatic period deliberately suppressed or excised to conceal some act (or acts) of collaboration, of which the town council was subsequently ashamed – and for which the community might be penalised? However, the council was careful to preserve the minutes (relating to cordwainers and carters) which enshrined judicial decisions with financial implications.

Damage to covenanter records and muniments by Montrose's marauding army was widely reported. This destruction was presumably a considered tactic intended to dislocate public and private legal, administrative and financial business: inconveniencing individuals, impeding trade, undermining the management of estates and hampering the collection of moneys that should have financed the covenanters' war effort. Alexander Brodie of Brodie petitioned the committee of estates on 6 August 1645 claiming, with plaintive hyperbole:

> I make no mentione of burning of houses landes cornezairds spoyleing of goods and cattell … Amonges the rest in this commone calamity the writes and evidentes quherby I have title to enjoy the small estate wherto I succeid are not in pairt but wholly destroyed. I am, throughe this loise and distruction of writes, evidentes, contractes, discharges, and others such lyke, exposed to ane hundredth yea many yeires troubles and pley[11]

It is difficult, however, to reconcile Brodie's claim with significant documentation predating the burnings of 1645, that still exists today among Brodie castle muniments.

As Montrose's men marched along Elgin high street, they would have seen little in the pattern of building to surprise them. Elgin's house-fronts presented an aspect that was a commonplace of Scottish townscape and medieval burgh planning. Houses stood on burgh feus pegged out with a standard (English) measure. Each feu measured ¼ acre in area (1 rood). Each rood was 1½ rods wide (24ft 9in), with an additional 9in representing the ploughed furrow with which each curving feu was originally marked out on the ground by the Norman kings' town planners. There were, originally, some four dozen burgage plots on each side of the burgh high street. A later medieval extension eastwards added a further 48 roods. In 1646 the burgh stent roll listed 211 individual property-holders liable for local taxation.

Burgh dwellings were typically built gable-on to the high street, nicely fitted to their narrow plots. Windows and doors opening directly onto the public street were initially forbidden and probably still rare in the 17th century. The main door – usually the only door – to a burgh dwelling opened onto a close (wynd). The feuholder guarded his close with a locked gate at the high street end.

The rood behind each burgh house was cultivated as a kitchen garden. Here the burgess kept his peats, horse and pigs, and the goodwife her geese and chickens. Curiously, no mention is made of the loss of burgh peat, poultry and pigs to Montrose's foragers; perhaps domestic fuel, chickens and swine were embraced by the economical catch-all 'household provision'.

Stone walls and fences preserved the boundaries between neighbouring feus, following the curving line traced by the precise plough of the medieval planners. At the foot of each feu, a substantial masonry wall marked the boundary of the rood and also of the royal burgh's liberties. These walls linked to form a curtain sufficient to keep out all but the most determined thieves and caterans. Beyond the walls ran a roadway (back gate or back passage) following the line of long-since slumped and rubbish-choked medieval earthwork defences.

Elgin did not possess a circuit of medieval masonry walls and bastions. Nor did the townsfolk throw up any defences in the face of the enemy. Perhaps, paradoxically, Elgin was spared the worst excesses of MacColla's Irish troops because the community offered no effective resistance. Certainly Aberdeen suffered horribly because, at the beginning of the conflict, the Gordons tried to deny the burgh to Montrose's covenanters, and subsequently because the inhabitants stoutly defied Montrose's royalists; the town councillors declaring with unwittingly prescient bombast that they would 'not abandone and render our toune so lightly' but would 'spend the last drope of our blood' to defend the burgh and Covenant.[12] At Dundee too an aspect of military preparedness seemed to inflame Montrose. The suburb of Bonnet Raw was burnt by a detachment of Irish infantry when the burgh refused to 'render' in 1644. During 1645 Dundonians constructed modern earthwork defences under the direction of a military engineer named Henry Young, and for this defiance the town was sacked when Montrose returned. Elgin was probably wise to make no military effort and to surrender without murmur.

Although the town of Elgin was open to the enemy, most of the houses were locked. (Neighbours were as mistrustful of one another in the 17th century as at any other time.) Montrose's men, however, felt entitled to enter all and any houses at will. The Elgin Depositions suggest that doors were comprehensively kicked in and keys routinely confiscated as the occupying troops came and went. The houses that they ransacked were typical burgh dwellings of all classes. Although no intact house of the period now survives in Elgin, fieldwork and inference allow us to visualise the housing stock of 1645.

The humblest class of burgh dwelling is nowhere visible. However, the footprints and foundations of peasant halls can be seen on abandoned settlement sites (deserted during the Moray clearances after 1766) throughout the north east. This simple style of house was also built in town – in snaking rows that straggled gable-to-gable along the roods of feuars with a taste for property development, or who needed housing for their dependants, journeymen, labourers and servants. Well-preserved remains of this style of house may be examined beside the Grant castle motte on Speyside or among numerous deserted townships in the Gordon country of Glen Avon. These dwellings were cruck-framed with turf walls perhaps raised on a low rubble base. These were structures that could be erected in a matter of days: the kind of house that Elizabeth Innes, Lady Echt, had built for her favourite preacher – the famous Moray minister, Mr James Allan. The house of a rural peasant or burgh labourer was more or less worthless. Turf walls and roof thatch were of value only as compost; though the roof timbers, door and door frames might be worth money – and these things typically belonged to the laird or landlord. Valuations on the estate of Stoneyforenoon, near Forres, in the 1720s show the paltry worth (while hinting at the insubstantial readily-replaceable structure) of a commonplace peasant house:

> Item Iohn Young's Fyre house Consisting of tuo Midduells and one Couplethe Couple worth one pound Ten sides worth four shillings each Door & door cheeikis worth fourteen shillings
>
> Iames Duncans fyre house Consisting of tuo Couples worth Four Merks Eighteeen sides worth four shillings each Door & Door Cheeckis worth fourteen shillingis[13]

The dwellings of rural peasants and burgh labourers comprised an undivided firehouse – a single room with a hearth on the earthen or cobbled floor. Chickens roosted on the rafters beneath the sooty thatch. Furnishings were few and functional, comprising at most a table with stools and benches, a dresser, and a box bed for the goodman and his bedfellow. In country dwellings the peasant family was joined by a milch cow or milking goat stalled at the lower end of the house. It seems likely that Elgin's Mosstowie tenants – and peasant subtenants who fell beneath the commissioners' notice – occupied simple cruck-framed turf-and-scantling homes of this type. The most valuable property of these rural husbandmen was their livestock. Indeed, one cow might be worth more than all a man's other plundered possessions put together. Patrick Grant in Mosstowie (claim 147) swore to the commissioners that he had:

> plunderit from him be the commone Enemie … insicht plenissing cloithes abuilziementis money wictual household provisione & wtheris of that kind abouwritin with ane young staige worth 14 lib' 13s 4d with ane Cow worth 12 lib'

Patrick Grant's total losses amounted to only £30 13s. 4d., of which the value of possessions other than animals was just £4 (Scots). When we consider that the town's soldiers were paid 42s. a week, and a parliamentary soldier received 4s. a day – we begin to appreciate how poor a tenant such as Grant might be, and how little he had to lose.

The dwellings of the middle class of Elgin's burgesses and master craftsmen are depicted in contemporary prints such as John Slezer's *Theatrum Scotiae* (1693). These houses were substantial hall-and-chamber structures with walls of harled clay-bonded rubble; a hearth with gable-end chimney; even a roof of local schistose tiles above the garret which housed children, servants, stores of food and stocks of material. A rare survivor of this style of house still stands in Forres high street, though much altered, notably by the enlargement of an original ground-floor window (with characteristic rolled moulding) into a doorway opening directly onto the public street. In Elgin, here and there, it is possible to see the sturdy jointed crucks of 17th-century dwellings built into the walls of later structures in the dank pends and curving closes that snake behind the 19th-century high-street façade of the burgh. Most of the Elgin claimants whose houses were looted of goods to the value of a few hundred pounds (Scots) occupied this middling class of dwelling, for example, Hew Hay, merchant burgess (claim 22), who had:

> taken avay from him be the common enemie … Insicht plenisching cloithis abuilziementis merchand wares money armor household provisione and wtheris of that kind … his loisses … To the soume of tuo hundredthe aucht pundis Sex shillingis aucht pennies mone

Prosperous merchant burgesses such as the (past and future) provost and commissioner to parliament, Mr John Hay, and Walter Smythe, messenger, burgess, and moderator of the kirk session (claim 150), occupied conspicuous masonry dwellings, recorded in The Elgin Depositions as 'ane fair Luidging of thrie houshight'. These three-storeyed lodgings, spreading over two or more roods, tower over the town in Slezer's engraved *Prospectus oppidi Elginae* (1693). The fair lodging of a merchant burgess was the architectural equal of a rural landowner's lairdly towerhouse. The vaulted ground floor of a large lodging was usually reserved for storage. At first-floor level was the main living room (hall), with a focal fireplace. Private chambers leading off the hall (some with fireplaces) contained the curtained beds of the master and mistress. Servants, children and apprentices slept in (usually unheated) rooms above the hall and in garrets under the stone-tiled roof.

No fair lodgings survive in Elgin's high street today. However, a single stair turret – relic of the lodging of Alexander Leslie and Jeane Bonyman (claim 5) – stands as evidence of the craze for forestairs that swept the burgh from the later 16th century onwards as multi-storey living became fashionable. Exemplary survivors such as Abertarff House in the old high street of Inverness, Provost Ross's House in Ship Row, Aberdeen, and the impressive lodging built at Fordyce by Robert Menzies, an Aberdeen burgess, all suggest the style to which 'theis of best qualitie' in Elgin might aspire. Elgin's best houses were cosily furnished (in the hall and the master's chamber at least) with wood panelling: 'weill plenischit with wanscott plenissing'. Prosperous burgesses also boasted 'glasen windowes', presumably installed by Alexander Forsyth, the glasswright (claim 34), who was also contracted to maintain the windows of the parish church – a public service that earned him his burgess-ship and 10 merks yearly in cash. Several merchants boasted 'buiths' (forebooths). These permanent shops were erected (compromising medieval building lines) in front of the merchants' houses, with town council permission and on payment of an additional feu duty.

The burgh of Elgin was entered by roads from the east, from the south (Moss Street) and the north (Lossie Wynd). The burgh was also entered by a road which skirted the royal castle motte on the western boundary of the town, to cross the Lossie by a ford near the Blackfriars' convent – or followed the riverbank to the newly-completed high arch of the Bow Brig. Each entrance to the town was guarded by a gate (port). Here the town's officers were posted to regulate traffic, collect tolls and exclude undesirables such as sturdy beggars, gypsies, lug-marked criminals and pregnant women without visible support. In a town without defensive walls, the gates and gatehouses at the ports were perhaps of more symbolic political than military significance.

A network of roads connected the town with its hinterland. Byways led to and threaded the ridged strips of arable burgh. A serviceable cart road connected Elgin with its port at Garmouth on the Spey. A web of roads linking parochial networks allowed landward peasants to reach the burgh market. Within this network rivers were crossed by fords and ferries, maintained by parochial authorities or private enterprise. Burghs erected bridges across the rivers that washed their boundaries. Elgin's stately Bow Bridge at the Old Mills was brand new when Montrose marched across it in 1645. Thus, although travel was slow – conducted at the walking-pace of an ambling nag – merchants and ministers, peasants, soldiers, lairds and craftsmen were able to move through the Moray landscape (and beyond) without significant difficulty.

Thus the burgh of Elgin was connected to the mainstream of Scottish cultural and commercial life. Coastal shipping allowed Moray merchants to reach the south of Scotland in relative comfort, and more than a few may have travelled further abroad in pursuit of merchant ventures – to England and (braving the notorious Dunkirk pirates) to the wondrous entrepôts of continental Europe.

Elgin folk were well aware of the major events of the day. News (good and bad) travelled fast. Inverness was just an easy day's ride away, Aberdeen could be reached, even in winter snow, within a couple of days, and Edinburgh was only a four day journey from Aberdeen. News and correspondence flowed rapidly and readily among lairds and merchants who enjoyed extensive networks of family and business interests. Official information came from the capital to the war committee. Matters of burghal interest were communicated through the convention of royal burghs, which cemented the nationwide sodality of Scottish burgesses – and to which Elgin usually sent a delegate. The press of printer/publisher Edward Raban, established at Aberdeen and subsidised with £40 a year from public funds, ensured that official polemic, proclamations (from parliament and the General Assembly) and other matters of common concern might be disseminated through the north east. Even if Elgin folk had no direct access to newsbooks and widely-circulating pamphlets, informal mechanisms were more than adequate for broadcasting rumour, propaganda and news.

The kirk played a key role. The usual parochial concerns were humdrum matters such as fornication, adultery, bastardy, poor relief, sabbath-breaking, superstition, fighting, swearing, prostitution and laughing in church, but in times of crisis the major political news of the day was transmitted to kirk sessions and announced from the pulpit. For example, on 26 July 1644 session minutes noted, 'The letter from the General Assembly was presented for ane thanksgiuing to God for the victorie our armie had in Ingland against Prince Rupert'.[14] This, of course, was a celebration of the decisive role played by Scottish cavalry, commanded by Sir David Leslie, in the pivotal parliamentary victory at Marston Moor (on 2 July 1644).

The economy of Elgin, as of all royal burghs, was founded on trade. Monopolies and privileges granted by medieval monarchs were jealously defended. Unfree (non-burgess) traders were rigorously prosecuted in burgh courts where Elgin burgesses sat as judge and jury. Thirty-two claimants among The Elgin Depositions are described as merchants; 20, designated simply as burgess, were also entitled to engage in trade. The humblest merchants were men such as John Hardie (claim 60). He claimed losses assessed at £180 15s. 0d., which suggests that his plundered goods represented little more than the stock of a small shopkeeper. Taken from him was 'insicht plenissing houshold provisione money wictual armor merchand wares & wtheris of that kynd'.

The most prosperous merchants operated on a large, even international scale: for example Robert Mertein, head of a five-horse household (claim 7). A few, such as the Calder family or Robert Gibson, bought country estates (Muirton and Linkwood respectively) and were accepted into the gentry. John Grant of Ballindalloch did not think it beneath his lairdly dignity to act as a witness along with Gibson of Linkwood, for Robert Dunbar (claim 10), a mere burgh merchant, though claiming substantial losses worth £1,416 11s. 4d.

Enterprising and adventurous Elgin merchants traded by land and sea with the rest of Scotland and, on occasion, also with England and continental Europe, particularly the Baltic and Netherlands. They trafficked in wine, wax, skins, fells, leather, pickled salmon, salt, timber, iron, cloth, spices, ceramics and other exotic goods.

Merchants engaged in the grain trade are indicated in The Elgin Depositions by losses of 'cornes'. Corn merchants may also be identified by references to kilns which were constructed at the foot of merchants' roods to minimise fire hazards, and used for drying grain or malting barley for ale and whisky.

Quantities of livestock were 'plunderit and avay Takin be the comonn Enemie'. The plundering of 91 horses represented a considerable loss to the town. No carters are mentioned in the Depositions; presumably these mobile businessmen had escaped with their vehicles, horses, oxen and household goods before the enemy arrived. Other losses of burghal livestock – of cows (31), bulls (2), oxen (26) and sheep (252) – were relatively small. This suggests that, by 1645, Elgin burgesses were no longer extensively engaged in agriculture. Presumably their commonfield strips and grazing rights on burgh lands were, by this time, enjoyed by peasant subtenants, who paid rent (probably in poultry and victual) leaving burgesses free to concentrate on commerce, trade and industry. This peasant tenandry was presumably plundered of livestock and crops, but fell beneath the notice of the Deposition commissioners.

The Elgin Depositions may give an uneven impression of Elgin's economic activity, by over-emphasising trades connected with the burgh's agricultural hinterland. Two groups of claimants are conspicuous. The Depositions refer to 29 individuals associated with leather-working: 15 skinners (dealers in skins and hides), three fleshers (butchers), two saddlers and notably nine cordwainers. This latter trade was a highly specialised craft ostensibly working in fine Cordova leather. This supple grade of leather, treated with alum ('almit ledder'), was used in the manufacture of gloves – a fashion essential, without which no self-respecting 17th-century man or woman could feel properly dressed.

A further 25 claimants were concerned in textile manufacture. These included a dyer and three litsters, who were all involved in producing coloured yarn ready for weaving. Twelve websters (weavers) were mentioned. Some of these were doubtless individual master craftsmen, working looms in their own cramped firehouses. Others, though, may have been entrepreneurs who set up looms in peasant houses outwith the burgh, or who operated workshops fitted up with several looms operated by a team of journeyman weavers. The nine tailors among the Depositions' claimants may also have included a mix of individual craftsmen working from home, and capitalists operating sweatshops where a crew of journeymen stitched together.

In suffering such specific plunder, Elgin's experience was similar to that of Aberdeen, where Alasdair MacColla's Irish troops:

> remained behind searching for cloaks and plaids in order to indulge their craving for cloth and fabrics. Although Alasdair whipped them out of town he appropriated £1440 worth of apparel himself[15]

Doubtless the Irish regiments boasted the best-dressed soldiers of the civil war. The wives, children and camp followers who marched with the army were decked out in plundered clothing, affecting the style of the most haughty burgess or wealthy merchant's wife. This vanity allowed dour presbyterians to recall the prophesies of Isaiah 3:16-24, confident that God would smite with ghastly vengeance the Irish soldiers' catholic doxies who strutted the covenanted high street of Elgin in a sartorial excess of stolen abulziements, and:

> take away the bravery of their … changeable suits of apparel and the mantles, and the wimples, and the crisping pins, The glasses, and the fine linen, and the hoods, and the vails … and instead of a girdle there shall be a rent; and instead of well set hair baldness; and instead of a stomacher a girding of sackcloth

The quantities of gloves, textiles and clothing that MacColla's men plundered were far more than any individual could need or carry, especially in an army which prided itself upon rapid marches and agile mobility. What did they do with these looted goods? It is plausible that the textiles stolen in Elgin, and the fine leather gloves and supple skins that were 'away takin', were not plundered for personal use, but to be sold on to support the King's cause. If such was the case, who were the merchants and middlemen who prospered from the trade in plundered goods? Was there a culture of connivance within the community of Scottish merchants that turned a blind eye to this traffic and allowed profiteers to function with impunity in a business that benefited everyone?

Other trades mentioned in The Elgin Depositions include a selection of specialist burgh crafts. There was an orilogeris (clockmaker) named John Andersone (claim 62), and a gunsmith, David Mailling (claim 39), who was plundered of 'Insicht plenissing cloithes muscottis gunes pistollis household provisione and wtheris of that kynd' – although, presumably, Mailling's stock of weapons was fairly limited as the whole value of his losses was only £178 9s 4d. The glasswright, Alexander Forsythe (claim 34), was a glazier rather than a glassmaker; his stock of lead (plundered to be melted down for bullets) would have been used to fix the diamond-shaped panes (losens) popular for domestic windows. Lead and glass most likely arrived by sea as trade goods, landed at the burgh port of Garmouth. The burgh's maltmen supplied raw material to be brewed into ale and distilled into aqua vitae (whisky) – though no brewers or distillers appear in the Depositions. Three law officers – William Thom, a notary (claim 182), and two messengers, Alexander Dunbar (claim 172) and Walter Smythe (claim 150) – attracted special attention from Montrose's troops; though the Depositions do not mention any spoiling or scattering of their protocol books and other records. Other members of Elgin's flourishing legal profession are not mentioned at all; perhaps they fled. Or perhaps, like careful lawyers, they preferred the discretion of collaboration and negotiation to the valour of defiance, and so were spared.

Several trades seem to be conspicuously under-represented in The Elgin Depositions. For example, only three smiths were plundered, and just one cooper. A mason, Alexander Anderson (claim 183), was plundered; the lime stolen from him may have been required to disinfect middens and graves as a precaution against disease (especially plague) in the royalist camp. Other trades are notably absent from the Depositions: these include baxters, bonnetmakers, brewers, candlemakers, carters, fullers, gardeners, innkeepers, lorimers, tallow chandlers, tavern keepers, turners and wrights. Most probably, these trades did not have anything that the various occupying armies wished to take. The absence of metal trades – smiths, cutlers, goldsmiths, pewterers, tinkers – cannot be readily explained. Perhaps unfree craftsmen, not incorporated in guilds, had such low status in the burgh community that their losses were beneath notice.

The town of Elgin – and indeed most royal burghs – was presbyterian and staunchly committed to the covenants. A protestant work ethic, reinforced by burghal instincts of frugality, self-discipline and self-government possibly meant that burgh merchants and craftsmen were naturally inclined towards muscularly radical presbyterianism and the representative institutions of the Calvinist kirk. Kirk session and town council worked in tandem to regulate burghal affairs. Service on the kirk session seemed a natural extension of service on the town council, and a convenient method of enhancing influence within the community. In most burghs, town councillors also sat on the kirk session. The leading names among the Depositions' claimants were members both of the session and town council. Elgin burgesses and Moray landowners were enthusiastic opponents of Charles I's religious reforms. Leaders of Elgin society 'entered into the Covenant with alacrity' and ordinary folk followed their betters.[16] On 30 April 1638:

the haill people was convened: Mr Andrew Cant stood up in the reader's desk, and made some little speech; therafter the provost, baillies, council and community altogether subscribed this covenant, very few refusing[17]

In the wider arena of the Province of Moray, Brodie lairds of Brodie and Lethen, Grant of Grant, Dunbar of Westfield, hereditary sheriff of the shire of Elgin, Innes of Innes, Hay of Lochloy, Kinnaird of Culbin, Rose of Kilravock and 'many other gentlemen of quality, the whole landed interests of Nairn and Moray, with few exceptions, signed the Covenant'.[18] The signatories, did not, of course, include the peasantry. Though many peasants could read and make a mark on a document – and also entertain an opinion on the religious and political issues of the day – their subscriptions were not required. Presumably rural tenants could be expected to follow their own self-interest in following their lairds. Nor did the 'haill people' include more than a handful of the most prominent women and probably none of the mass of labourers, servants and children who made up the burgh population.

Representatives from the province of Moray attended as deputies at the historic meeting of the General Assembly of the kirk at Glasgow in 1638. Elgin town council appointed bailie Robert Hardie as 'commissioner for this burghe of Elgin to pass to Glasgow again the 21 of November nixt to the General Assemblie'.[19] This assembly marked a watershed in the relationship between covenanters and the King: neither side was inclined to compromise and so war was inevitable. The General Assembly embraced the Covenant and proceeded to abolish '*Yooleday*, and Saints dayes … superstition and idolatrie … bone-fires, singing Carols' and especially all the 'practice of novations introduced in the worship of God', professing that:

> *We willingly agree in our conscience to the form of religion, of a long time openly professed by the kings majestie, and Whole body of this Realme in equal points, as unto Gods undoubted truth and verity, grounded upon his written word, and therefore abhor and detest all contrary religion and doctrine, but chiefly all kinde of papistrie*[20]

The General Assembly reconvened at Aberdeen on 28 July 1640. Delegates from Elgin and Moray joined in passing an 'Act anent the demolishing of Idolatrous Monuments', especially in the north of the country:

> many Idolatrous Monumants, erected and made for Religious worship, are yet extant, Such as Crucifixes, Images of Christ, Mary and Saints departed, ordaines the saids Monuments to be taken down, demolished, and destroyed, and that wtth all convenient diligence[21]

Moray covenanters took the Act to heart, though it was several months before they could organise the positive action that was required. The matter was discussed by the Elgin presbytery in September 1640,[22] and the parish minister was authorised to consult with the Earl of Moray. Perhaps there was a purpose in this delay and Elgin's covenanting hardliners timed their actions to have the added force of being taken during the despised and superstitious festival of Christmas. At all events, on 28 December 1640, in zealous obedience to the General Assembly's instruction, Alexander Brodie of Brodie went with his brother-in-law, the young Laird of Innes, and Gilbert Ross, Minister of Elgin, to the cathedral church.

The Lantern of the North (stripped of its lead roofing in 1567-8) was semi-derelict but nonetheless imposing, its presence and mouldering fixtures and fittings a chafing reminder of superstitious pre-reformation reverence. Brodie, Innes and the Minister arrived with a gang of workmen, probably pausing for prayers: Mr Ross's peroration perhaps inspired by 2 Chronicles 23:16-7:

> And Jehoiada made a covenant between him, and between all the people, and between the king, that they should be the Lord's people. Then all the people went to the house of Baal, and brake it down, and brake his altars and his images in pieces, and slew Mattan the priest of Baal before the altars

before the men stripped off their coats and set to work. The Minister and lairds would have watched with a grim satisfaction as the labourers tore down and dismembered the rood screen. Medievally this substantial decorated timber structure had supported a carved rood (from the Old-English *rod* meaning 'cross') – a calvary of Christ crucified, flanked by saints. The rood had long since been removed, but the screen remained as a hateful reminder of times when priests celebrated masses in the chancel, separated – indeed, all but hidden – from the people who congregated in the nave as scarcely more than spectators in the mystery of divine worship. Elgin's cathedral rood screen was also (despite neglect and exposure to the elements) covered with idolatrous images, including a conventional medieval doom. One side was: 'painted in excellent colours illuminated with stars of bright gold, the crucifixion of our blessed Saviour Lord Jesus ... on the other ... was drawn the day of judgement'.[23] No strict presbyterian could tolerate such things, and furthermore, the gilded screen was a continual temptation to idolaters and backsliders, who still crept guiltily into the mouldering relic of the cathedral for private prayer. Thus the screen was demolished. The wooden frames were dismembered and cut up for firewood; though legend insists that the sacred timber declined to burn in Gilbert Ross's presbyterian hearth.

This act of covenanting iconoclasm was punished with a response in kind (though not in scale) from Montrose when he occupied the burgh in February 1645. Royalist soldiers sacked the parish church of St Giles, though in a strict presbyterian place of worship there was little of monetary value to be looted. The Elgin Depositions recorded:

> Thair silver boulis for the Communione plundered Tuo Brasin Candill stick stickes within the kirk torin & pitifullie brokin The pulpitt robbed of a new grein cloth & many wther Sacriliges comitted[24]

During the autumn of 1643 the Solemn League and Covenant was agreed, bringing Scotland fully into the civil war on the side of the English parliament. On 11 October 1643, the kirk ordered all ministers to subscribe the Solemn League and Covenant. By Sunday 5 November 1643, parish elders had read a copy of the new covenant and were meeting with the Minister of Elgin to discuss the matter. All signed and agreed that the following Sunday should be 'a fast and that the whole parroch should sweare and subscrywe the League and Covenant'. On Sunday 12 November 1643 'the persone preached, whilk day the people, both men and woman, did swear and subscrywe the League and Covenant'.[25] Of course, it remains a matter for debate how many of the two or 3,000 adults in the parish actually subscribed the document, but clearly everyone who mattered signed – and signed with willing enthusiasm.

Elgin's enthusiasm for the Covenant cannot be doubted. The townsfolk refused to sign the Kilcumin bond when Montrose offered it – even though the town was at the mercy of MacColla's catholic Irish and savage highlanders. The leading burgh notary (and three-times provost) Mr John Hay, suffered 'grievous outrages and threatning reproachis … for not zeilding to subscryve ane paper [presumably the Kilcumin bond] … full of proud and reproachfull expressions … derogatorie of his oath of Covenant'.[26] The community followed Hay's steadfast example, preferring (after a little haggling) to pay a swingeing fine of 'Tuo Thousand thrie hundredth pund' in order 'to saiff our selffis from periurue being cruellie assalted to Subscryve a wreitt [the Kilcumin Bond] quhilk in effect was the Renunceing of our covenant'.[27] For burgesses, whose primary concern was making money, to part with it in payment of a fine rather than renounce the covenants, is surely evidence of sincere religious and political commitment. On the other hand, the money collected from individual townsfolk for this purpose was probably (like the 2,000 merks ransom paid to prevent Montrose burning the burgh and committing 'the inhabitantes to the mercie of his sojoris')[28] deemed a loan by individuals to the burgh, which the town council would repay when parliament reimbursed the community's losses.

The plundering of 1645-6 seems not to have dampened Elgin's ardour for the covenants. The town dutifully opposed the engagement with Charles I. This secret agreement was reached in December 1647 between moderate Scottish presbyterians and the King, who was by then a prisoner of the English parliament. The engagers' hopes of securing Charles I's freedom were crushed when their Scottish army was defeated at Preston in July 1648. Elgin declared unequivocal support for the kirk party against the engagers, though not until the engagement was clearly a lost cause. King Charles I was beheaded on 30 January 1649. In March 1649, Elgin kirk session ordered:

> all sojors of the late wnlawfull engadgment to be taken wp the nixt Fryday that they may confess their error and be received that they may have libertie to receive the Sacrament of the Lords Supper[29]

The following Friday the soldiers duly confessed their sin before the congregation and were then obliged to sign or make their marks upon a copy of the Solemn League and Covenant.

But even as they did so the cause of the covenants was lost. There would be further fighting, but not directly affecting the burgh of Elgin. Moray did, however, enjoy a further fleeting prominence. Brodie of Brodie was one of the commissioners who negotiated the return of the late King's son, the future Charles II. Brodie joined with gusto in bullying the heir to the Stuart crowns into signing the covenants. When Charles arrived on 23 June 1650 to claim his crown, he landed at Elgin's port of Garmouth at the mouth of the River Spey. Here the prince was greeted by old Sir Robert Innes (proprietor of the town) and his wife Grizzel Stuart. Charles dined in Innes's house at Garmouth, but he did not stay. He hurried southwards to Scone to be crowned by the covenanting Marquis of Argyll.

The sequel is well known. Charles's Scottish armies were crushed at Dunbar and Worcester and the King fled into exile. Scotland was embraced into the republican Commonwealth. Elgin played no significant part in these events – unless perhaps one or two Elgin men fought and died anonymously among the bristling pikes for Charles Stewart and 4s. (Scots) a day. The burgh played host to Crowellian soldiers during 1652. The behaviour of this force was copiously deplored in kirk session records.[30] Of course, there could be little objection to the stabling of the Commonwealth's cavalry horses in the cathedral, but the quakerish theological errors of the independents (baptists, anabaptists, fifth monarchists, millenarians, and old-style ranters and levellers) who filled the ranks of Cromwell's army, were deeply offensive to presbyterian sensibilities. The soldiers did not come for plunder, but, in between indulging a penchant for theological debate, the soldiers found, it seems, that Elgin quines offered one thing they did lack and (more alarmingly) vice versa.

Chapter 3

Waisted and Plundered All Within

Montrose and MacColla led King Charles's Scottish army into Elgin for the first time on 19 February 1645; on this the historians all agree. Among 17th-century commentators, George Wishart does not mention any plundering of Elgin in his *Memoirs of the … Marquis of Montrose* and Patrick Gordon, in his *Short Abridgement of Britane's Distemper*, does not mention Elgin at all. Both writers were royalists and so, perhaps, likely to understate the misery that the King's forces inflicted on his subjects. However, a third contemporary commentator, John Spalding, in his *History of the Troubles … in the Reign of Charles I* asserted that Montrose's soldiers 'plundered the town pitifully, and left nothing tursable uncarried away'.[1] But none of these writers travelled with the army. Their accounts are second-hand at best and always tainted by the political partiality of royalist sympathies.

The Elgin Depositions are the only first-hand account to have come down to us. Each claim represents an eye-witness account. In each claim, Elgin residents who watched the various armies arrive made declarations by 'great aith Solemnelie Suorne' as to what the soldiers did. In front of witnesses, each claimant did 'depone and declair' regarding losses sustained at the hands of the 'comonn enemie' and sometimes also from the depredations of friendly forces. The Elgin Depositions record the individual and communal sufferings of the royal burgh.

According to The Elgin Depositions:

> Wpon the Nyntein Day of Februar j^m vj^c fourtie five zeiris enterit Iames grahame sumtyme Erle of Montroise and … they … plunderit waistit & maid desloate the said Toune of elgin for the space of Ellewin Dayes[2]

Montrose threatened the town and its inhabitants. In the words of the Depositions, the Marquis threatened 'to burne the said burghe and to kill themselves'. In order to 'save the toun unburnt' – and to spare the people from the fate which their cousins in Aberdeen suffered when MacColla's Irishes were unleashed – Elgin paid a ransom. John Spalding believed that the sum exacted was 'four thousand merks' (£2666 13s. 4d.).[3] The Elgin Depositions contain a neat vignette of the negotiation that led to a settlement satisfactory to all. First, Montrose demanded the impossible sum of 10, 000 merks. Then the Lord Gordon appeared, pretending to be Elgin's friend. He suggested that the Marquis might be persuaded to accept a lower figure – say 2,000 merks. Most of the town council was unavailable. The senior councillors were defying the common enemy from the battlements of Spynie castle but enough influential burgesses remained for a negotiation to take place. Haggling came naturally to Elgin merchants; and a bargain was struck:

> Mair when the Enemie had waisted & plundered all within the toun the said Iames grahame callit for theis of best qualitie within the toune fewe of the magistrates and counsel being at home And chairgit them to ransome the toune at Ten Thowsand markis of else he wold burne the toun & comitt the inhabitantes to the mercie of his sojors quhilk he haid not faillit to hawe Done wnlese the wmquhill lord gordon advysit them that was at home to Schift Tuo Thowsand markis quhilk they war forcit to Borrowe & pay it to montroise[4]

Two thousand merks was worth £1,333 6s. 8d. How such a sum was raised after the town had been comprehensively plundered is something of a mystery. Of course, the canny folk who paid this protection money ensured that the payment was characterised as a loan – a debt which the town was expected to honour.

A further sum of £2,300 was extorted as Montrose perceived that Elgin burgesses were cleverer at hiding their silver than his soldiers were at finding it. A few well-targeted threats and arrests, however, – 'committing greivous outrages againes the magistratis & tounes people setting guairdis about them and threatning them with Imprissonment'[5] – were enough to send the fearful burgh folk scurrying to retrieve their cash from its hiding-places. The sum of £2,300 included, it seems, payment in lieu of signing the Kilcumin bond. Clearly the royalist commanders might, in some circumstances, put money before principle.

The community of Elgin claimed further losses totalling £1,800. The detail of this does not survive, though encompassed in the figure was the cost of quarters for the Gordons. Montrose also received 'moneyes Pretending leavies of hors & foott for the kingis service';[6] although whether any Elgin folk went as foot soldiers and troopers in the royal army is not recorded.

A niggling £20 was claimed for the cost of accommodating forced labour gangs brought in to work on the Gordons' siege works at Spynie. These 'poor Peopill', numbering 'Towardis ane hundreth men' stayed but a single night in Elgin, 'finding cauld intertainment'[7] as they were snubbed for their complicity – albeit unwilling – in Huntly's military operations. A significant element among the labourers was conscripted from Rothes in a measured reprisal for the covenanting zeal of the late 6th Earl of Rothes, John Leslie, who had died in 1641. By imperiously commanding the tenandry of the teenage 7th Earl (also John Leslie), Huntly affirmed the extension of Gordon influence into the fertile and prosperous covenanter territory of Lower Strathspey – and incidentally taunted the young Earl's powerful tutor, Archibald Campbell, Marquis of Argyll.

The surviving portion of the roll of The Elgin Depositions preserves claims by 202 individuals. Part of a final leaf (containing probably some half-dozen further claims) is certainly lost, as is an initial leaf (or leaves). Quite properly, leading burgesses head the list. Thus the first claimant is Johne Mylne, with his son James. Mylne was one of the Rhynie murderers, and his house was probably burnt. The portion of Mylne's claim that survives at the head of the roll of Depositions includes the loss of two fine horses worth £40 each, and a third horse belonging to his son which, with four head of cattle, was valued at £33 6s. 8d. (100 merks). Mylne's total claim was for 'Thrie Thowsand Tuo hundreth fourscoir pund ellevin schillingis four penneyes' (£3,280 11s. 4d.).

All claimants swore similar oaths, confirmed by the evidence of reliable witnesses, typically wives and servants. Independent witnesses were called to confirm claims in respect of livestock. Robert Dunbar, merchant, burgess of Elgin (claim 10) swore:

> that according to his avine certane knowledge and by sure Informatione of his wyff and servantis Thair was plunderit and takin avay from him be The comonn Enemie furth of his houssis buiths barnes cornzeaird and Sellar in the monethis of februarij and maij 1645 and in winter last when the gordones lay in murray of Insicht plenissing cloithes abuilziementis merchand wares wynes

> cornes wictuall moneyes houshold provisione and wtheris of that natur with plenissing broken and maid wnvsefull with fywe head of goodis pryce ane hundreth markis with ane cow with calff hoysit be the Enemie pryce – 22 lib' with sex peice of hors pryce – 186 lib' 13s 4d all plunderit and avay Takin from him be the Comon enemie …
>
> Extending the said Robert dunbar his loissis … To the soume of ane Thowsand Four hundreth Sextein pundis ellewin shillingis four penneyes [£1416 11s. 4d.]

A more modest and typical claim was made by Johne Andersone, merchant burgess of Elgin (claim 191):

> being deiplie suorne deponit that ther vas plunderit from him be the comon enemie in febraurij and maij 1645 and sincesyne of merchand wares Insicht plenisching money cold cunziet and wncunziet armor Insicht plenisching wictuall houshold provisione and wtheris of that kynd conforme to the particular [compt] giwin in theranent
>
> extending the said Iohne andersone his loissis to tua hundrethe thrie scoir sex pund [£266]

The smallest of burgh claims were for a few pounds-worth of household goods. James Matineasker in Elgin (claim 85), who had neither wife nor servants to confirm his oath, deponed:

> that ther was plunderit and avay takin from him be the comon enemie the tymes forsaidis of Insicht plenisching wictuall houshold provisione and wtheris of that kynd abowvrittin conforme to the particular compt
>
> Extending the said Iames matineasker his loissis abowwrittin to nyntein pundis money [£19]

The bureaucratic formula of the Depositions includes a reference to a 'particular compt'. This detailed account presumably itemised in detail the articles lost, giving also, perhaps, the weight and volume of victual and other foodstuff plundered and the composition, quantity and quality of trade goods taken away. Thus the commissioners might have accumulated in the course of compiling The Elgin Depositions, files of evidential papers (subscribed oaths, vouchers, declarations, correspondence) relating to each of the claimants. This supporting paperwork, however, has not survived. It was probably disposed of by the commissioners' clerks after it had served its purpose when the final version of the Depositions was complete.

Fourteen deponents claimed for the loss of gold and silver, coin (cunziet) and plate (uncunziet). Christane Kar, widow of Mr Dauid Philpe, Minister at Elgin (claim 161), uniquely, claimed for 'silver wark'. Christane's collection presumably included cups, dishes, spoons, candlesticks and perhaps items of jewellery. Some of this silverware may have been medieval church plate deconsecrated or remodelled for domestic use since the reformation.

With plenty of warning of Montrose's advance (in February if not in May), much of the burgh's gold and silver must have been safely hidden by the time the royalists arrived. It was usual to bury valuables in troubled times. Samuel Pepys famously recorded the interment of his office files, wine and other prized possessions in the face of danger from the great fire of London:

> 4th Sept. 1666. Sir W. Batten … did dig a pit in the garden … and I took the opportunity of laying all the papers of my office that I could not otherwise dispose of. And in the evening Sir W. Pen and I did dig another, and put our wine in it; and I my parmazan cheese, as well as my wine and some other things[8]

Elgin folk were probably just as clever in hiding their valuables: burying them in their roods, beneath the dunghill or in the pigstye; concealing them in secret crannies within the house or below the flagstones and cobbles of the floor, and yet, if the Depositions' claims are believed, the pillaging parties of enemy soldiers comprehensively looted the town of its domestic treasures. Or were the burgesses lying when they claimed that their silver and gold had been stolen? Who has not been tempted to gild the lily when compiling a compensation claim? Presumably some destruction of timber plenishing, wainscots, spars, deals and weirs, was the result of searches by MacColla's men and the Gordons for hidden money and plate. So too was damage to 'bandis of dores lockis and keyis taken away'. Perhaps indeed, the extent of losses of gold and silver was less a measure of an individual's wealth than of his adeptness at hiding his treasures.

When Samuel Pepys came to exhume his buried gold in October 1667 he was dismayed to find that:

> upon my lifting up the earth with the spudd, I did discern that I had scattered the peices of gold round about the ground among the grass and loose earth … I perceived the earth was got among the gold, and wet, so that the bags were all rotten … then W. Hewer and I, with pails and a seive, did … gather all the earth about the place into pails, and then sift those pails … just as they do for dyamonds.[9]

Similar scenes were probably played out in the privacy of the roods behind more than one high-street house when the soldiers at last left Elgin in 1646. Perhaps there are hoards beneath the floors of shops and houses in Elgin's burgh closes still waiting to be recovered.

The Elgin Depositions record that 92 households were plundered of arms or armour. Weapons and armour were taken to re-supply the Irish regiments and to equip the Gordon and highland levies; and confiscated simply to disarm the town. Armour was an expensive luxury, and while some townsfolk had loaned muskets, bandoliers, pikes and swords for the public good, none of the armour-owning class in Elgin was, it seems, willing to lend helmets and breastplates to equip the town's trained band. The Depositions record the losses of the town's armourer, John Alpein (claim 89), who claimed for goods worth a modest £302 3s. 4d.; while the burgh's gunsmith, David Mailling (claim 39) swore to losses worth £178 9s. 4d. Clearly neither craftsman held a large stock in his workshop. Presumably Alpein and Mailling made their livings chiefly by repairing and maintaining townsfolk's guns and armour, rather than from the more skilled and capital-intensive business of manufacturing new firearms and armour from raw metal.

The language and timbre of the Depositions change according to circumstance. Thus Montrose and the Gordons 'plunder'; covenanter forces merely 'take':

> Followis the loissis off horssis meares lambes wedderis and oxin Taken by argylls Troupers from the said robert gibsone and be the Comonn Enemie plunderit be them in februarij and maij 1645 (claim 6)

There is an explanatory and forgiving tone to depositions concerning actions by parliamentary soldiers:

> Wpon The aucht day of maij I^{m}vj^c fourtie Sex zeiris when general major middleton Came to relieve the seidge of Innernes of whois forces Thair was quarterit in Elgin Aucht hundreth or theirby for

ane nicht And when they returnit againe Four hundreth of his forces quarterit at Elgin Tua Dayes and tua nichtis And the reason that the quarter maisteris gave not tickettis conforme was the suddaine allarme of aberdein the expenssis heirof

Extending to the Soume of Ane Thousand pund [£1000][10]

The word 'plunder' was a new addition to popular vocabulary in the covenanter era. Previous generations might have spoken of rapine, pillage and sack; but in 1646 the new coining 'plunder' had eclipsed the old familiar words. 'Plunder' is first recorded in English in 1632, having entered the language in the context of the European wars of Gustavus Adolphus, King of Sweden. It seems possible that the word was imported directly into Scotland by Scottish soldiers who fought in the Swedish army and returned home to fight for the Covenant. It seems that clerks and claimants of the Depositions found conventional language insufficient to express the enormity of what had happened to Elgin and its sister burghs; a new word was required. The novelty of the word 'plunder' seems to be reflected in the relish with which it is used and reiterated in the course of The Elgin Depositions.

The claim that 'all within the toune' had been 'waisted and plundered' is probably an exaggeration. Other towns, notably Cullen, were indeed pillaged and put to the torch; but not Elgin. In other burghs, such as Aberdeen, there was significant loss of life; but not in Elgin. Furthermore, the 1646 stent roll for Elgin, which names the 215 individual burgh property-owners who were liable for local taxation (ultimately to maintain the covenanting armies), includes 89 names that do not appear as claimants in The Elgin Depositions. Clearly not everyone within the town claimed for losses. Poor folk, it is true, possessed little that was worth claiming for and were in any case beneath notice. The stented townsfolk, however, owned houses stocked with the usual plenishing and furniture as well as foodstuffs, clothing, arms and abulziements, with horses, milch cows, pigs, peat and chickens in the rood. This was all worth plundering – and there for the taking. Yet, it seems, many Elgin folk escaped the depredations of the common enemy; or at least they were willing to bear their losses without claiming compensation.

These fortunate individuals included property-owners from all levels. For example, Iohn Mcrae was a webster, assessed on the stent roll for the minimum amount of 3s., but not included among the Depositions' claimants. At the other end of the scale was the Laird of Pluscarden, with an assessment of 36s. He too made no claim – but of course Thomas Mackenzie of Pluscarden signed the Kilcumin bond.[11]

It is not clear how Elgin's fifth column of closet royalists signalled their allegiance and so protected their property when the common enemy entered the town bent on plunder. Was there a pre-arranged signal? Perhaps, imitating the Israelites, Elgin royalists painted their door cheeks, so that 'the Lord will pass over the door, and will not suffer the destroyer to come in unto your houses to smite you' (Exodus 12:23). Maybe the plundering was a careful and discriminating process, executed under military discipline, rather than an indiscriminate free-for-all of looting and wanton vandalism. Alternatively, everyone was plundered, but only a few merited compensation from parliament and inclusion on the roll of honour. Certainly the commissioners appointed to investigate losses were charged to take notice of the 'carriage and deservings' of those who made claims.[12] Perhaps then, the names missing from The Elgin Depositions are those of Elgin's unrepentant royalist sympathisers: the men who had thrown open the burgh ports to admit Montrose's army; men whose sufferings were a divine punishment rather than a crown of glory; men (and women) who did not deserve the immortality of inclusion on the great roll.

During Montrose's first visit to Elgin in February 1645, there was plundering but no burning. In May 1645, when Montose returned victorious from the battle of Auldearn, the houses of those suspected of murdering James Gordon of Rhynie were fired:

> because his son gave orders to kill James Gordon of Rhynie; Walter Smith's house, John Milne's house, Mr John Douglas' house of Murrieston, Alexander Douglas' house, all in Elgin were burnt, because some of themselves and some of their sons were at the killing[13]

It is not known how the culprits were identified. They might have been betrayed by Elgin royalists or by neighbours with undocumented grudges. At all events, the Depositions do not protest the innocence of these four prominent burgesses and their sons. Walter Smith, messenger, burgess (claim 150) lost:

> ane fair Luidging of thrie househight with wtterland and Inner Land brunt to him be montrois armie in maij 1645 becaus his sone wes capitanne of spynie …
>
> Extending to tua thousand thrie hundrethe threttie thrie pund 6s 8d [3500 merks, £2333 6s. 8d.]

The flames spread to neighbouring properties (and adjacent claimants). Christane Clerk (claim 149) lost her:

> Ludging of thrie hous height withe the Inner Land therof brunt to hir be montrois armie in maij 1645 the lois quherof with hir timber plenisching
>
> Extending to the soume of aucht hundrethe pundis money [£800]

Walter Smith's neighbour on the other side was a young man named Hew Sutherland (claim 151). Sutherland was identified as an indweller rather than a property owner or burgess – perhaps because he was a minor (under the age of 21) – but the conflagration was no respecter of youth or innocence; Sutherland was represented before the commissioners by the 'provest and bailzies' who:

> being suorne deponit that ther was ane pairt of ane hous of his brunt in elgin be montrois armie in maij 1645 with ane great pairt of his plenisching the loissis wherof
>
> Extending to ane hundreth thrie score pundis [£160]

The fires spread no further than the immediately adjacent feus. This suggests that Elgin was a well-built town whose houses were constructed from fireproof masonry with roof coverings for the most part of slate or stone tiles, rather than flammable thatch. In medieval towns the fire risk of thatched roofs was tackled with local statutes prohibiting its use and obliging builders to use slate or tile. Bylaws, however, were routinely flouted, and despite building regulations London was burnt in 1666; and less famously, Warwick in 1694. An Elgin bylaw of 16 November 1747 declared:

> That Whereas the Statutes formerly made for preventing fires have hitherto proven ineffectual … in all time coming no house shall be thatched withheather within this Burgh under penalty of Fifty pounds Scots money[14]

Elgin folk may well have thanked providence for preserving their town from a conflagration in 1645. The royalist historian Patrick Gordon, described the Irish soldiers led by Alasdair MacColla as:

> too cruell; for eueriewhere obserued they did ordinarely kill all they could maister of, without any motion of pitie, or any consideration of humanitie … and they were also, without all shame, most brutishlie giuen to vncleannes and filthie lust … there was no limites to their beastly appetites[15]

If Gordon's report was accurate, the Irish regiments were guilty of serious breaches of codes of conduct which had been long accepted if not always scrupulously observed in times of war. The Dominican scholar Francisco de Vittoria (*c*.1483-1546) advised that it was wrong to kill women, children 'harmless agricultural folk' and the 'peaceable civilian population'. Martin Luther, who declared it 'both Christian and an act of love to kill an enemy … to plunder and burn and injure him', added a caveat '… except that one must beware of sin, and not violate wives and virgins'.[16] Catholic moralists and soldiers might have embraced this view without compromising their faith, but codes of war are not readily enforced in the field, and theoretical moral codes are readily forgot in the heat of the moment; especially in civil wars and religious conflicts in which the enemy is an apostate or a detested neighbour.; and so Aberdeen was sacked and ravaged by MacColla's Irish soldiery.

There is little evidence, however, that MacColla's Irish regulars and highlanders (nor even the Gordons) behaved improperly by mistreating civilians (beyond threats and thefts) while in Elgin. The Elgin Depositions record only one act of personal violence – and this is included almost as an afterthought or incidental detail to claim 157:

> Followes the loissis of kathrein Annand relict of wmquhill Alexander Russell merchand burges of elgin who was Pittifullie murderit be Iames graham his armie goeing to Spynie in maij 1645

Nothing more is known of Alexander Russell's murder for the killing is not documented elsewhere.

The mass of poor unfreemen who made up the burgh population fell beneath the commissioners' notice because the main concern of The Elgin Depositions was financial. If the burgh's poor were mistreated, this is nowhere reported. Even the kirk session minutes are silent, recording none of the assaults, rapes, adulteries, fornication, prostitution, drunkenness and bastardy among working people that might be expected during a period of military occupation (and which was copiously deplored when the Commonwealth army visited the town in 1652). Perhaps the Irish soldiers' wives who travelled with the army reined in their menfolk, or maybe the burgh poor were simply not troubled by the common enemy. On the other hand, the burgh poor did not strictly belong to the burgh community which, properly, comprised only burgesses with full burghal freedom, and so, perhaps, the plundering of the burgh poor was of no account; the burgh poor simply did not matter.

It is extremely difficult to recover the authentic voices of ordinary working people. The burgesses and craftsmen speak clearly through the Depositions, albeit in voices modulated by the bureaucratic filter of the clerks' bland formulary. Ordinary folk are all but mute. A few humble husbandmen peer through, for example Patrick Grant, tenant in Mosstowie (claim 147), whose plundered household contents were valued at just £4 (Scots), but the burgh's tenants at Mosstowie are the only rural folk mentioned. Some of these, indeed, were men to be reckoned with – John Gordon in Mosstowie (claim 141) lost:

insicht plenissing cloithes abuilziementis money armor cornes wictual housholdi provisione …
with four scoir aucht head of sheip … ane meir …with whter tuo meiris … aucht head of goodis

Extending … to vjiij^{c}xij lib' viijd [£812 0s. 8d.]

Ordinary peasant husbandmen – such as the tenants who cultivated burgess's strips on the arable acres of common good lands – were not noticed, their losses were irrelevant. This is not unexpected: when Brodie of Lethen claimed from parliament for the loss of 'Eight hundreth oxin and kyne Eightene hundreth scheepe and goats two hundreth horses and meares' and the burning of standing crops, all was lamented as his own personal loss.[17] Brodie did not mention the peasant tenants to whom the cattle and crops directly belonged – and for whom the loss meant starvation. Similarly, burgh labourers and journeymen are invisible in the Depositions. Claimants' servants peep namelessly into the record only in the common-form 'by sure informatione of his … servantis' when dutifully giving oaths to confirm their masters' testimony. Presumably servants were plundered when their masters' houses were looted. The spare clothing and carefully hoarded cash that a servant lost may have represented his or her whole worldly goods, but that was not the commissioners' concern. If servants wanted compensation, they could always petition their masters.

Women too, for the most part, merely peep into the margins of The Elgin Depositions in the formula 'by sure Informatione of his wyiffe', confirming their husbands' claims. Thirty-seven women were mentioned by name; nine were widows, giving testimony as the relict of a plundered spouse. The losses of John Chalmer younger, skinner, burgess (claim 187) were 'givin wp be Elspet Chalmer his spous himselfe being from home'. Issobel Thayne (claim 9) appeared before the commissioners, 'hir husband being sick':

> sche by hir great aythe Solemlie suorne did depone and declair That acording to hir knowledge and by sure Informatione of hir husband and servantis Thair wes plunderit and takin avay fra theimm be the comonn enemie furth of thair houssis and buithis in elgin in the monethis of februarij and maij 1645 and at diverse tymes thairefter of Insicht plenisching cloithis abuilziementis merchand wares cornes wictuall armour household provisione …
>
> … that thair wes plunderit and away takin from thame ane hors … pryce ane hundrethe pundis money with ane wther hors plunderit be Lord Lues gordones men in winter Last pryce tuantie pundis money

Twenty-six women among the deponents were independent claimants. Issobell Forbes (claim 185) suffered collateral damage as a result of punitive burnings. She presumably did not own the dwelling she lived in, and so made no claim in respect of lost plenishings, which belonged to her landlord:

> the said Issobell being Deiplie suorne Deponit that ther was from hir … of Insicht money cloithes wictual household provisione & loissis be the burning of robert gibsones hous …

Extending the said Issobell forbes hir loissis to j^{c}iiij^{xx} lib' j s iiij d [£180 1s. 4d.]

Elgin's independent females ranged from the wealthy liferentix Christane Clerk (claim 149) to more humble women with no specific status, such as Elspet Gibsone (claim 105). Elspet was by no means the poorest, even of Elgin's property owners, with a tenement assessed in the stent roll at 7s. She was plundered of:

insicht plenissing cloithes abuilziementis wictuall money houshold provisione and wtheris of that kynd …

Extending … to iiij^{xx}9 lib' [£89]

Mariore Cuming, indweller (claim 201) was assessed in the stent roll 'for the land' at 8s.[18] She seems to have moved out of her own home following the February occupation of the burgh, and moved into Christane Clerk's three-storeyed lodging – a flitting she soon regretted. Mariorie moved in with a large cartload of possessions. Her losses were considerable:

the said mariore cuming being deiplie suorne deponit that ther was plunderit from hir be … montrois armie in februarij 1645 and be the burning of christane clerkis hous quherin sho duelt in maij therefter quhen they cam from auldearin of Insicht plenisching wictuall money airmes cloithes houshold provisione …

extending … hir loissis to sex hundreth tua pund iiij s [£602 11s. 0d.]

Mariore's case confirms that the initial plundering of February 1645 was less than comprehensive. Plenty remained for the army to take away when it returned in May, and for the Gordons to pillage in December.

Margaret Duncane (claim 154) does not appear on the stent roll. She lodged one of the smaller claims. Margaret lived beyond the burgh boundary in Oldmills, where she was possessed of a property that gave her an income and independence (and a status that merited the commissioners' notice) above that enjoyed by most 17th-century women:

margaret Duncane … Deponit That ther was plunderit from hir … of insicht plenissing cloithes abuilziementis wictuall money houshold provisione …

Extending … to thriescoir fyftein lib' 3s [£75 3s. 0d.]

The status of Christen Warden (claim 102) is noteworthy. The claim concerned 'the loissis of alexander Russell stabler in elgin and christen warden his spous'. However, only Christen was sworn to depone concerning losses and her deposition total contains no mention of Alexander Russell: 'Extending the said Christen wardene hir loissis abouwritin to fourscoir aucht pundis money' (£88). Similarly, Issobell Hardie, spouse to George Forsyth (claim 101), seems to have appeared for her husband, and so was credited with the family's joint losses as her own: 'the said Issobel hardie hir loissis abouwritin to threttein pund (£13).

In common with other burghs that the royalists occupied, Elgin was plundered, but arguably the plundering was deliberate and selective. Montrose had three concerns in plundering the burghs: to feed and re-equip his mobile force; to reward his followers (especially the ad-hoc levies of highlanders); and to punish covenanter populations. Arguably, Montrose was justified in expecting burghs to yield up all he required. After all, Montrose operated under a commission issued by Charles I, and the King was still the King. Surely the King's lieutenant-governor and captain-general, the Marquis of Montrose, should have been able to expect loyalty and support from the royal burgh of Elgin. As a royal burgh, Elgin constitutionally owed no allegiance to any lord beneath the king, indeed, the royal burgh owed its privileges and its very existence to the crown.

And yet, Elgin was a community in determined rebellion against the crown. Elgin had willingly embraced the National Covenant in opposition to Charles's religious policy. Elgin had contributed its share of money to parliament's war effort. Elgin folk had subscribed the Solemn League and Covenant and so become allies of the King's rebellious English subjects. Elgin had fulfilled its obligation to provide soldiers for parliament's armies to fight against the King's forces. Elgin had even taken up arms itself, fortifying Spynie castle, equipping a militia and murdering the King's loyal soldier, James Gordon of Rhynie.

Montrose's soldiers took money, gold and silver along with useable and saleable goods, notably textiles and leatherwork. They also took food, including grain and cattle as well as military equipment including armour, weapons and horses. This was nothing more than the parliamentary forces required from the burgh. The plundering perpetrated by the Gordons during their long stay in town during the winter of 1645-6 may have been somewhat more indiscriminate, though the Depositions suggest little distinction between Montrose's exactions and Huntly's. Apologists for the King might argue that plundering by the royalist forces was not malfeasant, but merely the collection of a justifiable mulct or tax. Covenanters might similarly justify parliament's regular demands for men and money – and the obligation to provide quarters to parliament's soldiers on demand (with or without 'tickettis').

Elgin's experience of occupation was not unique. Many burghs, especially in the north, suffered at the hands of Montrose and MacColla. Elgin suffered a good deal less than some. Aberdeen's suffering is well documented. Cullen, allegedly, was razed to the ground: in 1645, Cullen petitioned parliament complaining that 'our haill Toune is laitlie brunt be the enemy and all our goodes spoiled and takine from us So that we are wtterlie herried'.[19] It seems that the people of Elgin, despite a sturdy solidarity with the covenanting cause, got off relatively lightly. Parliament certainly believed so. For example, in March 1647, the list of those declared 'to be frie of the payment of ther proportionall pairtis of the monthlie maintenance for the armie' included Aberdeen, Inverness, Nairn, Forres, Brechin, Cullen, Dornoch and Banff. Elgin, however, was excused only a portion of its contribution: 'Frie of the payment of Fourscore pundis of their maintenance of ane hundereth threttie fyve pundis'.[20] The distressed burghs were granted further exemptions during 1648 and 1649 as parliament recognised the impossibility of enforcing payment and the political cost of alienating loyally covenanted communities by over-strenuous demands for money.

The total cost to the town of the various occupations during 1644-6 – including both communal and individual losses – was 'Ane hundreth fyve Thousand Aucht hundreth fourscoir fourtein pund four schillingis' (£105,894 4s. 0d.). For reasons that are not clear, this total was amended from a sum of perhaps £109,287 11s. 6d.[21] In either case it was a substantial sum. The claim was probably a good deal inflated by exaggeration and over-valuation (just like any other compensation claim) as people translated their sense of outrage into pounds, merks, shilling and pence. Sensible folk, meanwhile, knew that it did not really matter how much (or how little) they claimed. There was no chance that parliament would pay a penny in compensation to ordinary burgh folk; the best that could be hoped for was some relief from the burden of taxation. Of course, if Elgin's claimants gilded the lily a little, that was not necessarily dishonest. A little over-claiming would compensate for emotional distress: God knew what Elgin had suffered; God appreciated how faithful and steadfast Elgin was, and how willing its people were to suffer for their covenants and for the Lord Jesus Christ.

The Irish regiments at the core of the King's Scottish army were experienced professional soldiers, committed to the royalist cause. They were far from home, perhaps conscious too that their cause was doomed and that they had nothing to lose. Later commentators have allowed the horror of particular brutalities to colour their judgement of the whole campaign. On the other hand the liberal (and protestant) sympathies of modern historians have led to serious understatement of ghastly acts perpetrated by parliamentary forces. For instance, captured Irish soldiers (even unarmed men who had honourably surrendered) were routinely shot. There were atrocities on all sides; Spalding and Patrick Gordon were appalled by the 'savage Irishes' capacity for cruelty – and they were royalists. Arguably, atrocities committed by the army of Montrose were deliberate and targeted – though this probably makes the actions more reprehensible than rapine arising from simple indiscipline or the frenzy of battle. The Irish soldiers murdered, raped and pillaged under orders, following their orders with diligent intensity. They sacked Dundee because the town resisted; this was normal within the codes of medieval warfare. The Irish sacked Aberdeen because they were ordered to do so, as a punitive measure following the burgh's murderous breach of parley. Elgin's experience was very different. No rapes were recorded; and only one killing. Even the plundering was disciplined and targeted: on military equipment, foodstuffs and portable saleable goods. Damage to fixtures and fittings was the inevitable concomitant of searches for money to finance the King's war, foraging for firewood, and the casual carelessness of soldiers. The burnings were summary justice in the King's name; the punishment was a good deal less severe than the legal penalty usually paid by rebels and murderers.

    It is unlikely that Montrose's army actually quartered in the town. Doubtless the officers commandeered comfortable billets in the burgh's fair lodgings, but the ordinary soldiers were accommodated in the usual military manner. In order to establish a proper defensive posture and to maintain military discipline, it is most likely that the various regiments were camped extra-murally. There were several eligible sites for military encampments. The cathedral close was eminently suitable for guarding several fords across the River Lossie as well as the eastern approaches to the town. The area was enclosed with defensible walls up to 7ft thick and 12ft high and further protected by a loop of the river. The cathedral itself offered shelter and a focus for assembly. The canons' manses afforded comfortable lodgings for officers. Backing conveniently onto the south wall of the cathedral close, overlooking the east port of the royal burgh, stood the Marquis of Huntly's Elgin townhouse. This, presumably, was where Huntly and his sons set up headquarters, convened councils of war and entertained Montrose and MacColla. This also seems the likeliest setting for negotiations between the occupying forces and representatives of the townsfolk. The next fair lodging in this quarter was a burghal towerhouse belonging to the Laird of Pluscarden, Thomas Mackenzie. This brother of the Earl of Seaforth was no friend of the covenanters (though he too might be flexible in his loyalties as circumstances required). During the occupations of 1645-6, Pluscarden was probably happy to provide bed, board and every facility for officers of Montrose's army and the Strathbogie regiment.

    On the south side of Elgin, the Franciscan convent commanded the road from Speyside. Conventual buildings provided shelter for men and horses; and the derelict remains of the Greyfriars church may once again have witnessed the ancient rites of mass and confession. Adjacent to the Greyfriars, the medieval hospital of Maisondieu offered further accommodation for men, horses and equipment. Beyond the burgh's western boundary rose the towering bulk of the royal castle motte, crowned with substantial remains of the medieval stone keep. From this vantage point soldiers could both observe for the approach of enemies and overawe the burgh in its shadow. The undeveloped bailey area to the south was suitable for tented encampments. Defensible positions established in the remains of the Dominican (Blackfriars) convent on the haugh to the north of the castle accommodated men charged with the defence of the Hangman's Ford across the Lossie. Montrose's men at least were probably not 'Living at Randome'. The Strathbogie regiment and other Gordon forces, which occupied the town as a base from which to besiege Spynie, probably did commandeer dwellings in the burgh. The Gordon occupation was protracted, lasting several months from December 1645 until the spring of 1646, and it may be presumed that they did not live under suburban canvas but made themselves at home in the town.

The Elgin Depositions are a treasury of historical data, contemporary colour and personal experience, but this is not the most important aspect of the documents. The content of The Elgin Depositions is perhaps (and certainly was) less important than the meaning invested in the making and preservation of the roll of sworn testimony. It seems that no other burgh made such a deliberate and stately memorial. The people of Elgin self-consciously created a formal record of their suffering, remembering Isaiah 8:1-2:

> Moreover the Lord said unto me, Take thee a great roll, and write in it with a man's pen … and I took unto me faithful witnesses to record …

James Fraser of Brea, writing a generation later, articulated a sentiment that every Elgin covenanter appreciated: that 'great outward troubles … whether personal or publick quicken and revive our apprehension of eternity'.[22]

Uniquely, it seems, among Scottish royal burghs, Elgin preserved the record of its covenanting credentials and ensured its transmission down the centuries. Other burghs were able to put the past behind them and move on. A few, expecting little in the way of relief, nonetheless went through the motions of petitioning for assistance. For example, when the burgh of Montrose requested aid from the Convention of Royal Burghs, the war-ravaged community's record of sufferings consisted of a half-hearted five-line précis:

> It is evidently knowin that the Laird of drum vith ane vicked crew off the gordones came in Latly to our burgh killed some of our magistrats and vasted our vhoill burgh of all they wer able to transport vith them

> Iames grahame vith his bararous and bloody band Came thrie severall tymes to Monross and took avay that vhich the gordones had Left[23]

Arguably Elgin was compelled to create its own stupendous roll of losses by a collective sense of guilt and shame: guilt concerning the backsliders and closet royalists who had sullied the glory of the covenanted burgh's sufferings; shame that the community's comparatively slender suffering might be seen as evidence of lukewarm commitment to the covenants or a withdrawal of divine favour.

Indeed, Elgin was even passed over by the plague that swept through other towns in the wake of the armies: miraculously spared perhaps; or denied the love-gift of pestilence by an inscrutable providence. Montrose reported its burghal suffering in typical fashion:

> It is veill knowin to the kingdome that the road of the plague off pestilence did Ly this bygone yeir elevin Month vithout intermission in vhich space ther hes bein takin avay vith the violence theroff aboue four hunder and fyftie persones And thes vhom it pleased god to spare of the comon sort hes bein so burdensome to the burgh that it hes broucht sutch ane vnsuportable burding that being ready to sink vnder the weight theroff was Constrained to seik throuch out our province their charity for maintenance of thir puir ones[24]

Elgin's covenanters preserved a record of their sufferings because their royal burgh (and Moray generally) continued in commitment to fundamentalist presbyterianism long after Aberdeen and other communities had reverted to comfortable episcopalianism. James Allan, Moray's last covenanter – who was himself a native of Aberdeenshire – identified precisely the geographical boundary between the covenant and malignant prelacy:

> How soon we passed Spey I looked on all ye countrey befor us twixt that and Dundee as ye Devill's bounds in a speciall manner wherin he reynes with great power without any control[25]

It is surprising that no record of sufferings exists for the Forres division of Moray, though this may be explained by the ordinary vicissitudes of archival practice in the intervening centuries. It is, however, unsurprising that no similar record was created and preserved in northern communities outwith Moray – whose sufferings were deeper than Elgin's, but where commitment to the covenants was, arguably, more shallow and certainly less enduring.

The documents assembled by the Deposition commissioners for the burgh of Elgin were probably never refined into a final short version and despatched to Edinburgh. Certainly no copy is preserved among public records in the National Archives of Scotland. The penultimate version – a précis of sworn statements rendered into manageable common-form – was diligently assembled during the summer of 1646. The individual pages were trimmed and collated, then painstakingly pasted together to form the great roll of The Elgin Depositions.

The roll format is singular. There are no other records in roll format in the Elgin archives; indeed, rolls are very rare among local government records of the 17th century. Rolls were frequently preferred in the Middle Ages for civil, legal and administrative records: and although the codex was preferred for ecclesiastical archives, rolls might have biblical connotations:

> And when I looked, behold, an hand was sent unto me; and lo, a roll of a book was therein; And he spread it before me; and it was written within and without: and there was written therein lamentations, and mourning, and woe (Ezekiel 2:9-10)

Creating a record in roll form was eccentric, but understandable, investing a tedious bureaucratic exercise record with ponderous dignity. The marvellous scroll was enshrined in the burgh cadget. Here it rubbed shoulders with the community's precious ancient charters – preserved as a source of spiritual delight, solace and inspiration for posterity. The careful covenanters responsible for the record of their communal sufferings doubtless shared James Fraser's opinion:

> I have thought the disregarding of the Lord's providences to be one common great sin … All God's ways being wisdom and goodness, are worthy of observation; but especially those wherwith ourselves are exercised[26]

It was usual among 17th-century protestants to make written records of personal sufferings and evidences of divine grace. The Irish Depositions were such a testimony as well as an administrative and judicial record. Quakers are especially noted for their records of sufferings. Individual presbyterians such as Brodie of Brodie kept diaries in which they recorded and analysed the working of divine providence, and Moray nurtured two famous spiritual memoirs to illuminate the canon of Scottish literature, in the autobiographical works of James Fraser of Brea and James Allan. Elgin was in the mainstream of 17th-century culture; and so the ravaged community made a record of its sufferings.

Elgin's pious presbyterians did not seek the applause or reward of contemporaries; though the careless neglect of future generations might sadden the shades of the pious covenanters who, for a brief moment, dominated the burgh's polity. Nonetheless, Elgin's conscientious and zealous soldiers of the Lord rest quietly, lying at peace in the cathedral burying ground and beneath the cobbled plainstones of the high street. They do not care if heedless feet tramp over their graves for they died secure in the knowledge that they did not flinch in the face of the enemy, but performed all that was required of them by the god of the Covenant who was the ultimate judge of their faithfulness. In witness of his lovingkindness the covenanted burgh preserved the record of its triumph for posterity:

> it is well known that the best of God's people have so the praise of ye riches of his free grace marked & recorded his works & wayes of dealling with them – Even as the Lord also has a book of remembrance wherin is recorded (to speak after ye manner of men) any litle thing that by his own grace they do for him (Malachi 3:16); & … for strengthning their faith in a day of tryall[27]

Chapter 4

Tryell and Probatioun

Provenance and history
The early history and full provenance of The Elgin Depositions may be inferred from internal evidence and incidental circumstances.

Paper, ink, palaeography and language all fix the origins of the documents firmly in the mid-17th century.

The content, of course, establishes dates for the composition of The Elgin Depositions. The individual claims (Document A) and the account of the burgh's communal losses (Document B) relate to the occupation of Elgin by detachments of the Marquis of Huntly's Gordons (the Strathbogie regiment) and by elements of Montrose's army 'in the monethis of februarij and maij 1645 and at diverse tymes therefter'. The depositions relating to communal losses also refer to the quarterings and exactions of parliamentary forces in the armies of Argyll and Middleton during 1644-6. An endorsement provides the latest dated reference. This note, concerning Walter Smyth (claim 150), was added on 20 July 1646 – probably after the roll was made up.

The Elgin Depositions were sworn before commissioners appointed by parliament to take evidence on personal hurts and property damage. Parliament recognised that many individuals and communities had been impoverished by quartering, plundering and worse by its own forces as well as by the 'comonn enemie'. Parliament's main concern was to establish the extent of the plundering that had occurred; because many individuals and communities were claiming that, having been plundered, they could no longer afford to pay their dues – especially towards the maintenance of the Scottish army.

The first step in establishing the truth of these claims was the appointment of a 'Committie anent the Loisses' established under an Act of 15 January 1645.[1] An Act of 8 March 1645 charged 'the committie which goes with the Armie eftir due tryell To set downe ane roll or inventar of the particular landes or brughes … totallie Brunt wasted or possessed by the enemy'.[2] On that same day another Act appointed that 'eftire the tryell beis reported to the Committie that goes along with the Armie … the pairties shall have retentione proportionallie of their Loane money According to the quantitie of the skeath proven'.[3] A further commission to evaluate war damage and losses was appointed under an Act of 3 February 1646.[4] A commission 'For tryeing the Landis burnt or waisted be north the water of Tay' followed under an Act of 25 March 1647,[5] and on 11 May 1648 a committee was appointed specifically to investigate 'brunte and waisted landis within the shrefdome and burghis of Elgine and forres'.[6] The records of parliament do not list relevant particular instance papers preserved in connection with the work of these committees.

The 1646 Act established 'ane vniforme way throw the haill kingdome for tryell of Loisses baith be sea and Land That ... course may be taken for their reparatioune'. The commissioners enjoyed a wide remit to investigate losses 'ayther be the enemie or our awne forces'. The tenor and vocabulary of The Elgin Depositions reflect the language of the 1646 Act:

> And for the better clearing of the way of tryell ... that the partie grieved or complaining may prove be sufficient witnesses That he had in his posession Immediatlie befor the enemie come to his ground or hous such guidis and geir as he condiscendis vpon in his Complaint And that the enemie being thair They wer takine away and distroyed be the enemie and wer nevir sene thereftir in these places And for the insight and houshold plenissing and quhatsumevir vther guidis or vtheris wer in the complenaris hous That the servandis of the Complenaris be examined vpon oathe as witnesses theranent as ane adminicle of the probabtion[7]

In Moray, matters came to a head in January 1646 when the 'Heritors and commons of the shyres of Elgin and Nairne' lodged a formal collective protest against an assessment (cess) imposed on the war-ravaged province.[8] This national tax demand (the reason for the creation of burgh stent rolls) arrived while Elgin was still occupied by the Gordons. In a less committed community the assessment might have been a final straw to break the back of support for the covenants and the Scottish parliament's war effort. However, from Moray the response was a wail of despair rather than a roar of anger, which 'vnfoldit in a paper a pairt of the rage of the poor land ... with the wounds sores inieries sufferings necessities and anguish of heart of so many thousands'. Moray's petition spilled with plaintive (sometimes childlike) prolixity over four closely-written pages.

The document was addressed to the lords of council, appealing to their 'Lordships moderation and dew sense of our miseries', and since the civil war was fought by all sides in Scotland in the name of the King, Moray's petitioners also included a loyal reference to 'his hynes favor and Iustice' and to the King's 'proper Inclinatione to Iustice goodnes and compassionn to the people'. The petitioners expressed their satisfaction that, being able to negotiate 'with persones so Intelligent and full of honor', there was no need to 'enforce and strengthen our petition with arguments from commone Iustice, the lawis of god, and the morall bondis, which lye on them that rule over men, the practique of other nations, and reasones of state, compassion and suchlyke'. There is much in this diction that seems to betray the hand of Brodie of Brodie in its drafting. Brodie, of course, had a twofold interest in the matter: firstly he was one of Moray's leading covenanting heritors and chief sufferers; secondly he was numbered among the lords of council. Indeed, Brodie may be obliquely referred to in the penultimate paragraph, which draws attention to 'our ordinarie burtheins wherto some of the honorabll counsell ar not strangers'.

From the first paragraph the petitioners stoically declined to 'so mutch as mentione' their sufferings during 'sevintein yeiris ... of a grievous and bloodie warr, all the spoilings devastationes and burnings', because:

> It is true that the conscience of our dewtie, the hope of some notable and lasting advantage to us, and the generations to come with the daylie expectatione that a short tyme should finishe our troubles, did so animat and beir us upp that for many yeirs (albeit our bowellis wer consumed) yitt as if we had felt no paine we did quyetlie endure the misireis which so many changes did produce untill now the blood and vitall spirits being spent all estates families Incorporations and bodies of the land are deiplie and Irrecoverablie consumed and vorne to nothing, how many hundred of families ar ther within a litle compas (if honor and tendernes did not restraine them) who should willinglie turne ther back vpon all they have and bid farvell to ther native cuntrey And be content that ther acquaintance and dwelling places should know them no more

The writers continued with a doleful description of the heavy burden which the assessment imposed upon a war-weary community impoverished by plundering and quartering. They begged their lordships not to:

> measure our abilitie [to pay the cess] by our fervencie & Zeale in our Vndertaking great things In thir yeirs past. This hath so vasted and consumed the wholl land … Nay could it have bein Imagined our troubles could have runne this length men wold have shrunk and fainted ere they entered upon such difficulties

Inexplicably, no mention was made of the ongoing occupation of Elgin by the Gordons as the plea continued:

> For albeit the one half of the wholl assessments wer dischargit and the coall and candle and bedding with other suchlyke supervenient impositions, yitt (so great extremitie ar we redactit vnto) that we could hardlie subsist vnder the other half of the cesse

Civil war had brought the economy close to collapse, insofar as 'the revenue of Scotland mostlie consisting in cornes that commoditie … being brought to so low a rate it cane affourd us no money wer our extremities never so great & that we should sell att the halfe of the ordinarie availl'. Moreover, in addition to the cost of:

> coale and candle … beidis plaidis and all other domestic necessities … ther is a burdein superaddit wherby the pryces of Importit commodities ar expresselie raised and of native commodities so diminished that it affords no money

The petitioners appealed to history and precedent, naively failing to recognise that the world had changed and modern warfare could be financed only by tapping the resources of the whole country:

> neyther we nor our fathers (since the day that we wer acknowledged among the Nations of the earth) wer ever able to pay so mutch in two yeirs as now we pay in one month. for never did our late Kings or parliaments Raise abowe eight Thousand tuo hundreth pound sterling att once from this wholl nation … Lykas it is veil knowin to all that ar bot Indifferentlie versed in our affaires, that when we wer drawin to warrs our armies wer never Intertained by taxis and subsidies for albeit the people and Inhabitantes grew and wer never so numerous yitt did not our wealth bot we still remained iff not the fewest yitt the poorest of the kingdomes uponn the earth

The petitioners yearned for the time when:

> combustiones ar extinguished [and] we shall … enjoy … the great libertie & freedom which hath so oft bein holdin furth and promised … [when] great things may be done in Britaine as in former ages when Impositiones did not amount to the hundreth part of what we now live under

Finally the petitioners invited their lordships to 'compare our burtheins with any people or nation in Europe and it shalbe found ther is no address lyke ours'; and to look too nearer to home – to Scotland's neighbour and ally who perhaps was not suffering as much or contributing all it might:

> it is manifast that one shyre of England (as to value or revenue) is of more < *blotted word* > then all Scotland our sufferings have been no less then Englands … Nay many in England pay not the tuentie fyftt part of ther estate in assessment yeirlie

The response of the lords of council is not preserved. On 25 August 1646, however, a commission was appointed to take evidence of the losses of the burgh of Forres.[9] The commissioners comprised half-a-dozen west Moray lairds: Patrick Dunbar of Kilbuiack; James Dumbar of Dumphail; Patrick Campbell of Boithe; John Sutherland of Kinsteary; Robert Dumbar of Easter Bin; William Brodie of Tearie; and John Brodie of Woodhead. An Elgin baillie, Nicholas Dumbar, was included to provide a burghal perspective. The text of the Forres commission is reproduced in Appendix 2.

A few months later, on 21 November 1646, a 'Commission for trying the losses of Aberdein', consisting of 20 Aberdeenshire lairds and Aberdeen burgesses, was appointed.[10] The reports of the commissioners, finalised in December 1648, included a catalogue of claims in respect of the quartering of friendly troops and plundering by the enemy. This was followed by 'Compt of losses be sea'. The commissioners smuggled into the list of valuations of cast-away ships and lost cargoes, numerous claims unrelated to the nation's civil wars, including plunder by Dunkirk pirates and even ordinary commercial hazards such as bankruptcy. With these substantial additions a total of £1,582,910 3s. 10d. was claimed.[11]

On 10 December 1646 the names of Brodie of Brodie and John Hay, provost of Elgin, were added to the roll of the parliamentary committee appointed to investigate losses.[12] These appointments presumably gave a sharper focus to Elgin's sufferings. It is likely, however, that (perhaps in swift response to the heritors' petition of January) The Elgin Depositions were already well under way, if not complete, by the close of 1646.

The record of the names of the Elgin commissioners is not preserved. It is likely that Brodie and Hay were preoccupied with national politics and so were not among the commissioners who administered oaths and took evidence in Elgin. The commission comprised a selection of covenanting gentry, chiefly from the eastern (Elgin) division of the shire, including, presumably, several who also served on the local Committee of War. The local war committee consisted of: Duncan Forbes of Culloden; James Cuthbert of Draikes; Williame Mackintosh of Keillachie; William Dolles of Cantray; William Rosse of Clava; Hew Rosse of Kilravock; Alexander Brodie of Lethen; John Grant of Moyness; John Sutherland of Kinsteary; Alexander Dunbar of Boath; John Hay of Knockdowie; Thomas Mackenzie of Pluscarden; Alexander Dunbar of Westfield; Thomas Tulloch of Tannachie; Ninian Dunbar of Grangehill; Alexander Brodie of Brodie; Alexander Sutherland of Duffus; Sir Robert Innes of Innes; Mr John Hay, provost of Elgin; Patrick Campbell of Boath; James Grant of Freuchie and John Grant of Ballindalloch, younger – a Banffshire laird with Elgin interests who appears also as a witness (claim 10, Robert Dunbar).[13] A Forres bailie may have been among the Elgin commissioners to provide burghal balance. The local interest of these Moray men may have been tempered by the participation of outsiders, such as the men commissioned (in 1648) to investigate 'brunte and waisted landis' in the shire and burghs of Elgin and Forres: Alexander Ogilvie of Kincardine; Alexander Abercrombie elder of Birkinboige; Dr Alexander Dowglas in Banff; Thomas Abercrombie of Skeath; Gilbert Mair, baillie of Banff; and Robert Wilsone, sheriff depute of Banff.[14]

The documents assembled by the commissioners to the burgh of Elgin were probably never despatched to Edinburgh. Perhaps the careful commissioners and their clerks felt that they had sufficiently discharged their duties by taking depositions and making a record of the iniquity of the 'comonn enemie'. Arguably, bureaucratic inertia conspired with an appreciation of the improbability of compensation to dissuade the commissioners from the pointless exercise of transmitting the Elgin Depositions to the capital. Certainly, parliament could never have hoped to make good all the devastation suffered in town and country during Scotland's civil wars. Other burghs, such as Aberdeen, had more influence and had suffered more grievously than Elgin, and Elgin – where loyalty to the covenants had never wavered and losses totalled only £105,894 4s. (Scots) – was never likely to become parliament's priority.

Some compensation was paid and some relief granted to those whose sufferings came to parliament's attention, but payments were made in a piecemeal manner and not always from parliament's own purse. For example, in 1645 the burgesses of the burgh of Cullen in Banffshire begged plaintively for 'some support to rebuild our houss and menteane us in our present necessitie'. The response was not an immediate grant of money, but an Act of Parliament, passed on 6 August 1645, authorising 'ane voluntar contribution … from all persones duelling be North the water of Forth … Provyding … that the same contributione … shall not exceed the soume of Fourtie thousand pundes scotts'.[15] Parliament need not have troubled to add the caveat for Cullen's plight did not excite the charitable sympathy of the people north of the Forth to anything like that extent – if at all. Subsequently, on 16 March 1647, parliament was obliged to renew the Act for a voluntary collection.[16]

Also in March 1647, the sum of £20,000 sterling, received from the English parliament, was allocated 'To be given to the haill frie royall burrowis of this kingdom Towardis the reparatioune of their Loisses'.[17] Presumably Elgin received a share of this bounty, but even divided equally among all burghs, Elgin's portion could not have exceeded £500 sterling; and allocated in proportion either to the burgh's size or to its supposed losses, Elgin's share might have been as little as a few hundred pounds (Scots).

The distressed state of various communities was recognised by parliament in the form of periodic relief from the burden of monthly payments towards the maintenance of the army. Aberdeen maintained a steady barrage of protestations and petitions: pleading poverty, seeking redress and begging for the removal of friendly troops quartered upon its war-ravaged population. The general distress of northern burghs was recognised, for example in March 1647, when the list of those excused payments of monthly maintenance included Aberdeen, Inverness, Nairn, Forres, Brechin, Cullen, Banff, Dornoch and Elgin. Exceptionally, among these poverty-stricken communities, Elgin was excused only a portion of its contribution: 'Frie of the payment of Fourscore pundis of their mantenance of ane hundereth threttie fyve pundis'.[18] Elgin and other distressed burghs were granted further exemptions during 1648 and 1649 as parliament sensibly recognised the practical impossibility of enforcing payment, and the political danger of alienating loyally covenanted communities by over-strenuous demands for money.

In March 1649, the Scottish parliament noted Aberdeen's still-outstanding claim for compensation in the sum of 927,120 merks, but allocated only £1,000 sterling (£12,000 (Scots), 18,000 merks) towards the town's losses; and the main motive for this meagre payment was to bolster the shaky loyalty of the burgh.[19] Five years later the provost and bailies of Aberdeen were still bewailing the distressed condition of their community – forlornly claiming the sum of £1,470,350 (Scots) from 'his heines the Lord Protector'.[20]

Elgin never received specific compensation for its losses during the *annus horribilis* of 1645: not for its communal losses, nor for the plunderings suffered by individual townsfolk. Neither, probably, did neighbouring burghs such as Forres and Nairn, which may have suffered no less at the hands of the common enemy, but whose depositions are not preserved in local archives.

Reimbursements in respect of the cost of quartering troops were made to various burghs although records of payments to Elgin are not preserved. Nor are any of the tickets granted by friendly commanders who quartered in the town. Some commanders, such as Middleton, 'gave not Tickettis', whereas other tickets were perhaps destroyed when the burgh's 'registeres & evidentis ... war Pittifullie spoyled and Scattered'. Others again have almost certainly been destroyed according to weeding policies for which Moray custodians are sadly notorious. A few scant notes made by the treasurer of Forres seem to be all that survives to record parliamentary quarterings in Moray:[21]

> Ane not of ye expenssis quhilk ye brughe of forres depursit induring ye aboyd of ye pirsoneris within ye brughe the 9. 10. 11and 12 dayes of May 1649 after the ficht at Balvenzie
>
> Item aught gentillmen truperis for ye space of thrie dayes and their horssis ilk ane per diem 20sinde 24 lib'
>
> Item to Collonell Ker & Lieutenant Collonell Frachir their horssis forane night 20s
>
> Item to fourtteine soieris of ye garisone of spynie for ye space of four dayes at sex shillingis ye soiger per diem 16 lib' 16s

Aberdeen archives, however, preserve numerous tickets, for example:

> I, Patrick Kuningham capitane in the Earl of Glencairns regiment grants me to heve receaved quarteris and interteinment of the toune of Aberdeen forthrie scoir sodgers fra seterday at nicht the 14 Junii instant to Wedensday at tuel houris .... Total: 48 lib. scots[22]

Although most plunderings went uncompensated, there were notable exceptions; parliament was careful to look after its own members. Brodie of Brodie, parliamentary commissioner for Elginshire, benefited from several Acts recognising the poverty of his estate 'brunt and waisted by the barbarous rebellis'. Brodie was formally indemnified against claims resulting from the burning of his title deeds and other writs, and also (by way of financial recompense) exempted from 'bygane taxt and Loane'.[23] Among other covenanting lairds who were rewarded for their loyalty and compensated for their losses was Alexander Brodie of Lethen, commissioner to parliament for Nairnshire. Lethen's losses were considerable:

> his hous of Lethem wes beseidged be James grahame and his adherentis Wha not able to prevaill brunt his haill barnes barneyairdis and cornes Plunderit the haill insight and plenissing of his Barronie and took away Eight hundreth oxin and kyne Eightene hundreth scheepe and goats two hundreth horses and meares[24]

Parliament responded positively to the petition, granting to the loyal Laird of Lethen, in 1649, a cash sum of £10,000 (Scots) and 'the baillierie of the regalitie of Kinlosse Whilk belongit of befoir to the Laite Marques of Huntlie'.[25]

The same round sum (£10,000 (Scots)) was voted by parliament, on 25 March 1647, to Sir Robert Innes of Innes, 'for his present subsistence and towardis the reparatioune of his Loisses'. The sum was 'To be payed to him out of the readiest moneyis .... But prejudice of the payment of the armie'. The record does not show whether the financial demands of the army did in fact leave any cash spare to honour the obligation to Innes. However, the extravagant renovation of Innes house (completed in 1653 at a cost of £15,266 (Scots)) provides some evidence that the money was paid and tastefully invested in the family's property.[26]

Johne Grant of Ballindalloch was compensated for the plundering and burning of his three Speyside houses and estates – at Petcash (Pitchaish), Foyness (Phones), and Balnadalachs (Ballindalloch). The compensation in this case cost the nation nothing and also punished the malignant Gordons. In March 1647 parliament recognised the Ballindalloch's 'Loisses and sufferingis and his constant affection and carriage to the caus and cuntrie against the rebellis and enemies of the same'; and the Grant laird was awarded a charter of infeftment granting the superiority formerly pertaining to 'george gordoun late Marques of Huntlie … his declared enemie', in respect of the 'Landis of Morinsh and chaiplanrie of pitchais and fones'.[27]

An Act of 27 March 1647 accepted the petition of William Dumbar (Dunbar), provost of Forres and also the royal burgh's commissioner to parliament. Dumbar complained of his 'present hard condition' – the result of 'being frequentlie plundered' and also of a ransom paid when he was kidnapped by 'the capitan of the Clanronnald'. Parliament allowed the unfortunate provost 1,000 merks (Scots) from fines levied upon malignants.[28] Two days previously, an Act had allocated the same sum to Mr Johne Hay, provost of Elgin and also the burgh's commissioner to parliament.[29] But this was merely to tide him over. On 29 June 1649 Hay received generous additional recompense in the sum of £3,008 6s. 8d.[30] No copy of Hay's petition and no itemised claim survives either in Elgin or Edinburgh. Provost Hay is the only Elgin resident known to have received specific compensation.

Under the Commonwealth and Protectorate all hope of compensation evaporated. The Scottish parliament ceased to exist. The English independents who governed the country despised presbyterianism. There was no one officially to applaud or reward Elgin's faithfulness to the covenants. The Elgin Depositions were, however, preserved as a testimony to the community's suffering and as evidence of its gracious state. The covenanted burgh's roll of honour was carefully placed – reverently enshrined – in the burgh cadget.

Elgin merchants and craftsmen, meanwhile, buckled down to the business of making money – recouping their losses through agricultural enterprise, trade and industry. The town managed to recover its fortunes during the uncertain generation that saw the death of Cromwell and the restoration of the Stuarts – and with them the reimposition of episcopacy. Elgin folk were not conspicuous among those who supported conventicles and godly guerrilla warfare during the killing times – though support for the presbyterianism of the Covenant remained strong in west Moray. Elgin, however, maintained a quiet faithfulness to the presbyterianism of the covenants. The royal burgh prospered, and by the 1680s a spasm of rebuilding was beginning to dignify the burgh high street with polite stone houses, whose jettied upper storeys, supported on stumpy doric columns, shaded arcaded piazzas for pedestrian traffic and market-day stalls.

Repression and royal indulgences under Charles II and James VII broke the back of old-style presbyterianism and crushed the spirit of its surviving supporters. The revolution of 1688 removed the Stuarts and restored presbyterianism. Old men (and women, too) were doubtless nostalgic for the heady dangerous days of the 1640s. The young, though, were probably bored rather than inspired by their grandparents' reminiscences of godly suffering in the good old days of the Covenant; and they were indifferent to the glorious scroll of depositions that preserved the record of the burgh's suffering. The keynote of resurrected presbyterianism was moderation. The new laird of Brodie was typical of his generation – flexibly willing to conform, compromise and conciliate under King William's regime. Few of the older generation of ministers survived; and those that did were past their zealous prime. The restored General Assembly was packed with pragmatists and practical managers. If the new generation of presbyterian ministers venerated the theocratic fundamentalism of its predecessors, it did so quietly, without prejudicing parochial career prospects. One notable youngster did take up the fading torch of the covenants: but a latter-day covenanter, such as the remarkable James Allan, was already an anachronism – embraced by a few and succoured by the daughters of Innes, but shunned and suspected by sensible folk as a dangerous firebrand, a Cameronian, a madman, or worse.

Meanwhile, The Elgin Depositions sank to the bottom of the burgh cadget and were at last forgotten.

During the 18th century, in the pursuit of prosperity and Britishness, Elgin folk looked to the future. Rebuilding continued apace, given a fillip as the profits of reformed agriculture flooded into the burgh following the Moray clearances of 1766. Progress and perspective did, however, gild the past with a glamour that caught the interest of a rising generation of antiquarians and historians, but early investigators only shallowly excavated among the upper strata of Elgin's uncatalogued administrative archives. The Elgin Depositions were not seen by Lauchlan Shaw whose *History of the Province of Moray* appeared in 1775; nor by Isaac Forsyth who published a *Survey of the Province of Moray* in 1798. William Cramond prepared stupendous editions of Moray archives, though his two-volume *Records of Elgin* (1903 & 1908) focused upon the bound-codex series of burgh court records, kirk session and town council minutes. Cramond made no mention of the Depositions. Robert Young's *Annals of the Parish and Burgh of Elgin* (1879) and the enlarged edition of Shaw's history (edited by J.F.S. Gordon, 1882) similarly make no notice of The Elgin Depositions.

It seems surprising that, in a century whose ecclesiastical landscape was reshaped by catholic emancipation and the schism of the Disruption, the conflicts of the age of the covenants did not engage the enthusiasm of historians. Perhaps the liberal instincts of 19th-century academics were repelled rather than aroused by the fundamentalism and fanaticism of the covenanting era. Indeed, though the Forres commission was certainly noticed among the burgh's archives during the 19th century, its significance was entirely overlooked. An antiquarian's note attached to the document shows how little the events of 1645-6 were understood. The note refers to 'waste lands appertaining to the different burghs ... because ... Corns had been burnt ... by the different clans who were at feud with each other'.[31] The full text of this note – and of the commission itself – is contained in Appendix 2.

Ecclesiastical history and the political convolutions of the 17th century remained unfashionable among historians – indeed increasingly distasteful as the 20th century progressed. However, a happy consequence of this academic neglect was that The Elgin Depositions remained obscurely out of sight, deeply buried within the mass of unsorted inaccessible burgh muniments jealously guarded by Elgin's secretive town clerks. Subsequently, the Depositions were spared the destructive attentions of antiquarian collectors, tidy-minded local bureaucrats and travelling teams of Scottish Record Office weeders.

The Elgin Depositions were eventually recognised in 1975, when the archives of the newly defunct royal burgh were transferred to the Moray District Record Office at the Tolbooth, Forres following local government reorganisation. The documents containing the Depositions were catalogued under reference ZBEl C699/646/1. The classification recognised 1646 as the latest date on the documents. The roll of individual claims was illustrated in D. Iredale & J. Barrett, *Discovering Local History* (1999).[32]

Sadly, one page of the Depositions has been lost. The first page of the town's losses (Document B) survives only in typed transcripts prepared by Moray Council archivists during the early 1980s. The original of this leaf dropped from sight, possibly during weeding of archive collections by Moray Council library staff under Scottish Record Office direction in 1986. It can still be hoped, though, that the page was misplaced rather than destroyed: perhaps misfiled during internal reorganisation following closure of the local authority's professional archive service in 1998 and subsequent transfer of archives to the local heritage service at Grant Lodge, Elgin; or mislaid when services were relocated to Elgin Public

Library after fire gutted the heritage centre in 2001. The surviving documents comprising The Elgin Depositions are currently in the custody of the Moray Council Heritage Service at East End School, Elgin.

The present edition makes The Elgin Depositions fully accessible for the first time since they were sworn more than three centuries ago.

The Format

The Elgin Depositions are contained in two documents. Document A comprises a substantial paper roll containing a manuscript record of sworn testimony concerning the losses of over 200 individual claimants. Document B comprises a single original paper manuscript page and two versions (three pages and four pages) of typed transcript of a lost leaf. Document B describes general losses of the community. Neither document is complete.

Document A comprises paper leaves pasted together to form a continuous roll some 30ft long (ending part way through claim 198, Marjorie Winchester) containing sworn testimonies concerning individuals' losses. A further fragment approximately 6½in long completes claim 198 and continues to tail off in a ragged edge at the end of claim 202 (Alexander Petrie). The significance of this singular format is discussed in chapter three above.

The surviving text begins with a damaged sheet. The first line records a total valuation (£2,000) – presumably of Johne Mylne's burnt house and his losses of insicht, plenishing, fixtures and fittings, merchant wares, armour, valuables and personal possessions. Following the total, complete text describes the plundering of three horses from Johne Mylne and his son James.

At least one preceding page is amissing. It seems likely that no more than a couple of pages are lost, though two pages would hardly have been sufficient to itemise the most grievous losses of four individuals whose houses were burnt in retribution for the Rhynie murder: George Donaldson, Alexander Douglas, John Douglas of Morriston and George Sutherland.[33] Nor would a single page be sufficient to record testimony concerning the plunderings suffered by two other leading burgesses notably absent from the roll: Mr John Hay and Mr Gavin Douglas.

The detached and damaged fragment with which the roll ends (preserving claims 198-202) represents the upper portion of a leaf which, if complete, might have contained a further half-dozen short entries.

The surviving roll comprises 30 sheets (including the detached fragment). Each is 12in wide between deckle edges. The sheets are pasted together head-to-foot. The foot of each sheet is trimmed with a knife to a clean (but not always straight) edge. This trimmed lower edge is pasted over the untrimmed top edge of the succeeding sheet, overlapping it by up to one inch. Occasionally the overlap partly obscures a line of text. Most of the pages that form the roll are complete sheets, trimmed to between 12in and 15in in length. Five smaller sheets are pieced in. The make-up of the roll is as follows:

probable missing page(s):

sheet number	depositions	overall length
1	1-2	12 inches
2	2-6	15
3	6	3
4	6-7	14
5	8-10	15

6	10-14	14¾
7	14-9	14
8	19-25	15
9	25-31	15
10	31-7	14¾
11	37-44	14
12	44-51	14¾
13	51-7	14¼
14	58-67	15¼
15	68-78	15½
16	79-90	15
17	90-101	14¾
18	101-11	15
19	112-22	15
20	122-31	15
21	132-40	15
22	141-48	15
23	49-151	4
24	152-7	13½
25	158-66	15
26	167-76	15
27	177-82	7¾
28	183-87	6½
29	187-98	14
30 (fragment)	199-202	6

Discolouration, damage and other physical evidence on the latter part of the roll – including the presence of a titling endorsement – suggest that the final surviving tattered (detached and fragmentary) part page was probably the final sheet of the original document, forming the outermost turn of the roll.

The hand of the endorsement is different from the hands of the depositions. It is also different from the hands of Document B. The endorsement reads: 'Toun of Elgynn [the]r loiss[is] in montrose tyme'. The spelling of the place-name 'Elgynn' is unusual and hints that the clerk who wrote the endorsement may not have been an Elgin (or Moray) man.

If a hint can be inferred from the numbering of the marginal notes which head each of the two pages of Document B, then we might tentatively suggest that perhaps only one leaf is amissing from the 30-page roll comprising Document A. Thus the whole of The Elgin Depositions (including both Documents A and B) perhaps originally comprised 34 sheets, and that the surviving text is almost complete. In this case it might be presumed that depositions relating to the houses that were targeted for burning – and also of the most prominent townsfolk including Mr John Hay and Mr Gavin Douglas – did not form part of the roll of Depositions. Perhaps these leading burgesses preferred to make their claims separately and by other means. Certainly, John Hay claimed (and received compensation) directly from parliament, though there is no record of his fellow sufferers following this course.

Document B itemises the costs of various quarterings and communal losses. The text begins in mid-sentence with an account of losses sustained 'at Iames Grahame and Mckdonoldis handes in februarij & maij 1645'. This beginning suggests that Document B was once longer, by at least one page – or that the first surviving entry commenced on the lost fragment of the foot of the last page of Document A. The two pages of Document B commence with numbered notes: '32 throughe to the closure'; and '33 nixt the closure'. A detailed analysis of the make-up of Document B and its relationship with Document A is hampered because the first page survives in only two annotated typescripts. Some aspects of the transcription of this text are necessarily tentative. The second page of Document B is, though, an original 17th-century manuscript. Document B concludes with a (much corrected) grand total – of £105,894 4s. 0d. – suggesting that this was the final entry of The Elgin Depositions.

Pages and text, which do not survive among Elgin burgh archives and have not been traced elsewhere, were probably amissing at an early stage. An endorsement in a 17th-century hand recognises that the two pages represent only 'ane pairt of the loiss[is] of elgin', implying that other material was already detached or lost.

The third and fifth paragraphs of page '33 nixt the closure' are cancelled with heavy crossed penstrokes. It is possible, too, that a paragraph of the typescript page was similarly cancelled. Thus it might be suggested that Document B comprises an early draft, revised and recopied during the creation of a final fair copy, or edited into a standard form required by the commissioners. During final revision of the text a marginal insertion was added to emphasise the grievousness of the oppression that the burgh had suffered. The insertion is untidily written, in a smaller hand, perhaps by a different clerk.

The leaf comprising the one surviving manuscript page of Document B is 12in wide between deckle edges and 13¾in long. The sheet has been trimmed with a knife to give clean (but not straight) edges at the head and foot. This trimming has partly cut away a calligraphic flourish at the foot of the page. The convoluted mark, suggestive of a notary's sign manual, includes the letters *Io* (perhaps for the Christian name John).

The town's losses are written in a confident, clear 17th-century hand. The first word of each paragraph is writ large and dignified with a flourished initial letter. The clerk uses few abbreviations. Two minor errors are corrected by over-writing. The sums of money in the final paragraph are notably corrected, with crossings-out and interlinear insertions in a smaller hand – the result of arithmetical afterthought and recalculation rather than copyist's error.

The Four Clerks

The 202 surviving depositions of Document A were written by three clerks, each with a distinctive hand and personal quirks in spelling and abbreviation. These clerks were not involved in the writing of Document B, which is the work of a fourth writer and several additional editors. All four principal deposition writers were clearly competent administrative clerks and skilled copyists, cooperating closely on the compilation of The Elgin Depositions. Occasionally, in Document A, a clerk relieved his colleague in the middle of a testimony – indeed even in mid-sentence (for example claim 70, Michaell Andersone). This seems to confirm that the record of testimony was compiled as a team effort by copying and editing from source materials prepared earlier. Clerk I wrote a bold black upright hand evident in 97 depositions. Clerk II wrote a bold sloped (and sometimes careless) attacking hand evident in 57 depositions. Clerk III wrote a small (sometimes tiny) upright hand evident in 52 depositions. Clerk IV wrote a confident clear script with letters somewhat squared, distinctively prominent tall sloped *f* and long *s*, and notable large capitals to open new paragraphs. A fifth writer is identifiable in the small black and abbreviated script of the marginal addition '[com]mitting grievous out rages … the loiss[is] [whe]rof being' added to the Document B page headed '33 nixt the closure'. At least one further clerk may have been responsible for correcting the arithmetic in Document B. The division of labour among the four principal clerks was as follows:

> Clerk I claims 1-57, 70-8, 101-22, 158-66
> Clerk II claims 58-70, 132-48, 152-57, 167-87
> Clerk III claims 79-101, 122-31, 149-51, 187-202
> Clerk IV Document B

The Modern Edition

The transcription of The Elgin Depositions has been contrived to present an accessible text, faithful to the original, with minimal editorial intervention. Brief headings (with modest editorial modernisations) and numbering of individual depositions have been inserted to divide the text and assist the reader.

The variation in writing styles among the hands of the four clerks – small or large, careful or careless – is within the usual range for the time. The scripts employed are legible, every-day business hands, except for the initial words of paragraphs in Document B, which are dignified in an angular formal noncurrent legal hand. The principal scripts are characterised by the usual secretary-hand letter-forms, typified by a straggle-tailed *h*, high rolled-back *e*, single-stroke *d* and *x*, convoluted *k*, and distinctive forms of long, double and terminal *s*. There is no evidence of the humanistic letter-forms that were already commonplace on the mainland of Europe and in England. In this the commissioners' clerks were in the Scottish mainstream – and almost a century behind the most modern bureaucratic practice.

Sentences, paragraphs and proper names commence variously with ordinary small letters, small letter-forms writ large, and convoluted large forms clearly intended to possess the dignity conveyed by a capital in modern usage. The use of capital and lower case type in the transcription reflects the editors' personal appreciation of the original clerks' intentions – and doubtless will be open to quibble.

The clerks' punctuation is sparse if not non-existent. This defect does not hamper the sense of a text that is clearly written with careful consistency and correct syntax. The grammar and vocabulary employed is typical of the businesslike prose of skilful bureaucrats. The consistent layout – especially in respect of paragraph divisions and indented material – further clarifies a text from which punctuation is hardly missed. The formula adopted for Document A represents an elegant solution to the chaos represented by the different claims and emphases of over 200 ordinary (perhaps unlettered) folk – some in a state of shock, some dismayed and angered – all clamouring for recognition and redress.

The clerks occasionally made mistakes. Most of these are minor errors, such as the words 'Extending the said barbara his loissis' in the account of Barbara Dunbar's deposition (claim 189). Scribal deletions are indicated as < *deleted* > in the transcription. Diamond brackets are also used to indicate <*damage*> to the manuscript and words editorially interpolated to fill lacunae. The busy clerks' occasional lapses – dittographies, anticipations and omissions – are reproduced as they appear in the original. The nature of these small clerical errors suggests that Document A was compiled from earlier drafts. For example, in claim 141, where the value of cattle totals £106 13s. 4d., the clerk wrote j^{c}iij^{xx} lib' 13s. 4d. (£160 13s. 4d.) – arguably as a result of miscopying as the weary clerk lost concentration for a moment.

Seventeenth-century spelling is occasionally disconcerting to modern readers, though each commissioners' clerk is remarkably consistent, and a thoughtful reading overcomes occasional difficulties. Because 17th-century spellings were not standardised, clerks adopted phonetic approaches, which allow the sensitive modern reader to hear the authentic accents of the time. The plural termination *-is* and the rendering of words such as *maisteris* 'masters', *aucht* 'eight', *nichtis* 'nights', *sex* 'six', *wreitt* 'writ', *saiff* 'save', *threittie* 'thirty' and *brunt* 'burnt' convey with astonishing clarity the timbre of Scottish voices silent for more than three centuries. The use (and non-use) of double letters and the addition (or omission) of terminal *e* may be unfamiliar but are not incomprehensible; nor is terminal *ie* where modern usage prefers *y*. Here and there, though, the clerk's preferred spelling may momentarily bemuse even the most confident scholar – as for instance with a word such as *gliffis*.

Scottish syntax preserved Old-English and Middle-English *-es* and *-is* plural and possessive terminations. These archaic usages, which may seem quaint or couthy to modern eyes are, nonetheless, correct. The possessive apostrophe was introduced into English writings only during the later 17th century. It does not occur in The Elgin Depositions where clerks employed the prevailing form of possessive in 'Iames myllis loissis', or the usual, but illiterate, affectation of 'William Thom his loissis'.

The Depositions contain vocabulary and idioms that may be unfamiliar to the nonspecialist. These include words that have fallen from everyday use and specific terms connected with particular trades (such as leatherworking) or with livestock (notably sheep and horses). Troublesome words and phrases are explained in a short glossary at Appendix 4. Other difficulties may be resolved and meanings amplified by reference to the *Oxford English Dictionary* with support from the *Scottish National Dictionary* and *Dictionary of the Older Scottish Tongue*.

The use of *quh* where modern convention prefers *wh* – for example in *quhilk* for 'which' and *quhais* for 'whose' – was usual in Scottish vernacular writing, perhaps reflecting an aspirated pronunciation closer to Old-English than to modern standard English. This spelling began to fall from use during the 17th century, though flourishing into the 18th century as a convenient abbreviative in q^c, q^t and q^n for 'which', 'what' and 'when'.

The use of large and small *z* in words now commonly spelled with *y*, derives from the runic letter *yogh* which represented a guttural sound lost to standard English. The commissioners' clerks clearly wrote *z*, not *yogh*, in *zet* 'yet', *zeiris* 'years', *zairne* 'yarn' and *zounger* 'younger', and this is reproduced in the transcription.

Also a rune derivative is the use of *y* to represent the *th* sound of the runic letter *thorn*. By the 17th century *thorn* was widely used as a shorthand, usually with further contraction or superscript letters, for example *ye*, y^t and oy^r for *the*, *that* and *other*. In all cases *y* is silently expanded to *th* in the transcription. The inconsistencies of clerks' spellings – *ther*, *thair*, &c., used promiscuously for 'their' and 'there' – are resolved in the transcription by preferring the simplest variant *ther* when extending abbreviated forms.

At the time of the Depositions, letter *j* had not yet emerged into widespread Scottish use as a distinct consonant. The commissioners' clerks did not use consonantal *j* at all. Thus large initial *I* and small *i* might be either a vowel or a consonant. The initial vowel of *Item* and the initial consonant of *Iames* are written identically, and small *i* serves as both vowel and consonant in *periurie* 'perjury'. Small *i* was used as a Roman numeral, clerks being careful to insert the correct number of dots above confusible multiple letters, and to use a long-form *i* (transcribed as *j*) for the final unit.

The 17th-century alphabet did not clearly distinguish among *u*, *v* and *w*, which might be regarded as different forms of the same letter and used promiscuously as either vowel or consonant. Thus the commissioners' clerks offer, among other intriguing spellings, *siluer*, *avay*, *wseit*, *wtheris*, *vther*, *induellar*, and *ellewin*, for 'silver', 'away', 'used', 'others', 'other', 'indweller' and 'eleven'.

Abbreviation was a usual convention employed to assist both reader and writer. In this edition abbreviations have been silently expanded following, as far as practicable, the clerk's original intention and usual practice.

Abbreviation by contraction – omitting one or more letters – might be highlighted by use of superscript letters. Typically, personal names are contracted to forms such as *Ro^{t}sone*, *Io^n*, *Straq^n* and *Wm* for 'Robertsone', 'Iohn', 'Straquhan' and 'William'. Frequently recurring words, too, are contracted: *sd* and *forsd* for 'said' and 'forsaid'; *mo^{ey}* (with the superscript letters convolved into a diphthong) for 'money'. An all-purpose arching mark above the affected word indicates contraction, usually by omission of a letter or letters, typically from a word with numerous minims occurring together. Thus a letter *m* is frequently dropped from *commone*. In contracted words missing letters have been editorially restored without comment and without the pedantic clutter of square brackets.

Clerks drew upon a repertoire of conventional abbreviative symbols to speed their task. Specific signs representing particular recurrent letter groups were, for the most part, evolved or borrowed from medieval Latin scribal practice. Among the more notable symbols in the Depositions is a slashing penstroke standing for *er*, *ir*, *re*, abbreviating *servandis* 'servants' and, with some further convolution, *abouwrittin* 'above written'. A symbol devised originally for the Latin prefixes *com* and *con* was widely used in vernacular writing – and frequently in Document A – to abbreviate *common* and *conforme*. A hooked flourish standing for terminal *es* or *is* in plurals and genitives hangs from the head of the final long *s* in *horss[is]*, *loiss[is]* and *witness[is]*. Occasionally, however, the commissioners' clerks added this tag to the terminal long *s* of a word that is certainly singular, for example *ane horss'*, in which case the mark has been interpreted as a scribal affectation and ignored. Words abbreviated by conventional signs are editorially extended without comment or square brackets.

The clerks' use of ampersand – a symbol derived from a conventional convolution of Latin *et* 'and' – seems to represent no difficulty and is preserved in the transcription as an ordinary & sign.

The Elgin Depositions were sworn at a time when accounting practice was undergoing radical reform as a result of the widespread adoption of Arabic numerals (*1, 2, 3, 4, 5, 6, 7, 8, 9* and *0*) and the new arithmetical methods they facilitated. The commissioners' clerks used both Roman numerals (*i, ij, iij, iiij, iv, v, vj, vij, viij, ix* and *x*, with *l* or *L* for 50, *c* for 100 and *m* for 1,000) and Arabic numerals, as well as spelling out numbers in words – sometimes all in the same valuation.

Money was expressed, of course, in *pundis*, *schillingis* and *penneyes*, 'pounds', 'shillings' and 'pennies'. The score (20) was much favoured. Merks (valued at two thirds of one pound – 13s. 4d.) were also used, adding slightly to the arithmetical challenges. Clearly, many folk preferred to reckon in merks – hence the many valuations ending in 3s. 4d., 6s. 8d. and 13s. 4d. This popular preference led to a clerical error in the account of George Carmichall's losses (claim 165) which were valued at 'iiij^{c}4 markis 16s 8d' where, surely, the clerk intended £404 16s. 8d. On one rare occasion (claim 118, Thomas Andersone) a careless clerk became arithmetically entangled when changing from merks to pounds, but in misconverting the value of two horses at 50 merks each to threescore and thirteen pounds six shillings and eight pence (£73 6s. 8d. – which should, of course, have been £66 13s. 4d.) – he incidentally raises the intriguing suggestion that he was writing from dictation as he transposed and jumbled the figures.

Abbreviations assisted the clerks in expressing sums of money, and these have been rationalised into a conventional *s* and *d* for shillings and pence, except where the context seems to require expansion of the abbreviation. The abbreviated form of Latin *libra(e)* 'pound(s)' has been allowed to stand as *lib'*. The usual abbreviation for one thousand, conventionally written to appear like *jaj*, has been restored editorially to a numerically correct I[m]. Readers should have little difficulty with the superscript abbreviations: [c] for Latin *centum* 'hundred' and [xx] representing *viginti* 'twenty' for 'score'.

The Elgin Depositions

Document A
Individual Claims

The surviving text begins with a damaged leaf from which the initial paragraph is missing. It is likely that one or more full sheets, detailing losses of major claimants preceding Johne Mylne, have been lost.

1. Johne Mylne
    particular comp<t --------------------->
    Extending the loiss[is] of the s<aid ----------->
availl to the Soume of Tuo Thowsan<d --------->
    Follouis the loissis of horssis and goodis plunderit be <the Comonn Enemie fra the said Iohne> mylne in the moneth of februarij and mai 1645 <---------->

Imprimis the said Iohne mylne being Interrogat and examinat be the saidis Comissionars he being deiplie and solemnelie suorne did depon and declair that ther was plunderit and away takin fra him tuo horssis In februar 1645 pryce of the peice – 40 lib' Inde – iiij xx lib' mo[n]ey with ane hors taken from his sone Iames myln wnforisfamiliat duelling with himselff with four head of goodis pryce of them all – 33 lib' 6s 8d

    Extending the loissis of the saidis horssis and goodis to the Soume of
    Extending the said Iohn myln his haill loissis abouwritin to the soume of Thrie Thowsand Tuo <hund>reth fourscoir pund ellevin schillingis four penneyes
    Follouis a declaratione of the witnessis quha wer wseit for probatione of the particular loissis sustenit be the said Iohn mylne of the horssis and goods abouwritin According to thair seuerall depositiones in presens of the saidis Comissioneris

    Imprimis Androw Annand merchand burges of elgin being examinat and Interrogatt wpon his aith deiplie suorne did depone and declair that ther was plunderit from the said Iohne myln the first tuo horssis abou mentionat Thomas warrand merchand burges ther being Suorne & examinat did declair and depone conforme to the said androw Annand his depositione in all poyntis Iohn Forsyith officir burges in elgin being Suorne and axaminat did declair and depone that said hors was plunderit from the said Iames Milne sone to the said Iohne and that the saidis four head of goodis war plunderit fra the said Iohne myln and Iames fairrer smyth induellar In elgin being Suorne and examinat did declair and depone conforme to the said Iohne forsyith his depositione in all poyntis

2. William Robertsone, skinner, burgess of Elgin

Follouis the loissis sustenit be william Robertsone skinner burges of elgin in his insicht plenissing cloithes abuilziementis and wtheris wnderwritin

Imprimis the said william Robertsone being interrogat and examinat be the saidis Comissioneris he by his great aith solemnelie suorne did depone and declair that according to his awin certaine knowledge and by Sure Informatione of his wyffe and servantis thair was plunderit and away takin fra the said william Robertsone be the Comonn Enemie furth of his houssis and buithis in elgin in the moneth of februar 1645 and at diverse tymes therefter insicht plenissing cloithes abuilziementis merchand wares cornes wictuall armer gold siluer cunziet and wncunziet <hous>hold provisione and wtheris of that kynd with Timber plenissing broken and maid wnvsefull bandis of dores lockis and keyis takin away glasen windowes brokin conforme to the particular compt giwin in to the saidis Comissioneris

Extending the forsaidis loissis to the Soume of

Follouis the loissis of the horssis and goodis plunderit be the Comon Enemie fra the said william Robertsone in the moneth of december 1645 when the marqueis of huntlie and his forses lay in Murray

Imprimis the said william Robertsone being interrogat and examinat be the saidis Comissioneris <being> solemlie suorne did depone and declair that their was plunderit and away takin from him at the tyme forsaid Tuo horssis pryce of the peice 50 markis Inde – 66 lib' 13s 4d with tuo oxin pryce of Both – 26 lib 13s 4d

Extending the loissis of the saidis horssis and goodis to the Soume of fourscoir thretten pund sex shillingis aucht penneyes

Extending the said william his haill loissis abouw[ri]tin To the Soume of sex hunder four scoir Tuell pundis

Folouis the declaratione of the witnessis quha wer wseit for probatione of the particular loissis sustenit be the said william Robertsone of the horsis and goodis abouwritin

Imprimis walter Hay merchand burges of elgin being axaminat and Interrogat wpon his aith deiplie Suorne did depone and declair that ther was plunderit from the said william Robertsone the tyme forsaid the forsaid tuo hors and tuo oxin and alexander Russell elder being Suorne and examinat did depone conforme to the said walter hay his dispositione in all poyntis alexander dunbar messenger burges of elgin being suorne and examinat did depon and declair That ther was plunderit from the said william Robertsone the said tuo oxin and alexander Sinclar sone to George Sinclar in the colledge of elgin being Suorne and examinat did declair and depone conforme to the said alexander dunbar his dispositione in all poyntis

3. William Falconer, burgess of Elgin

Followis the loissis of william falconer burges of elgin of his insicht plenissing cloithes abuilziementis mer[chan]d waires and wtheris wnderwreattin

Imprimis the said william falconer being interrogat and examinat be the saidis comissioners he by his great aith Solemnelie Suorne did depone and declair that according to his owin certaine knowledge and by sure informatione of his wyffe and servantis thair was plunderit and avay Takin from the said william falconer be the Comonn enemie furth of his houssis and Buithes in elgin in the moneth of februar 1645 and at diverse Tymes ther efter of Insicht plenissing cloithes abuilziementis merchand wares cornes wictuall armor gold Siluer Cunziet and wncunziet and wther houshold provisione of that kynd conforme to the particular compt giwin in to the saidis Comissioners

Extending the said william falconer his loissis abouwritin To the Soume of

The Elgin Depositions: Document A

4. Alexander Lesley, merchant, burgess of Elgin

Followis the loissis sustenit be wmquhill alexander Lesley merchand burges of elgin of his Insicht plenissing merchand wares goodis Insicht plenissing abuilziementis cloithes and wtheris wnderwritin

Imprimis the said wmquhill alexander Leslie befor his deceis Subscriuit wpon his aith befor his deceis that ther was plunderit and avay Takin fra him befor his deceis furth of his houssis and buithes in elgin in the moneth of februarij 1645 and at divers Tymes ther after of Insicht plenissing cloithes abuilziementis merchand wares cornes wictuall armor gold siluer cunzeit and wncunzeit houshold provisione and wtheris of that kynd with tuo hors plunderit and avay takin from the said wmquhill befor his deceis conforme to the particular compt Subscriuit be the said wmquhill alexander givin in to the saidis comissioners

Extending the said wmquhill alexander Leslie his loissis abouwritin To the Soume of

5. Jeane Bonyman, relict of Alexander Leslie, merchant, burgess of Elgin

Followis the loissis of Ieane Bonyman relict of the said wmquhill alexander Leslie Since the said wmquhill alexander his deceis of ane hors taken from hir be Generall major Middletonnes Trouperis when they went to The releiff of the Seidge of Innernes in maij Last by past

Imprimis The said Ieane Bonyman being Interrogat and examinat Be the saidis Comissioners and deiplie and Solemnlie Suorne did depone and declair That the forsaidis persones Tuik fra hir at the said Tyme ane broun naige worth Fourtie pundis money

Extending the loissis of the said wmquhill alexander Leslie and Ieane Bonyman his relict To the Soume of

Follovis the loissis of the said umquhill alexander Leslie and Ieanne Bonyman his Spous thair loissis be declaratione of the witnessis wnderwritin quha was wseit for probatione therof according to their Severall despositiones in presens of the saidis Comissioners

Imprimis Iohne mckeane maltman burges of elgin being examinat and Interrogatt Wpon his aith deiplie Suorne did depone and declair That thair was plunderit and avay fra the said wmquhill alexander Leslie The tyme forsaid The saidis Tuo horssis abouwritin and Thomas Murdoche Taillzeor burges of elgin being Suorne and examined did declair and depone conforme to the said Iohne mckean his depositione and william Laying Baillzie burges of elgin being Suorne and examinat did declair and depone That the wther hors abouwritin was Taken fra the said Ieane Bonyman in maner abouspecifeit Item the said Thomas Murdoche being again Suorne and examined did declair and depone Conforme to the said william Laying his depositione

6. Robert Gibsone of Linkwood, burgess of Elgin

Followis the loissis of Robert Gibsone of Linkvoodes burges of elgin of his Insicht plenissing Cloithes abuilziementis and wtheris wnderwritin

Imprimis the said Robert Gibsone Being Interrogat and examinat be the saidis Comissioneris he by his great aith solemnelie Suorne did depone and declair That according to his awne certaine knowledge and by sure Informatione of his wyiff and seruantis Thair was takin away from him be the Marqueis of argyill his Troup in the moneth of 164 yeiris and plunderit and avay taken from him be the Comonn Enemie furth of his awin houssis in the colledge of elgin In the moneth of februarij 1645 and at wtheris tymes ther efter of Insicht plenissing cloithes ornamentis abuilziementis cornes wictuall airmour gold Siluer cunziet and wncunziet houshold provisione and wtheris of that kynd of Timber plenissing broken and maid wnvsefull Bandis of dores lockis and keyes taken avay conforme to the particular Compt givin in to The saidis Comissioners

Extending the said Robert Gibsone his loissis abouwritin To the Soume of 144 lib' money

Followis the said Robert Gibsone his loissis of the burning of ane fair ludgeing within the toun of elgin be montrois armie in maij 1645

Imprimis the said Robert gibsone being Interrogatt and examinat be the saidis comissioneris he by his grait Aith Solemnelie suorne did depone and declair that montrois armie at the tyme forsaid did burne the said ludgeing off thrie hous height with the Inland therof all new plenissit with beddis and buirdis and wther necessary plenissing The worth therof Far exceiding ane Thowsand markis money quhilk was lykwayes provin be the magistratis off elgin Conforme to the particular Compt givin in to the saidis Comissioneris

Extending the loissis of the said burnt ludgeing and wthers abouwritin far within the availl To the Soume off ane Thowsand markis money

Followis the loissis off horssis meares lambes wedderis and oxin Taken be argylls Troupers from the said robert gibsone and be the Comonn Enemie plunderit be Them in februarij and Maij 1645 and at diverse wthers tymes ther efter

Imprimis the said Robert gibsone being Interrogatt and examinat be the saidis Comissioneris he Being deiplie and Solemnlie Suorne did depone and declair that ther was takin from him be the marqueis of argyllis Troupers in the moneth of   164 foir hors pryce – iiij^{xx} lib' And that thair was plunderit from him be montrois armie in the moneth of februar 1645 The number of tuentie ane oxin tuo ky with calffe pryce of the peice – 8 libs' money Inde – 414 lib' money with ane paiced hors pryce ane hundrethe markis money with ane wther black younge hors pryce – 53 lib' 6s 8d money with tua meiris pryce of both – 40 libs' money with four oxin pryce of the peice – 10 libs' money Inde – 40 lib' money plunderit and avay be the marqueis of huntlies forces and his forces Lord Lodovickis forces quhen they Ley in murray in winter Last bypast with sex Lambis pryce – 6 lib' money with four wadderis pryce – 8 lib' money lykvayis taken be thame at the said tyme Conforme to the particular compt giwin in to the said comissioneris

Extending the said Robert gibsone his loissis of the horssis guidis and wtheris abowewrittin To The soume of

Followis The declaratione of the witnessis quha were wseit for probatione of the particular loissis Susteinit be the said Robert gibsone of the horssis meiris guidis and wtheris abowe writtin according To thair severall depositiones in presens of the saidis comissioneris

Imprimis Iames gibsone in the colledge of elgin being examinat and Interrogat wpon his aith deiplie suo<rne> did depone and declair the forsaid four hors was takin from the said robert gibsone at the tyme abowewrit<in> be marques of argyillis trouperis and that the haill remanent hors meiris oxin ky wedderis lambis and wtheris rextive forsaid wer plunderit and avay takin from the said Robert gibsone be the comonn enemies abow specifeit at the tymes rextiue abow exprest and george sinclair in the colledge of elgin and Iames Lillie ther being deiplie suorne did depone and declair

7. Elizabeth Douglas, spouse of Robert Mertein, merchant, burgess of Elgin

Follouis the loissis of umquhill Robert mertein merchand burges of elgin and Elizabeth douglas his spous of thair Insicht plenisching cloithes abuilziementis and wthers wndervrittin

Imprimis the said Elizabeth douglas being Interrogat and examinat be the saidis comissioneris schee by hir great ayth Solemnelie suorne did depone and declair That according to hir owne certane knowledge and by sure Informatione of hir wmquhill husband and thair servantis thair wes plunderit and takin avay fra thamme be the comonn Enemie furth of thair houssis kill and buith in elgin in the monethis of februarij and maij 1645 and thairefter be the markes of Huntlie and his sones their armie lying in murray Betuixt the fyfteint day of december 1645 and the monethe of maij last by past of Insicht plenisching cloithis abuilziementis merchand wares cornes wictuall armour gold silver cunziet and wncunziet houshold prowisione and wthers of that kynd with Timber plenisching brokin and maid wnusefull sparres deallis buirdis of dores lokes and keyis takin avay demolisching of glasin windowis Stanchellis weiris keassis bredis cruikis of dores and wtheris of that kynd Conforme to the particular compt giwin in to the saidis comissioneris

Extending the said Elizabeth douglas & hir said wmquhill husband thair loissis abowevrittin To the soume of

Followis the loissis of horssis and guidis plunderit from the said Elizabethe and hir Wmquhill husband Be the comonn enemie in the monethis of februar and maij 1645 at wtheris divers tymes therefter

Imprimis the said Elizabethe being Interrogat and examinat be the saidis comissioneris and deiplie and Solemnelie suorne did depon and declair That thair wes plunderit and avay taken from hirselffe and <hir> wmquhill husband at the tyme forsaid fywe hors wherof tua of thame ware wurth a hundreth pund the peice and <ane> wther thrie wurth ane – hundrethe markis the peice Inde – 400 lib' Item tuantie four head of guidis <wurth> Tuantie markes the peice Inde – 302 lib' Item tuo younge beastis at four pund the peice Inde – 8 lib'

Extending the loissis of the saidis horssis and guidis to the some of

Extending in the haill the lossis of the said wmquhill robert martein and the said Elizabeth douglas abow writtin to the soume of

Followis the declaratione of the witnessis quha wer wsit for probatione of the forsaid horssis and guidis according to thair severall depositionis in presence of the saidis comissioneris

Imprimis robert Lamb indueller in elgin being examinat and Interrogat wpon his aithe deiplie suorne did depone and declair that thair wes plunderit from the said Robert mertein and the said Elizabeth douglas his spo<us> The said fywe peice of horssis tuentie head of guidis and tuo young guidis alexander watsone flescher indueller in elgin and and Iohne wood Skinner burges of elgine being suorne and examined Being deiplie suorne did depone and declair conforme to the said Robert Lambe his depositione in all poyntis

8. Androw Key, litster, burgess of Elgin

Followis the Loissis of androw key litster burges of elgin of his litster wair insicht plenissing cloithis abuilziementis and wtheris wnderwrittin

Imprimis the said androw key being Interrogat and examinat be the saidis comissioneris he by his great aythe Solemlie suorne did depone and declair that according to his avine certane knowledge and by sure Informatione of wyiff and servantis thair wes plunderit and avay takin fra the said andro be the comon enemie furth of his buiithis warkhous and housis In elgin in the monethis of februarij and maij 1645 & at wtheris tymes theirefter of litster wair littit yairne clothis stuffis Insicht plenissing clothis abuilziementis cornes wictuall armour gold silver cunziet and wncunziet houshold provisione and wtheris of that kynd conforme to the particular compt giwin in to the saidis comissioneris

Extending the said androw kay his loissis To the soume of

Followis the said androw kay his loissis of a hors plunderit be the comon enemie fra the said andro at <the> tyme forsaid

Imprimis the said androw key being examined and Interrogat be the saidis comissioneris and deiplie and Solemlie suorne did depone and declair that thair wes plunderit and avay takin from him Be the comonn ene<mie> at the tyme forsaid ane hors wurth threttie pundis money

Extending the said androw kay kay his loissis abowwrittin To the soume of

Followis the declaratione of the witnessis quha ware wseit for probatione of the said hors according to thair severall depositionis in presens of the saidis comissioneris

Imprimis george baxter litster burges of elgin being examinat and Interrogat wpon his aith deiplie suornes did declair that the said hors wes plunderit fra the said androw key and william milne burges of elgin being suorne and examinat did declair and depone conforme to the said george baxter his depositione

9. Thomas Murdoche, tailor, burgess of Elgin and Issobell Thayne his spouse

Followis the loiussis of Thomas murdoche tailzor burges of elgin and Issobell thayne his spous of thair Insicht plenisching merchand wares and wtheris wnderwrittin

Imprimis The said Issobell Thayne hir husband being sick being Interrogat and examinat be the saidis comissioneris sche by hir great aythe Solemlie suorne did depon and declair That according to hir knowledge and by sure Informatione of hir husband and servantis Thair wes plunderit and takin avay fra theimm be the comonn enemie furth of thair houssis and buithis in elgin in the monethis of februarij and maij 1645 and at divers tymes thairefter of Insicht plenisching cloithis abuilziementis merchand wares cornes wictuall armor houshold provisione and wtheris of that kynd Conforme to the particular compt Giwin In to the saidis comissioneris

Extending the said Thomas murdoche and Issobell Thayne thair loissis abowe writtin To The soume of

Followis The said Thomas murdoche and Issobell Thayne his spous of thair Loissis of horss < *deleted* Insicht plenisching merchand wares > plunderit be the comon enemie in the monethe of februarij 1645 and at wther tymes thereftir

Imprimis the said Issobell being Interrogat and examinat be the saidis comissioneris and deiplie and Solemnelie suorne did depone and declair that thair wes plunderit and away takin from thame <ane> hors Be montrois armie in februar 1645 pryce ane hundrethe pundis money with ane wther hors plunderit <be> Lord Lues gordones men in winter Last pryce tuantie pundis money

Extending the loissis of the saidis horssis to ane hundrethe and tuantie pundis money

Extending the said Thomas murdoche and Issobell Thayne thair haill loissis abowvrit<tin> To the soume of

Followis the declaratione of the witnessis quha war wseit for probatione of the want of the saidis thrie hors according To thair severall depositionis In presens of the saidis comissioneris

Imprimis williame Laynge bailzie burges of elgin being examinat and Interrogat wpon his aythe deiplie suorne did depone and declair that thair was plunderit fra the said Thomas murdoche and his spous Be montrois armie in februarij 1645 tuo hors and be Lord Lues gordones men in winter last ane hors and robert dunbar officer burges of elgin being deiplie suorne declairit and deponit conforme to the said williame Laynge his depositione

10. Robert Dunbar, merchant, burgess of Elgin

Followis the Loissis of Robert dunbar merchand burges of elgin of his Insicht plenisching and wndervrittin

Imprimis the said robert dunbar being Interrogat and examinat be the saidis comissioneris he by his great aythe Solemlie suorne did depone and declair that according to his avine certane knowledge and by sure Informatione of his wyff and servantis Thair was plunderit and takin avay from him be The common Enemie furth of his houssis buithis barnes cornzeaird and Sellar in the monethis of februarij and maij 1645 and in winter last when the gordones lay in murray of Insicht plenissing cloithes abuilziementis merchand wares wynes cornes wictuall moneyes houshold provisione and wtheris of that natur with plenissing broken and maid wnvsefull with fywe head of goodis pryce ane hundreth markis with ane cow with calff hoysit be the Enemie pryce – 22 lib' with sex peice of hors pryce – 186 lib' 13s 4d all plunderit and avay Takin from him be the Comon enemie in the monethis of februarij and maij 1645 yeirs conforme to the particular compt givin In to the Saidis Comissioners

Extending the said Robert dunbar his loissis abouwritin To the soume of ane Thowsa<nd> Four hundreth Sextein pundis ellewin shillingis four penneyes money

Followis the declaratione of the witnessis qua war wseit for probatione of the saidis horssis and goods according to ther seuerall depositiones in presens of the saidis Comissioners

Imprimis Iohne grant of Ballandalloche be his missive did depone and declair that the first fywe head of goods was plunderit from the said Robert dunbar Robert gibsone of Linkvoods being Suorne deponit conforme to the said Iohne grant his depositione martein moreis in the colledge of elgin being suorne deponit wpon the cow and four hors Robert zewnie and william Nicoll and william zewnie being suorne deponit and declairit conforme to the said martein moreis his depositione Iohne Smyth in elgin being suorne deponit wpon the wther tuo hors Thomas clerk ther being Suorne deponit conforme to the said Iohne Smythis depositione

11. Patrik Chalmer, skinner, burgess of Elgin

Followis the loissis of patrik Chalmer skinner burges of elgin

Imprimis the said patrik being Interrogatt and examinat be the saidis Comissioners he by his grait aith Solemnlie Suorne did depone and declair That according to his awne certaine knowledge and by Sure Informatione of his wyff and servantis Thair was plunderit and avay takin from him be the comonn Enemie in februarij and in maij 1645 and in winter last when the gordones lay in murray of Insicht plenissing cloithes cornes wictuall armor money houshold provisione and wthers of that kynd with tuo hors pryce ane hundreth marks money with tuo kye pryce – 32 lib' with Fyiftein head of Sheip – 30 lib' wther kow – 12 lib' with ane wther hors – 40 lib' money with ane wther cow pryce – 12 lib' money conforme to the particular compt givin Into the saidis Comissioners

Extending the said patrik chalmer his hoill loissis abouwritin To the Soume of allewin hundreth fourtie ane pundis Sextein shillingis fouir penneyes money

Followis the declaratione of the witnessis quha war wseit for probatione of the loissis of the said patrik his horssis goods and Scheip abouwritin

Imprimis Iames wilsone in elgin being Interrogat and examinat wpon his aith deiplie suorne did depone and declair That ther was plunderit from the said patrik the hoill horsis kye and Sheip abouwritin and Iames Symsone ther being suorne and examinat did depone and declair conforme to the said Iames wilsone his depositione

12. William Lesley, merchant, burgess of Elgin

Follovis the loissis of william lesley merchand burges of elgin

Imprimis the said william leslie being Interrogatt and examinat be the saids Comissioners he by his great aith Solemnelie Suorne did depone and declair That their was plunderit and avay taken fra the said william be the comonn Enemie furth of his houssis in elgin in the monethis of februarij and maij 1645 and at divers tymes theirefter of Insicht plenissing cloithes abuilziementis Ornamentis merchand wares cornes wictuall armor money gold siluer cunziet and wncunziet houshold provisione and wtheris of that kynd conforme to the particular compt givin in to the saidis Comissioneris

Extending the said william leslie his loissis abouwritin To the Soume of Sex hundreth threttie pundis threttein shillingis four penneyes money

13. Alexander Urquhart, surgeon, burgess of elgin

Followis the loissis of alexander wrquhart Chirurgiane burges of elgin

Imprimis the said alexander wrquhart being Interrogatt and examinat be the saidis Comissioners he by his great aith solemnelie Suorne did depone and declair That ther was plunderit and avay taken fra the said alexander be the comonn Enemie Furth of his houssis in elgin in the monethis of februarij and maij 1645 and at diverse tymes therefter of insicht plenissing cloithes abuilziementis Ornamentis wynes drogges cornes wictuall Armor houshold provisione and wtheris of that kynd with ane hors – 50 lib' money conforme to the particular compt givin In to the saidis comissioners quhilk hors was Instantlie provin be Thomas calder baillzie burges of elgin and patrik chalmer skinner burges

Extending the said alexander wrquhart his loissis abouwritin To the Soume of ane thowsand thrie hundreth fourtie four punds Sex shillingis aucht penneyes money

14. William Milne younger, burgess of Elgin

Followis the loissis of william milne zounger burges of elgin

Imprimis the said william Milne being Interrogatt and examinat be the saidis Comissioners he by his grait aith Solemnelie suorne did depon and declair that ther was plunderit and avay takin fra the said william be the Comonn Enemie Furth of his houssis in elgin in the monethis of februarij and maij 1645 and at diverse tymes therefter of Insicht plenissing cloithes abuilziementis cornes wictuall Armor money gold siluer cunziet and wncunziet houshold provisione and wtheris of that kynd with fywe peice of hors pryce – 100 lib' money with ane hors at ther cuming fra auldearne worth – 13 lib' 6s 8d money with ane hors plunderit be Capitane gordone in winter last pryce – 53 lib' 6s 8d with ane hors Taken be lord lewes gordone pryce – 20 lib' money with thrie head of goods pryce – 20 lib money conforme to the particular compt giwin in to the saidis comissioners

Extending the said william milne his hoill loissis abouwritin To the soume of Sex hundreth ane pund thretein shillingis four pennes money

Followis the depositiones of the witnessis wseit for probatione of the horssis and goodis abouwritin

Imprimis thomas grant burges of elgin being Suorne deiplie and Interrogat be the saidis Comissioners did d<epone> and declair That the Fywe hors abouwritin wer plunderit fra the said william milne and Iames milne burges ther being Suorne and examinat did depone conforme to the said Thomas grant his depositione Nicholas dunbar baillzie burges ther being suorne deponit That ther was ane hors plunderit fra the said william when montrois came from auldearne alexander dunbar his sone being Suorne deponit That ther was ane hors plunderit from the said william be Capitan Iohne gordone and thomas calder baillzie burges of elgin proveit That ther was ane hors plunderit fra the said william be lord lowes gordone and the said thomas grant deponit that the said thrie head of goods was plunderit and Iohn Mindheart in elgin being suorne deponit conforme to the Said Thomas grant his deposition

15. Elspet Falconer, relict of James Key, burgess of Elgin

Followis the loissis of elspet falconer relict of wmquhill Iames key burges of Elgin

Imprimis the said elspet being Interrogatt and examinat be the saidis comissioners she by hir great aith Solemnelie suorne did depone and declair that according to hir awin certain knowledge and by Sure Informatione from hir servantis that ther was plunderit and avay takene from hir be the comonn enemie in the moneth of februarij 1645 and at diverse tymes therefter of Insicht plenissing cloithes abuilziementis cornes wictuall gold siluer cunziet and wncunziet houshold provisio<ne> and wtheris of that kynd conforme to the particular compt giwin in to the saidis comissioners

Extending the said Elspet falconer hir loissis To the Soume of Tuo hundreth aucht punds sextein shillingis money

16. James Dunbar, merchant, burgess of Elgin

Followis the loissis of Iames Dunbar merchand burges of elgin

Imprimis the said Iames being Interrogatt and examinat be the saidis Comissioners he by his great aith Solemnlie suorne did declair and depone that according to his awin certain knowledge and by Sure informatione off his wyff and servantis that ther was plunderit and avay taken from him be the comonn enemie in the moneth of februarij and maij 1645 and at diverse tymes therefter of insicht plenissing cloithes abuilziementis merchand wares money houshold provisione and wthers of that kynd conforme to the particular compt giwin in to the saidis Comissioners

Extending the said Iames dunbar his loissis abouwritin to the soume of Tuo hundreth four scoir Fy<ft>eine punds Sewin shillingis money

17. James Milne, merchant, burgess of Elgin

Followis the loissis of Iames milne merchand burges of elgin

Imprimis the said Iames milne being Interrogatt and examinat be the saidis Comissioners he by his great aith Solemnelie suorne did depone and declair that according to his awine certain knowledge and by sure informatione of his wyff and servantis that ther was plunderit and avay takin from the said Iames milne be the comonn enemie in the monethes of februarij and maij 1645 and at diverse tymes ther efter of Insicht plenissing cloithes abuilziementis merchand wares money houshold provisione and wtheris of that kynd conformne to the particular compt giwin in to the saidis Comissioners

Extending the said Iames milne his loissis abouwritin To the Soume of Thrie hundreth allwein pundis money

18. James Feldonne, maltman, burgess of Elgin

Followis the loissis of Iames feldonne maltman burges of elgin

Imprimis the said Iames feldonne being deiplie suorne and examinat be the saidis comissioners did depone and declair that according to his owin certain knouledge ther was plunderit and avay takin fra him be the comonn Enemie at the tymes forsaid of insicht plenissing cloithes wictuall and armor houshold provisione and wthers off that kynd conforme to the saidis Comissioners

Extending the said Iames feldonne his loissis abouwritin To the Soume

19. Thomas Carmichaell, merchant, burgess of Elgin

Followis the loissis of Thomas Carmichaell merchand burges of elgin

Imprimis the said Thomas carmichaell being Interrogatt and examinat be the saidis comissioners he by his great aith Solemnelie Suorne did depone and declair That according to his owin certaine knowledge and By sure Informatione of his wyffe and servantis That Thair was plunderit and avay tackin from the said Thomas Carmichaell be the comon enemie in the monethis of februarij and maij 1645 and at diverse tymes thairefter of Insicht plenisching cloithes abuilziementis merchand wares almit ledder houshold provisione and wtheris of that kynd Conforme to the particular compt giwin in to the saidis comissioneris

Extending the said Thomas Carmichaell his loissis abowwrittin To the soume of tu hundreth nyntein pundis

20. William Tarres, merchant, burgess of Elgin

Followis the loissis of William tarres merchand burges of elgin

Imprimis the said william tarres being Interrogat and examinat be the saidis Comissioneris he by his great ayth Solemlie suorne did depone and declair That according to his aine certane knowledge and by sure informatione of his wyffe and servantis that thair wes plunderit and avay takin from the said williame tarres be the comon enemie in the moneth of februarij and maij 1645 at diverse tymes theirefter of Insicht plenisching cloithis abuilziementis merchand wares armor houshold provisione and wtheris of that kynd with ane paiced hors pryce – 46 lib' money conforme to the particular compt giwin in to the saidis comissioneris Quhilk hors was prowin be willliame Laynge burges of elgin and Iohne andersone skinner burges ther being deiplie suorne To Tat effect

Extending the said William tarres his haill loissis abowrittin To the soume of ane Thousand Sex hundrethe tuantie thrie pundis fourtein shillingis

21. Walter Hay, merchant, burgess of Elgin

Followis the loissis of walter hay merchand burges of elgin

Imprimis the said walter hay being Interrogat and examinat be the saidis comissioneris he by his great ayth Solemlie suorne did depone and declair that according to his owne certane knowledge and by sure Informatione of his wyiff and servantis that thair was plunderit and avay takin from him be the comon enemie in the moneth of februarij and maij 1645 & at diverse tymes theirefter of Insicht plensiching cloithis abuilziementis merchand wares armor houshold provisione and wtheris of that kynd Conforme to the partiular compt giwin to the saidis comissioneris

Extending the said walter hay his loissis abowe writtin To the soume of ane hundrethe Ten pundis fyftein shillingis aucht pennies money

22. Hew Hay, merchant, burgess of Elgin

Followis the loissis of hew hay merchand burges of elgin

Imprimis the said hew hay being Interrogat and examinat be the saidis comissioneris he by his great aythe Solemlie Suorne did depone and declair That according to his avne certane knowledge and by sure informatione of his wyiff and servantis that thair wes plunderit and avay takin from him be the comon enemie in the monethis of februarij and maij 1645 & at diverse tymes therefter of Insicht plensiching cloithis abuilziementis merchand wares money armor houshold provisione and wtheris of that kynd Conforme to the particular compt giwin in to the saidis comissioneris

Extending the said Hew Hay his Loissis abowwrittin To the soume of tuo hundrethe aucht pundis Sex shillingis aucht pennies money

23. Patrik Murdoche, indweller in Elgin

Followis the loissis of patrik murdoche induellar in elgin

Imprimis The said patrik murdoche being Interrogat and examinat be the saidis comissioneris he by his great aythe Solemlie suorne did depone and decalir That according to his aune certane knowledge and by sure Informatione of his wyiff and servantis that thair wes plunderit and avay takin from him be the comon enemie in the monethis of februarij and maij 1645 and at diverse tymes therefter of Insicht plenisching cloithis abuilziementis merchand warres money armor houshold provisione and wtheris of that kynd Conforme to the particular compt giwin in to the saidis conissioneris

Extending the said patrik murdoche his loissis abowwrittin To the soume of ane hundreth fourscoir threttein pund Sevin shillingis aucht pennies money

24. Frances Dunbar, saddler, burgess of Elgin

Followis the loissis of frances dunbar saidler burges of elgin

Imprimis the said frances being Interrogat and examinat be the saidis comissioneris he by his great aythe Solemlie suorne did depone and declair that according to his avne certane knowledge and by sure Informatione of his wyffe and servantis that thair was plunderit and avay takin from the said frances dunbar be the comon enemie in the monethis of februar and maij 1645 and at diverse tymes therefter of Insight plensiching cloithis money armor wictuall saidles saidle graythe houshold provisione and wtheris of that kynd Conforme to the particular compt giwin in to the saidis comissioneris

Extending the said frances dunbar his Loissis abowwrittin To the soume of ane hundrethe thriescore sex pundis fywe shillingis money

25. James Gordone, indweller in Elgin

Followis the loissis of Iames gordone induellar in elgin

Imprimis The said Iames gordone being Interrogat and examinat be the saidis comissioneris he by His great aith Solemnlie Suorne did depone and declair that according to his awne certane knowledge and by sure imformatione of his wyffe and servantis that thair was plunderit and avay taken fra the said Iames gordone be the comonn enemie in the monethis of febr[uar]ij and maij 1645 and at diverse tymes therefter of Insicht plenissing cloithes money shoos barkit ledder money armor and wtheris houshold provisione and wtheris of that kynd conforme to the particular compt giwin in to the saidis comissioners

Extending the said Iames gordone his loissis abouwritin To the Soume of Thrie scoir Ten punds fourtein shillingis aucht penneyes money

26. Johne Wynchester, tailor, burgess of Elgin

Followis the loissis of Iohne wynchester tailzor burges of elgin

Imprimis the said Iohne wynchester being Interrogatt and examinat be the saidis Comissioners he by his grait aith Solemnelie suorne did depone and declair that according to his owine certaine knowledge and by Sure informatione off his wyff and servantis that ther was plunderit and away Takin from the said Iohne wynchester be the comonn enemie in the monethes of februarij and maij 1645 and at diverse tymes therefter of Insicht plenissing cloithes abuilziementis money armor houshold provisione and vtheris of that kynd conforme to the particular compt giwin to the saidis Comissioneris

Extending the said Iohne wynchester his loissis abouwritin to the Soume of Thrie Scoir Sewinteine pund fourtein shillingis money

27. Helen Innes, relict of Johne Muirone, tailor in Elgin

Followis the loissis of helen muirone relict of wmquhill Iohne muirone teilzeor in elgin

Imprimis the said helein Innes being Interrogatt and examinat be the saidis Comissioners shee by hir great aith Solemnelie Suorne did depone and declair that according to hir owne certaine knowledge and by Sure Informatione of hir husband that ther was plunderit and avay takin from the said Helen Innes be the comonn Enemie in the monethis of februarij and maij 1645 and at diverse tymes therefter of Insicht plenissing cloithes abuilziementis money houshold provisione and wtheris off that kynd conforme To the particular compt giwin in to the saidis Comissioners

Extending the said Helen Innes hir loissis abouwritin To the Soume of Fourtie four pundis nyne shillingis aucht penneyes

28. Alexander Philp, webster in Elgin

Followis the loissis off alexander philp webster in elgin

Imprimis the said alexander philp being Interrogatt and examinat be the saidis Comissioners he by his grait aith Solemnelie suorne did depone and declair that according to his owen certaine knowledge and by sure Informatione of his wyff that ther was plunderit and avay taken from the said alexander philp be the comonn enemie in the monethes of februarij and maij 1645 and at diverse tymes therefter of insicht plenissing cloithes abuilziementis money houshold provisione and wtheris of that kynd conforme to the particular compt giwin in to the saidis Comissioners

Extending the said alexander philp his loissis abouwritin To the Soume of Thrie Scoir Ten punds money

29. Johne Thomsone, flesher in Elgin

Followis the loissis off Iohne Thomsone flescher in elgin

Imprimis the said Iohne Thomsone being Interrogatt and examinat be the saidis Comissioneris he by his great aith Solemnelie Suorne did depone and declair that according to his owen certaine knowledge and by Sure Informatione of his wyff and servantis that thair was plunderit and avay taken from him of Insicht plenissing cloithes abuilziementis money armor houshold provisione and wtheris off that kynd conforme to the particular compt giwin in to the saidis Comissioners

Extending the said Iohne Thomsone his loissis abouwritin to the Soume of Tuo hundreth pundis money

30. Thomas Grant, tailor, burgess of Elgin

Followis the loissis off Thomas Grant Tailzeor burges of elgin

Imprimis the said thomas grant being Interrogatt and examinat be the saidis Comissioners he by his great aith Solemnilie suorne did depone and declair that according to his owne certaine cnowledge and by sure informatione of his wyff and servantis that ther was plunderit and avay taken from him of insicht plenissing cloithes abuilziementis money houshold provisione & wtheris of that kynd conforme to the particular compt givin in to the saidis comissioneris

Extending the said thomas grant his loissis abouwritin to the Soume of ane hundreth thretie Sewin pundis money

31. Johne Forsyth younger, burgess of Elgin

Followis the loissis of Iohne forsyth zounger burges of elgin

Imprimis the said Iohne forsyth being Interrogatt and examinat be the saidis Comissioners he by his great aith solemnlie suorne did depone and declair that according to his owne certaine knowledge and by Sure informatione off his wyff that ther was plunderit and avay taken from the said Iohne forsyith of Insicht plenissing Cloithes wictuall armes money houshold provisione and wtheris of that kynd conforme to the particular compt giwin in to the saidis comissioneris

Extending the said Iohne forsythe his loissis abowwrittin To the soume of sex scoir pundis

32. Robert Smythe, indweller in Elgin

Followis the loissis of Robert smythe indueller in elgin

Imprimis the said Robert smythe being Interrogat and examinat be the saidis comissioneris he by his great aythe Solemlie suorne did depone and declair That according to his awne certane knawledge and by sure Informatione of his wyiff that thair was plunderit and avay takin from the said Robert smythe be the comon enemie in the monethis of februarij and maij 1645 and at diverse tymes thairefter of Insicht plensiching cloithis abuilziementis cornes wictuall houshold provisione and wtheris of that kynd conforme to the particular compt giwin in to the saidis comissioneris

Extending the said Robert smythe his loissis abowwrittin To the soume of ane hundrethe tuentie nyne pundis 13s 4d

33. George Purse, burgess of Elgin

Followis the loissis of george purse burges of elgin

Imprimis The said george being examinat and Interrogat be the saidis comissioneris he by his great aythe Solemlie suorne did depone and declair That according to his awne knowledge and by sure Informatione of his wyiffe and servantis that ther was plunderit and avay takin from the said george purse be the comon enemie in the monethis of februarij and maij 1645 and at diverse tymes therefter of Insicht plensiching cloithis abuilziementis cornes wictuall armor houshold provisione and wtheris of that kynd conforme to the saidis comissioneris

Extending the said george purs his loissis abowe writtin to the soume of ane hundrethe Sevin punds tuell shillingis

34. Alexander Forsythe, glasswright, burgess of Elgin

Followis the loissis of alexander forsythe glasen wricht burges of elgin

Imprimis the said alexander forsythe being interrogat and examinat be the saidis comissioneris he by his great aythe Solemlie suorne did depone and declair that according to his awne certane knawledge and by sure Informatione of his wyffe and servantis that ther was plunderit and avay takin from the said alexander forsythe be the comon enemie in the monethis of februarij and maij 1645 and at diverse tymes thairefter of Insicht plensiching cloithis abuilziementis cornes wictuall money glass lead houshold provisione and wtheris of that kynd Conforme to the particular compt giwin in to the saidis comissioneris

Extending the said alexander forsythe his loissis abowe writtin to the soume of ane hundrethe fourscoir ane pund thrie shillingis 8d

35. Robert Pringill, burgess of Elgin

Followis the loissis of Robert pringill burges of elgin

Imprimis the said robert pringill being Interrogat and examinat be the saidis comissioneris he by his great aythe Solemlie suorne did depone and declair That according to his awne certane knowledge and by sure Informatione of his wyiff and servantis That thair was plunderit and avay takin from the said robert Be the comon enemie In the moneth of februarij & at diverse tymes thairefter of Insicht plenisching cloithis cornes wictuall almit ledder gliffis houshold provisione and wtheris of that kynd conforme to the particular compt giwin in to the saidis comissioneris

Extending the said robert pringill his loissis abowwrittin to the soume of Sex score ten pundis mone\<y\>

36. James Walker

Followis the loissis of Iames walker

Imprimis the said Iames walker being Interrogat and examinat be the saidis comissioneris he by his great aythe Solemlie suorne did depone and declair that according to his awne certane knowledge and by sure Informatione of his wyffe and servantis that ther was plunderit and avay takin from the said Iames valker be the comon enemie in the monethis of februarij and maij 1645 and at diverse tymes ther efter of Insicht plenisching cloithis abuilziementis cornes wictuall money houshold provisione and wtheris of that kynd with tua hors pryce – 100 lib' with ane cow pryce – 13 lib' 6s 8d with sex head of scheape at 33s 4d the peice Ind – 60 lib' quhilkis horssis cow and scheipe wes prowin be Richard Walker and alexander walker induelleris in elgin they being suorne To that effect conforme to ane particular compt giwin in to the saidis comissioneris

Extending the said Iames walker his loissis abowwrittin To the soume of tuo hundrethe pundis ten shillingis aucht pennies money

37. James Duncane, maltman in Elgin

Followis the loissis of Iames duncane maltman in elgin

Imprimis the said Iames ducane being Interrogat and examinat be the saidis comissioneris he by his great aythe Solemlie suorne did depone and declair that according to his awne certane knawledge ther wes plunderit and avay takin fra the him comon enemie in the monethis of februarij 1645 of Insicht plenisching cloithis wictuall malt houshold provisione and wtheris of that kynd conforme to the particular compt giwin in to the saidis comissioneris

Extending the said Iames Duncane his loissis abouwritin To the Soume of Thrie Scoir Sex pund threttein shillingis four penneyes money

38. James Warden, indweller in Elgin

Followis the loissis of Iames warden indueller in elgin

Imprimis the said Iames warden being interrogatt and examinat be the said Comissioners he by his great aith Solemnlie Suorne did depone and declair that according to his awne certaine knovledge and by sure informatione off his wyff and servantis that ther was plunderit and avay taken from the said Iames warden be the comonne enemie in the moneth of februarij and maij 1645 and at diverse tymes therefter of insicht plenissing cloithes abuilziementis almit ledder houshold and provisione and wtheris off that kynd conforme to the particular compt givin in to the saidis Comissioners

Extending the said Iames warden his loissis abouwritin to the Soume of Thrie scoir Sewintein pundis 13s 4d

39. David Mailling, gunsmith in Elgin

Followis the loissis off david mailling gunsmith in elgin

Imprimis the said david mailling being Interrogatt and examinat be the saidis Commissioneris he by his great aith solemnlie Suorne did depone and declair that according to his owne certaine knowledge That ther was plunderit and avay takin from him be commonn enemie in the monethes of februarij and maij 1645 and at diverse tymes therefter of Insicht plenissing cloithes muscottis gunes pistollis houshold provisione and wtheris of that kynd conforme to the particular compt givin in to the saidis comissioneris

Extending the said david mailling his loissis abouwritin to the Soume of ane hundreth thrie scoir auchteine pund 9s 4d

40. Patrik Mirrisone, cordwainer in Elgin

Followis the loissis off patrik mirrisone cardoner in elgin

Imprimis the said patrik mirrisone being interrogatt and examinat be the saidis comissioneris he by his great aith solemnlie suorne did depone and declair that according to his owne certaine knowledge that ther was plunderit and avay takin from the said patrik mirrisone be the comonn enemie in the moneth off februarij and maij 1645 and at diverse tymes therefter of insicht plenissing cloithes abuilziementis armor money Barkitt ledder houshold provisione and wtheris of that kynd conforme to the particular Compt givin In to the saidis Comissioners

Extending the said patrik mirrisone his loissis abouwritin To the Soume of Four Scoir punds aucht Shillingis money

41. James Paull in Elgin

Followis the loissis of Iames paull in elgin

Imprimis the said Iames paull being interrogatt and examinat be the saidis Comissioneris he by his great aith Solemnelie Suorne did depone and declair that according to his aune certaine knowledge and by sure informatione of his wyff and servantis that ther was plunderit and avay takin from the said Iames paull be the Comon enemie in the monethes of februarij 1645 and at diverse tymes therefter of insicht plenissing cloithes armor houshold plenissing and wtheris of that kynd conforme to the particular compt givin In to the saidis comissioneris

Extending the said Iames paull his loissis abouwritin to the Soume of Tuentie four pund 12s 4d

42. Thomas Cok, indweller in Elgin

Followis the loissis of Thomas Cok indueller in elgin

Imprimis the said thomas cok being interrogatt and examinat be the saidis comissioners he by his great aith Solemnelie Suorne did depone and declair that according to his owne certaine knowledge and by sure informatione of his wyff and servantis that thair was plunderit and avay takin from the said thomas Cok be the Comonn enemie in the monethes of februarij & maij 1645 and at diverse Tymes therefter of insicht plenissing armor houshold provisione and wtheris of that kynd conforme to the particular compt givin in to the saidis Comissioners

Extending the said Thomas Cok his loissis abouwritin to the Soume of Thrie scoir fyiftein punds 7s 8d

43. Alexander Smyth, smith in Elgin

Followis the loissis of alexander Smyth Smyth in elgin

Imprimis the said alexander Smyth being interrogatt and examinat be the saidis Comissioneris he by his great ayth Solemnelie Suorne did depone and declair that according to his owne certaine knowledge and by sure informatione of his wyff and Servantis that ther was plunderit and avay takin from the said alexander Smyth be the comon enemie in the monethes of februarij and maij 1645 and at diverse tymes therefter of insicht plenissing cloithes abuilziementis cornes wictuall coals Irone wark houshold provisione and wtheris of that kynd conforme to the particular compt Givin In to the saidis Comissioneris

Extending the said alexander Smyth his loissis abouwritin to the Soume of ane hundreth tuentie fywe punds nyntein shillingis four penneyes

44. Androw Layng, cordwainer in Elgin

Followis the loissis of androw layng cardoner in elgin

Imprimis the said androw layng being interrogatt and examinat be the saidis Comissioneris he by his great ayth Solemnlie Suorne did depone and declair that according To his owne certaine knowledge and By Sure informatione of his wyffe that thair was plunderit and avay takin from the said androw layng be the comon enemie in the monethis of februarij and maij 1645 and at diverse tymes thairefter of Insicht plenisching cloithis hayd<is> armor houshold provisione and wtheris of that kynd conforme to the particular compt giwin in to the saidis comissioneris

Extending the said androw laynge his loissis abowwrittin to the soume of fyftie aucht pundis 6s 8d

45. Johne Kleis, tailor in Elgin

Followis the loissis of Iohne Kleis Teilzour in elgin

Imprimis the said Iohne Kleis being Interrogat and examinat be the saidis comissioneris he by his great othe solemlie suorne did depone and declair according to his owne certane knawledge and by sure Informatione of his wyffe and servantis that thair wes plunderit and avay takin fra the said Iohne Kleis be the comon enemie in the monethis of februarij and maij 1645 and at divers tymes therefter of Insicht plenisching plaiding houshold provisione and wtheris of that kynd conforme to the particular compt giwin in to the saidis comissioneris

Extending the said Iohne Kleis his loissis abowwrittin to the soume of fourscore ane pundis money

46. Alexander Innes, cordwainer, burgess of Elgin

Followis the loissis of alexander Innes cordoner burges of elgin

Imprimis the said alexander Innes being Interrogat and examinat be the saidis comissioneris he by his great oathe solemlie suorne did depone and declair That according to his awne certaine knowledge and by sure Informatione of his wyffe and servantis that thair wes plunderit and avay takin from the said alexander Innes be the comon enemie in the monethis of februar and maij 1645 and at diverse tymes therefter of Insicht plenisching cloithis cornes wictuall Barkit haydis schoone money houshold provisione and wtheris of that kynd conforme to the particular compt giwin in to the saidis comissioneris

Extending the said alexander Innes his loissis abowe writtin to the soume of tuo hundreth 4 lib' 13s 4d

47. George Watsone, indweller in Elgin

Followis the loissis of george watsone indueller in elgin

Imprimis the said george watsone being Interrogat and examinat be the saidis comissioneris he by his great oathe solemlie suorne did depon and declair that according to his owne certane knowledge and by s<ure> Informatione of his wyffe That thair was takin from the said george watsone be the comon enemie In the monethe of maij 1645 and at diverse tymes theirefter of Insicht plenisching cloithes wictuall money houshold provisione and wtheris of that kynd conforme to the particular compt giwin in to the saidis comissioneris

Extending the said george watsone his loissis abowwrittin to the soume of thriescoir Sex pundis 15s 4d

48. Johne Stronache, flesher in Elgin

Followis the loissis of Iohne stronache flescher in elgin

Imprimis the said Iohne stronache being Interrogat and examinat be the saidis comissioneris he by his great oathe Solemnlie suorne did depone and declair that according to his owne certane knawledge and by sure Informatione of his wyffe that ther was plunderit and avay takin from the said Iohne stronache be the comon enemie in the monethis of februarij and maij 1645 and at diverse tymes thairefter of Insicht plenisching cloithis abuilziementis cornes wictuall haydis houshold provisione and wtheris of that kynd conforme to the particular compt giwin in to the saidis comissioneris

Extending the said Iohne stronache his loissis abowvrittin to the soume of tuo hundrethe aucht pundis aucht pennies money

49. Robert Malice, merchant, burgess of Elgin

Followis the loissis of Robert malice merchand burges of elgin

Imprimis the said robert malice being Interrogat and examinat be the saidis comissioneris he by his great oathe Solemlie suorne did depon and eclair that according to his awne certane knowledge and by sure informatione of his wyiff and servantis that thair wes plunderit and avay takin from the said robert malice be the comon enemie in the monethis of februarij and maij 1645 and at diverse tymes therefter of insicht plensiching cloithis merchand wares armor houshold provisione and w<theris> of that kynd conforme to the particular compt giwin in to the saidis comissioneris

Extending the said robert malice his loisis abowwrittin to the some of fyftie nyne pundis sex schillingis aucht pennies money

50. Alexander Peterkin, webster in Elgin

Followis the loissis of alexander peterkin webster in elgin

Imprimis the said alexander peterkin being Interrogat and examinat be the saidis comissioneris he by his great aythe Solemlie suorne did depone and declair that according to his aune certane knawledge and by sure Informatione of his vyiff thair vas plunderit and avay takin from the said alexander petterkin be the comon enemie in the monethes of februarij and maij 1645 and at diverse tymes thairefter of Insicht plensiching cloithis plaiding houshold provisione and wtheris of that kynd Conforme to the particular compt giwin in to the saidis comissioneris

Extending the said alexander peterkin his loissis abowvrittin to the soume of threttiesevin pundis sevintein schillingis aucht pennies money

51. Alexander Smythe, merchant, burgess of Elgin

Followis the loissis of alexander smythe merchand burges of elgin

Imprimis the said alexander smythe being Interrogat and examinat be the saidis comissioneris he by his great oath Solemlie suorne did depone and declair that according to his awne certane knawledge and by sure Informatione of his wyiffe and servantis that ther vas plunderit and avay takin from the
Said alexander Smyth be the Comon enemie in the moneth of februarij and may 1645 and at diverse tymes therefter of cloithes Insicht plenissing money armor cornes wictuall merchand wares houshold provisione and wtheris of that kynd conforme to the particular compt givin in to the saidis comissioneris

Extending the said alexander Smyth his loissis abouwritin to the Soume of Sewin Scoir ane pund money

52. Alexander Boynd, merchant, burgess of Elgin

Followis the loissis off alexander Boynd merchand burges of elgin

Imprimis the said alexander Boynd being interrogat and examinat be the saidis Comissioneris he by his great ayth Solemnelie suorne did depone and declair that according to his awin certaine knowledge that ther was plunderit and avay taken from him be the comonn enemie in the moneth of februarij and maij 1645 and diverse tymes therefter of insicht plenissing cloithis abuilziementis armor merchand wares houshold provisione and wtheris of that kynd Conforme to the particular Compt givin in to the saidis Comissioneris

Extending the said alexander Boynd his loissis abouwritin to the Soume of Fywe hundreth fourtie aucht pund sex schillingis aucht penneyes money

53. Grissell Lermonth, indweller in Elgin

Followis the loissis of Grissell lermonth indueller in elgin

Imprimis the said grissell lermonth being interrogatt and examinat be the saidis Comissioneris she by hir great aith Solemnelie suorne did depone and declair that according to hir awen certaine knovledge that ther was plunderit and avay takin fra hir be the comonn enemie in the moneth of februarij 1645 and at diverse tymes therefter of cloithes insicht plenissing wictuall houshold provisione and wtheris of that kynd conforme to the particular compt givin In To the saidis Comissioneris

Extending the said Grissell Lermonth hir loissis abouwritin to the Soume of ane hundreth ane pund threttein shillingis four pennes money

54. Robert Dunbar elder, burgess of Elgin

Followis the loissis of Robert dunbar elder burges of elgin

Imprimis the said Roberit dunbar being interrogat and examinat be the saidis Comissioneris he by his great ayth Solemnelie Suorne did depone and declair that according to his owne certaine knowledge by sure informatione of his wyff and servantis that ther was plunderit and avay takin from the said Robert be the comon enemie in the monethes of februarij and maij 1645 and at diverse tymes therefter of cloithis abuilziementis insicht plenissing wictuall money armor houshold provisione and wtheris of that kynd Conforme to the particular compt givin in to the saidis Comissioneris

Extending the said Robert dunbar his loissis abouwritin to the Soume of tuo hundreth fovr Scoir sevin pund auchtein shillingis money

55. James Malice, merchant, burgess of Elgin

Followis the loissis of Iames malice merchand burges of elgin

Imprimis the said Iames malice being interrogatt and examinat be the saidis Comissioneris he by his great ayth Solemnelie Suorne did depone and declair that according to his certaine knowledge thair was plunderit and avay takin from him be the comonn enemie in februarij and maij 1645 sensyne of insicht plenissing cloithes merchand wares houshold provisione and wtheris of that kynd conforme to the particular compt givin to the saidis Comissioneris

Extending the said Iames malice his loissis abouwritin to the Soume of ane hundreth aucht pund threttein shillingis four penneyes

56. Robert Sinclar, indweller in Elgin

Followis the loissis of Robert Sinclar indueller in elgin

Imprimis the said Robert Sinclar being interrogat and examinat be the saidis comissioneris he by his great ayth solemnelie suorne did depone and declair < *deleted* and depone > was plunderit and avay takin from him be the Comonn enemie in februarij and maij 1645 and sensyne of insicht plenissing wictuall money armor cloithes houshold provisione and wtheris of that kynd conforme to the particular compt givin in to the saidis comissioneris

Extending the said Robert Sinclar his loissis abouwritin To the Soume of vj^{xx}4 lib' 13s 4d

57. Kathrein Stronache in Elgin

Followis the loissis of kathrein Stronache in elgin

Imprimis the said kathrein being sworne and examinat be the saidis comissioneris did depon that ther was plunderit and avay takin from hir be the comonne enemie in februarij and maij 1645 and sensyne of insicht plenissing cloithes abuilziementis houshold provisione & wtheris of that kynd conforme to the particular compt Givin in to the saidis Comissioneris

Extending the said kathrein Stronache hir loissis abouwritin To the Soume of ane hundreth thrie scoir fywe pund thrie shillingis aucht pennes

58. James Boynd, webster in Elgin

Followis the loissis of Iames Boynd vobster in elgin

Imprimis the said Iames boynd being Deiplie suorne Deponit that ther was plunderit from him be the commone Enemie at the tymes forsaid < *deleted* to the soume > of insicht plenissing houshold provisione money armor cloithes abuilziementis & wtheris of that kynd abouwritin conforme to the particular compt

Extending the said Iames Boynd his loissis abouwritin to – 1^{c}iij^{xx}12 lib' 14s

59. Thomas Dauidsone in Elgin

Followis the loissis of thomas dauidsone in elgin

Imprimis the said thomas dauidsone being Deiplie suorne Deponit that ther was plunderit from him be the commone Enemie at the tyme forsaid of insicht plenissing cloithes money wictuall houshold provisione & wtheris of that kynd abouwritin conforme to the particular compt

extending the said thomas dauidsone his loissis abouwritin to – 1^{c}xlviij lib'

60. John Hardie, merchant, burgess of Elgin
Followis the loissis of Iohn hardie merchand burges of elgin

Imprimis the said Iohn hardie being Deiplie suorne Deponit that ther was plunderit from him be the commone Enemie at the tymes forsaid of insicht plenissing houshold provisione money wictual armor merchand wares & wtheris of that kynd abouwritin conforme to the particular compt

Extending the said Iohn hardie his loissis abouwritin to – 1^c iiij^{xx} lib' xv s

61. George Readhead in Elgin
Followis the loissis of george readhead in elgin

Imprimis the said george readhead being Deiplie suorne Deponit that ther was plunderit from him be the commone Enemie at the tyme forsaid of Insicht plenissing cloithes wictual money barkit ledder houshold provisione & wtheris of that kynd conforme to the particular compt

Extending the said george readhead his loissis abouwritin to – 25 lib' 6s 8d

62. John Andersone, clockmaker
Followis the loissis of Iohn Andersone orilogeris

Imprimis the said Iohn Andersone being Deiplie suorne Deponit that ther was plunderit from him be the commone Enemie at the tyme forsaid of insicht plenissing cloithes money armor merchand wares houshold Provisione & wtheris of that kynd conforme to the particular Compt

Extending the said Iohn andersone his loissis abouwritin to – xliij lib' vij s

63. Agnes Chalmer in Elgin
Followis the loissis of Agnes chalmer in elgin

Imprimis the said Agnes being Deiplie suorne Deponit that ther wes plunderit from hir be the commone Enemie of insicht plenissing cloithis money wictual houshold provisione & wtheris of that kynd abouwritin conforme to the particular compt

Extending the said agnes chalmer hir loissis abouwritin to – iij^{xx} lib'

64. Thomas Schipherd in Elgin
Followis the loissis of Thomas Schipherd in elgin

Imprimis the said thomas being Deiplie suorne Deponit that ther wes plunderit from him be the Comone Enemie of insicht plenissing cloithes abuilziementis money wictual houshold provisione & wtheris of that kynd abouwritin conforme to the particular Compt

Extending the said Thomas Schipheird his loissis abouwritin to xxxix lib' 12s

65. Patrick Pettindreiche, merchant, burgess of Elgin
Followis the loissis of Patrick Pettindreiche, merchand burges of elgin

Imprimis the said Patrick being Deiplie suorne Deponit that ther was plunderit from him be the commone Enemie at the tyme forsaid of insicht plenissing cloithes money merchand wares wictual houshold provisione & wtheris of that kynd abouwritin conforme to the particular compt

Extending the said patrick pettindreiche his loissis abouwritin to – ij^c vj lib' xiiij s

66. George Innes, burgess of Elgin
Followis the loissis of george Innes burges of elgin

Imprimis the said george Innes being Deiplie suorne Deponit that ther was plunderit from him be the comone Enemie at the tyme forsaid of insicht plenissing cloithes abuilziementis cornes wictual merchand wares & wtheris of that kynd abouwritin conforme to the particular compt

 Extending the said george Innes his loissis abouwritin to – iiij^{xx}j lib'

67. James Innes, skinner, burgess of Elgin

 Followis the loissis of Iames Innes skinner burges of elgin

 Imprimis the said Iames Innes being Deiplie suorne Deponit that ther was plunderit from him be the Comon Enemie at the tymes forsaid of insicht plenissing cloithes abuilziementis money wictuall gliffis almit ledder houshold provisione & wtheris of that kynd abouwritin conforme to the particular compt

 Extending the said Iames Innes his loissis abouwritin to – 1^c xlix lib' x s

68. John Pitterkin in Elgin

 Followis the loissis of Iohn pitterkin in elgin

 Imprimis the said Iohn being deiplie suorne Deponit that ther wes plunderit from him be the commone Enemie at the tyme forsaid of insicht plenissing cloithes abuilziementis money armor houshold provisione & wtheris of that kynd abouwritin conforme to the particular compt

 Extending the said Iohn his loissis abouwritin to – xxviij lib' xviij s

69. Agnes Jamesone in Elgin

 Followes the loissis of Agnes Iameson in elgin

 Imprimis the said Agnes being Deiplie suorne Deponit that ther was plunderit from hir be the commone Enemie the tymes forsaid of insicht plenissing cloithes abuilziementis money wictuall houshold provisione & wtheris of that kynd abouwritin conforme to the particular compt

 Extending the said Agnes hir loissis abouwritin to – 1^{c}iij^{xx}xv lib' xvj s

70. Michaell Andersone in Elgin

 Followis the loiss of michaell andersone in elgin

 Imprimis the said michaell being deiplie suorne Deponit that ther was plunderit from him be the commone Enemie of insicht plenissing cloithes abuilziementis houshold provisione and wtheris of that kynd conforme to the particular compt

 Extending the said michaell andersone his loissis abouwritin to the Soume of Sevintein pund 2s 8d

71. George Pitterkin, indweller in Elgin

 Followis the loissis of george pitterkin indueller in elgin

 Imprimis the said george piterkin being deiplie Suorne deponit that ther was plunderit from him be the comone enemie the tyme forsaid of Insicht plenissing cloithes abuilziementis money wictuall houshold provisione and wtheris of that kynd abouwritin conforme to the particular compt

 Extending the loissis of the said george pitterkin to fourie sewin pundis money

72. James Sibbald in Elgin

 Followis loissis of Iames Sibbald in elgin

 Imprimis the said Iames being deiplie suorne did depon that ther was plunderit from him be the comonn enemie the tyme forsaid of insicht plenissing wictuall money armor houshold provisione and wtheris of that kynd abouwritin conforme to the particular compt

    Extending the said Iames Sibbald his loissis abouwritin to fyiftie 5 lib' 6s 8d

73. Patrik Littlejohn in Elgin

    Followis the loissis of patrik littleIohn in elgin

    Imprimis the said patrik littleIohn being suorne deponit that ther was plunderit from him be the comonn enemie the tyme forsaid of cloithes armor houshold plenissing and wtheris of that kynd abouwritin conforme to the particular compt

    Extending the said patrik littleIohne his loissis abouwritin to Sextein pund 18s 4d

74. William Patersone in Elgin

    Followis the loissis of william patersone in elgin

    Imprimis the said william patersone being deiplie suorne deponit that ther was plunderit from him at the tyme forsaid of cloithes armor houshold provisione and wtheris of that kynd conforme to the particular compt

    Extending the said william patersone his loissis abouwritin to thrie Scoir pund thrie shillingis 4d

75. Issobell Warden, indweller in Elgin

    Followis the loissis off Issobell warden indueller in elgin

    Imprimis the said Issobell warden being deiplie suorne deponit that ther was plunderit and avay takin from hir be the comonn Enemie at the tyme forsaid of insicht plenissing cloithes abuilziementis money wictuall houshold provisione and wtheris of that kynd abouwritin conforme to the particular compt

    Extending the said Issobell warden hir loissis abouwritin to ane hundreth fourtie nyn lib' 6s 8d

76. Johne Pairker, indweller in Elgin

    Followis the loissis of Iohne pairker indueller in elgin

    Imprimis the said Iohne pairker being deiplie Suorne did depon that ther was plunderit from him the tyme forsaid be the comonn enemie off insicht plenissing cloithes abuilziementis cornes wictuall money houshold provisione and wtheris of that kynd abouwritin conforme to the particular compt

    Extending the said Iohn pairker his loissis abouwritin to four Scoir sewin pund 3s 4d

77. Margaret Geddes, indweller in Elgin

    Followis the loissis of margaret geddes indueller in elgin

    Imprimis the said margaret geddes being deiplie suorne deponit that ther was plunderit from hir be the comon enemie at the tyme forsaid of insicht plenissing cornes wictuall cloithes abuilziementis money houshold provisione and wtheris of that kynd abouwritin conforme to the particular compt givin in to the saidis comissioners

    extending the said margaret geddes hir loissis abouwritin to ij^c lib' 3s 4d

78. Alexander Watsone, indweller in Elgin

    Followis the loissis of alexander watsone indueller in elgin

    Imprimis the said alexander watsone being deiplie suorne deponit that ther was

The Elgin Depositions: Document A

plunderit from him at the tyme forsaid be the comonne enemie of insicht plenissing corns wictuall cloithes abuilziementis money armor houshold provisione & wtheris of that kynd abouwritin conforme to the particular compt

  extending the said alexander watsone his loissis abouwritin to jͨi9 lib' 9s 8d

79. Johne Murray, webster in Elgin

  Followis the loissis of Iohne murray webster in elgin

  Imprimis the said Iohne murray being deiplie suorne deponit that ther was plunderit and takin avay from him be the comon enemie at the tyme forsaid of Insicht plenisching cloithis abuilziementis armor money wictuall houshold provisione and wtheris of that kynd abowewrittin conforme to the particular compt

  Extending the said Iohne murray his loissis abow writtin to fiftie fyw pund

80. James Syme, smith in Elgin

  Followis the loissis of Iames syme smythe in elgin

  Imprimis the said Iames Syme being deiplie suorne deponed that ther was plunderit and avay takin from him at the tymes forsaidis of Insicht plenisching cloithis abuilziementis wictuall money armor houshold provisione and wtheris of that kynde abowvrittin Conforme to the particular compt

  Extending the said Iames syme his loissis abowwrittin to ane hundrethe ten pundis tuo shillingis 8d money

81. Janett Warden in Elgin

  Followis the loissis of Ianett warden in elgin

  Imprimis the said Ianett warden being deiplie suorne deponed that their wes plunderit and avay takin from hir at the tyme forsaid be the comon enemie of Insicht plenisching cloithis abuilziementis and wtheris of that kynd abowwrittin conform<e> to the particular compt giwin to the saidis comissioneris

  Extending the said Ianett warden hir loissis abowuritin to the soume of tuantie aucht pundis 6s 8d

82. Alexander Sutherland, flesher in Elgin

  Followis the loissis of alexander sutherland flescher in elgin

  Imprimis the said alexander sutherland being deiplie suorne deponit that ther vas plunderit and avay takin from him be the comon enemie the tymes forsaidis of Insicht plenisching cloithis abuilziementis money wictuall armor houshold provisione and wtheris of that kynde abowvrittin conforme to the particular compt

  Extending the said alexander sutherland his loissis abowewrittin to threttie sex pundis tuell schillingis

83. James Geddes, webster in Elgin

  Followis the loissis of Iames geddes webster in elgin

  Imprimis the said Iames geddes being deiplie suorne did depone that ther was plunderit and avay takin from him Be the comon enemie at the tymes forsaidis of Insicht plenisching cloithis abuilziementis wictuall money houshold provisione and wtheris of that kynd abowwrittin in conforme to the particular compt

  Extending the said Iames geddes his loissis abow writtin to fiftie thrie
  <deleted shillingis > pundis tuell shillingis money

84. Iissobell chalmer, indweller in Elgin
Followis the loissis of Iissobell chalmer indueller in elgin

Imprimis the said Iissobell being deiplie suorne did depone that ther was plunderit and avay takin from hir be the comon enemie at the tymes forsaidis of Insicht plenisching merchand wares money cloithis abuilziementis houshold provisione and wtheris of that kynd abowe writtin conforme to the particular compt

Extending the loissis of the said Issobell chalmer abow writtin to fourtie aucht pund 7s 8d money

85. James Matineasker in Elgin
Followis the loissis of Iames matineasker in elgin

Imprimis the said Iames matineasker being deiplie suorne deponit that ther was plunderit and avay takin from him be the comon enemie the tymes forsaidis of Insicht plenisching wictuall houshold provisione and wtheris of that kynd abowrittin conforme to the particular compt

Extending the said Iames matineasker his loissis abowwrittin to nyntein pundis money

86. Androw Wilsone, cooper in Elgin
Followis the loissis of androw wilsone couper in elgin

Imprimis the said androw wilsone being deiplie suorne did depone that ther vas plunderit and avavay takin from him be the comon enemie of Insicht plenisching cloithis abuilziementis money armor wictuall houshold provisione and vtheris of that kynd abowevrittin conforme to the particular compt

Extending the said androw wilson his loissis abowewrittin to fourtie four pundis 15s money

87. Williame Towrie in Elgin
Followis the loissis of williame towrie in elgin

Imprimis the said william towrie being deiplie suorne deponed that ther was plunderit from him be the comon enemie at the tyme forsaid of Insicht plenisching cloithis money merchand wares houshold provisione and wtheris of that kynd abowvrittin conforme to the particular compt

Extending the said william toruie his loissis abowwrittin to fourtie fywe pund i7s 4d money

88. Margarat Andersone in Elgin
Followis the loissis of margarat andersone in elgin

Imprimis the said margarat andersone being deiplie suorne did depon that thair was plunderit from hir be the como<n> enemie at the tyme forsaid of Insicht plenisching cloithis abuilziementis money wictuall houshold provisione and wtheris of that kynd abowewrittin conforme to the particular compt

Extending the loissis of the said margarat andersone abowvrittin to ane hundrethe Sex pund 15s 4d

89. Johne Alpein, armourer in Elgin
Followis the loissis of Iohne alpein armorar in elgin

Imprimis the said Iohne alpein being deiplie suorne did depone that thair was plunderit from him be the comon enemie the tymes forsaidis of Insicht plenisching cloithis abuilziementis money armor wictuall houshold provisione and wtheris of that kynd abowwrittin conforme to the particular compt

Extending the said Iohne alpein his loissis abowe writtin to thrie hundrethe tuo pund iii s iiij d

90. Johne Purs younger, in the colledge of Elgin

Followis the loissis of Iohne purs younger in the colledge of elgin

Imprimis the said Iohne purs being deiplie suorne did depone that ther was plunderit from him be the comon enemie the tyme forsaid of insicht plenisching abuilziementis stuffis money armor wictuall houshold provisione and wtheris of that kynd abowewrittin conforme to the pairticular compt

Extending the said Iohne purs his loissis abowwrittin to ane hundrethe fourtie 8 lib'money

91. James Murray, skinner in Elgin

Followis the loissis of Iames murray skinner in elgin

Imprimis the said Iames murray being deiplie suorne deponit that thair was plunderit from him be the comon enemie of Insicht plenisching cloithis gliffis almit ledder money armor houshold provisione and wtheris of that kynd abowwrittin conforme to the particular compt

Extending the said Iames murray his loissis abowewrittin to thriscore tuell markis money

92. Agnes Collie in Elgin

Followis the loissis of agnes collie in elgin

Imprimis the said agnes collie being deiplie suorne deponit that ther was plunderit from hir be the comon enemie at the tymes forsaidis of Insicht plensiching cloithis abuilziementis houshold provisione and wtheris of that kynd abowwrittin conforme to the particular compt

Extending the said agnes collie hir loissis abowwrittin to threttein pundis money

93. William Wilsone, cordwainer in Elgin

Followis the loissis of william wilsone cordiner in elgin

Imprimis the said william wilsone being deiplie suorne deponit that ther was plunderit from him be the comon enemie at the tymes forsaid of Insicht plenisching cloithis abuilziementis shone almit ledder houshold provisione and wtheris of that kynd abowe writtin conforme to the particular compt

Extending the said william wilsone his loissis abowe writtin to threttie four pund 14s money

94. William Gibsone in Elgin

Followis the loissis of william gibsone in elgin

Imprimis the said william gibsone being deiplie suorne deponit that ther was plunderit from him be the comon enemie at the tymes forsaid of Insicht plenisching cloithes abuilziementis armor money cornes wictuall houshold provisione and wtheris of that kynd conforme to the particular compt giwin in to the saidis comissioneris

Extending the said william gibsone his loissis abowwrittin to ane hundrethe nyne pund 6s 8d

95. Alexander Riache in Elgin

Followis the loissis of alexander riache in elgin

Imprimis the said alexander riache being deiplie suorne deponit that ther was plunderit from him be the comon enemie at the tymes forsaid of cloithis and abuilziementis with ane cow pryce – 10 lib' 13s 4d quhilk cow was sufficientlie provin be alexander nicoll and Iames < deleted tailyor > fairer induelleris in elgin they being suorne for that effect conforme to the particular compt giwin in to the saidis comissioneris

Extending the said alexander riach his loissis abowewrittin to Sextein pund sevintein shillingis 4d money

96. Agnes Forsythe in Elgin

Followis the loissis of agnes forsythe in elgin

Imprimis the said agnes forsythe being deiplie suorne deponit that ther wes plunderit for hir be the comon enemie the tymes forsaid of Insicht plenisching cloithis abuilziementis and wtheris of that kynd houshold provisione and wtheris of that kynd abowe writtin with four head of scheape pryce ten markis money quhilk scheip was sufficientlie provin be david forsythe in elgin he being suorne for that effect conforme to the particular compt

Extending the said agnes forsythe hir loissis abowewrittin to tuentie ane pund 2s 4d

97. James Fayrer, smith in Elgin

Followis the loissis of Iames Fayrer smythe in elgin

Imprimis the said Iames fayrer being deiplie suorne deponit that ther was plunderit from him be the comon enemie at the tymes forsaid and sensyne of cloithis abuilziementis cornes wictuall hors schone money Insicht plenisching houshold provisione and wtheris of that kynd abowewrittin with tuantie four head of scheip at 30s the peice or head Inde – xxxvj lib' money quhilk scheip was sufficientlie prowin be alexander nicoll alexander riache and Thomas andersone Induelleris in elgin they being suorne for that effect conforme to the particular compt

Extending the said Iames fayrer his loissis abowewrittin to ane hundrethe 12 lib' 5s money

98. Marjore Murray, relict of Johne Cok

Followis the loissis of mariore murray relict of wmquhill Iohne cok in elgin

Imprimis the said mariore murray being deiplie suorne deponit that ther vas plunderit from hir be the comon enemie the tymes forsaid of Insicht plenisching cloithis abuyliementis wictuall houshold provisione and wtheris of that kynde abowewrittin conforme to the particular compt

Extending the said mariore murray hir loissis abowwrittin to fourscoire nyne pundis 6s 8d money

99. Margarat Troupe, indweller in Elgin

Followis the loissis of margarat troupe indueller in elgin

Imprimis the said margarat troupe being deiplie suorne deponed that ther was plunderit from hir be the comon enemie the tymes forsaid of Insicht plenisching cloithis abuilziementis houshold provisione and wtheris of that kynd abowwrittin to the particular compt

Extending the said margarat troupe hir loissis abowwrittin to 24 lib' xvi iij d money

The Elgin Depositions: Document A

100. Johne Harivood, indweller in Elgin

Followis the loissis of Iohne harivood indueller in elgin

Imprimis the said Iohne being deiplie suorne deponed that ther was plunderit from him be the commone enemie the tymes forsaid of Insicht plenissing cloithes abuilzementis money merchand wares houshold provisione & vtheris of the kynd abouewritin conforme to the particular compt

Extending the said Iohn herivood his loissis To 97 lib' 4s 8d

101. Issobell Hardie, spouse to George Forsyth in Elgin

Followis the loissis of Issobell hardie spous to george forsyth in Elgin

Imprimis the said Issobell being deiplie suorne deponit that ther wes plunderit from hir be the commoune enemie at the tyme forsaid of Insicht plenissing clothes abuilzementis houshold provisione and vtheris of that kynd That kynd abouwritin conforme to the particular Compt

Extending the said Issobel hardie hir loissis abouwritin to threttein pund

102. Alexander Russell, stabler in Elgin, and Christen Warden, his spouse

Followis the loissis of alexander Russell stabler in elgin and christen warden his spous

Imprimis the said christen warden being deiplie suorne deponit that ther was plunderit from hir be the comonn enemie the tymes forsaid of insicht plenissing money wictuall cloithis abuilziementis houshold provisione and wtheris of that kynd abouwritin conforme to the particular compt

Extending the said Christen wardene hir loissis abouwritin to fourscoir aucht pundis money

103. Alexander Nicoll in Elgin

Followis the loissis of alexander Nicoll in elgin

Imprimis the said alexander Nicoll being deiplie suorne deponit that thair was takin from him be the comonn enemie the tymes forsaidis of insicht plenissing cloithes abuilziementis wictuall money houshold provisione and wtheris of that kynd abouwritin with tuentie four head sheip at – 40s the peice Inde – 48 lib' money quhilk sheip was sufficientlie provin be alexander Nicoll and alexander riache induelleris in elgin they being suorne deiplie for that effect conforme to the particular Compt

Extending the said alexander Nicoll his loissis abouwritin to ane hundreth pundis money

104. Johne Dunbar younger in Elgin

Followis the loissis of Iohne dunbar zounger in elgin

Imprimis the said Iohne dunbar being deiplie suorne deponit that thair was plunderit from him be the comonn enemie the tymes forsaid of cloithes abuilziementis insicht plenissing cornes wictual money armor household provisione and wtheris of that kynd abouwritin with ane hors pryce – 54 merkis money with ane cow worth – 10 lib' quhilkis hors' and cow was sufficiantlie provin be thomas andersone in elgin and thomas Schipherd ther they being deiplie Suorne for that effect conforme to the particular compt

Extending the said Iohne dunbar his loissis abouwritin to four scoir nyn pundis 13s 4d

105. Elspet Gibsone in Elgin

Followis the loissis of Elspet gibsone in elgin

Imprimis the said elspet gibsone being deiplie suorne deponit that thair was plunderit from hir be the comonn enemie at the tymes forsaid of insicht plenissing cloithes abuilziementis wictual money houshold provisione and wtheris of that kynd abouwritin conforme to the particular compt

Extending the said Elspet gibsone hir loissis abouwritin to iiij^{xx}9 lib'

106. William Hay, webster in Elgin

Followis the loissis of william hay wobster in elgin

Imprimis the said william hay being deiplie suorne deponit that thair was plunderit from him be the commonn enemie the tymes forsaid of insicht plenissing clothes abuilziementis wictual houshold provisione and wtheris of that kynd abouwritin conforme to the particular

Extending the said william hay his loissis abouwritin to iij^{xx}i8 lib' 13s 4d

107. James Gordone, tailor in Elgin

Followis the loissis of Iames gordone teilzeor in elgin

Imprimis the said Iames gordone being deiplie suorne deponit that thair was plunderit from him be the commonn enemie the tyme forsaid of insicht plenissing cloithes abuilziementis armor money wictual houshold provisione and wtheris of that kynd abouwritin conforme to the particular compt

Extending the said Iames gordone his loissis to thriescoir ten pund 8s 8d

108. Johne Corbane, webster in Elgin

Followis the loiss[is] of Iohne Corbane wobster in elgin

Imprimis the said Iohne corbane being deiplie suorne deponit that thair was plunderit from him be the comonn enemie the tymes forsaid of insicht plenissing cloithes abuilziementis armor money wictual houshold provisione and wtheris of that kynd < *deleted* wnder > abouwritin conforme to the particular compt

Extending the said Iohne Corbane his loissis abouwritin to fyiftie fywe pundis

109. Issobell Geddes in Elgin

Followis the loissis of Issobell geddes in elgin

Imprimis the said Issobell geddes being deiplie suorne deponit that thair was takin and plunderit from hir be the comonn enemie the tyme forsaid of insicht plenissing cloithes abuilziementis money wictual houshold provisione and wtheris of that kynd abouwritin conforme to the particular compt

Extending the said Issobell geddes hir loissis abouwritin to iij^{xx}15 lib' 10s

110. Johne Paull in Elgin

Followis the loissis of Iohne paull in elgin

Imprimis the said Iohne paull being deiplie suorne deponit that thair was plunderit from him be the comon enemie the tyme forsaid of insicht plenissing cloithes abuilziementis money wictual houshold provisione and wtheris of the kynd abouwritin conforme to the particular compt

Extending the said Iohne paull his loissis abouwritin to 37 lib' 5s 4d

111. William Donaldsone, cordwainer in Elgin
Followis the loissis of william donaldsone cordoner in elgin

Imprimis the said william donaldsone being deiplie suorne deponit that thair was plunder from him be the commonn enemie at the tyme forsaid of insicht plenissing clothes abuilziementis shoes barket ledder wictual money Armor household provisione and wtheris of that kynd abouwritin conforme to the particular compt

Extending the said william Donaldsone his loissis abouwritin to 27 lib' 9s

112. Johne Fraser, indweller in Elgin
Followis the loissis off Iohne Fraser Indueller In elgin

Imprimis the said Iohne Fraser being deiplie suorne deponit that thair wald plunderit from the comonn enemie the tymes forsaidis of insicht plenissing cloithes abuilziementis cornes wictual money armor houshold provisione and wtheris of that kynd abouwritin conforme to the particular compt

Extending the said Iohne fraser his loissis abouwritin to vij^c lib' 13s 4d

113. James Nauchtie in Elgin
Followis the loissis of Iames Nauchtie in elgin

Imprimis the said Iames Nauchtie being deiplie suorne deponit that thair was plunderit from him be the comonn enemie at the tymes forsaid of insicht plenissing cloithes abuilziementis armor money wictual houshold provisione and wtheris of that kynd abouwritin conforme to the particular compt

Extending the said Iames Nauchtie his loissis abouwritin to iij^{xx}xj lib' iij s 4d

114. Alexander Edvard, tailor in Elgin
Followis the loissis of alexander edvard teilzeor in elgin

Imprimis the said alexander edvard being suorne and examinat deponit that thair was plunderit from him be the comon enemie the tymes forsaid of insicht plenissing cloithes abuilziementis money wictual houshold provisione & wtheris of that kynd abouwritin conforme to the particular compt

Extending the said alexander edvard his loissis abouwritin to iiij^{xx}iij lib' iij s 4d

115. William Edvard in Elgin
Followis the loissis of william edvard in elgin

Imprimis the said william edvard being svorne deponit that ther was plunderit from him be the comon enemie at the tyme forsaid of insicht plenissing cloithes abuilziementis cornes wictual houshold provisione & wtheris of that kynd abouwritin conforme to the particular Compt

Extending the said william edvard his loissis abouwritin to 55 lib' 13s 4d

116. James Nicoll, webster in Elgin
Followis the loissis off Iames Nicoll wobster in elgin

Imprimis the said Iames nicoll being deiplie suorne deponit that ther was plunderit from him be the comon enemie the tyme forsaid of insicht plenissing cloithis abuilziementis money armor wictual houshold provisione & wtheris of that kynd abouw[ri]tin conforme to the particular compt

Extending the said Iames Nicoll his loissis abouwritin to 35 lib' 7s 8d

117. Thomas Duncan, webster in Elgin
Followis the loissis off Thomas Duncan wobster in elgin

Imprimis the said thomas duncan being deiplie suorne deponit that ther was plunderit from him be the comon enemie of insicht plenissing cloithes abuilziementis armor money wictual houshold provisione & wtheris of that kynd abouwritin conforme to the particular compt

Extending the said thomas duncan his loissis abouwritin to – 25 lib'

118. Thomas Andersone in Elgin
Followis the loissis of thomas andersone in elgin

Imprimis the said Thomas andersone being deiplie suorne deponit that ther was plunderit from him be the comon enemie at the tymes forsaidis of insicht plenissing cloithes abuilziementis money cornes wictual houshold provisione & wtheris of that kynd with fywe zewis with lamb pryce of the peice 53s 4d Inde – 13 lib' 6s 8d with tuo wadders at – 40s the peice Inde – iiij lib' with tuo hoges at – 26s 8d the peice Iende – iij lib' with tuo hors at L merkis the peice Inde iij^{xx}xiij lib' 6s 8d quhilkis zewis wedderis hoiges and horssis was sufficientlie provin be the alexander nicoll & Iames fairer induelleris in elgin they being deiplie suorne For that effect conforme to the particular compt

Extending the said thomas andersone his loissis abouwritin to j^{c}45 lib' 9s 8d

119. George Watt, webster in Elgin
Followis the loissis of george watt wobster in elgin

Imprimis the said george watt being deiplie suorne deponit that ther was plunderit from him be the comon enemie at the forsaidis tymes of insicht plenissing cloithes abuilziementis houshold provisione and wtheris of that kynd abouwritin conforme to the particular comp

extending the said george watt his loissis abouwritin to 14 lib'

120. William Purse, webster in Elgin
Followis the loissis off william purse wobster in elgin

Imprimis the said william purse being deiplie suorne deponit that ther was plunderit from him be the comon enemie at the forsaid tymes of insicht plenissing cloithes abuilziementis money armor wictual houshold provisione & wtheris of that kynd abouwritin conforme to the particular compt

extending the said william purse his lossis abouwritin to ij^{c}34 lib' 16s

121. Androw Rosse, webster in Elgin
Followis the loissis of androw Rosse wobster in elgin

Imprimis the said androw Rosse being deiplie suorne deponit that ther was plunderit from him be the comone enemie at the forsaidis tymes of insicht plenissing money cloithes abuilziementis wictual houshold provisione & wtheris of that kynd abouwritin conforme to the particular compt

extending the said androw Rose his loissis abouwritin to ij^{c}42 lib' 3s 4d

122. William Petrie, cordwainer in Elgin
Followis the loissis of william petrie cordoner in elgin

Imprimis the said william being deiplie suorne deponit that ther was plunderit from him be the comon enemie of insicht plenissing clothis abuilziementis cornes wictuall shoine barkit ledder armor money wictuall houshold provisione and wtheris of that kynd abowewrittin conforme to the particular compt

Extending the said william pettrie his loissis abowewrittin to tuo hundrethe fyftie tuo pund 7 schillingis

123. Jeane Michell in Elgin

Followis the loissis of Ieane michell in elgin

Imprimis the said Ieane michell being deiplie suorne deponit that ther was plunderit from hir be the comon enemie at the tymes forsaid of cloithis abuyiliementis insicht plenisching houshold provisione and wtheris of that kynd abo<we> writtin conforme to the particular compt

Extending the said Ieane michell hir loissis abowewrittin to tuentie aucht pund i8s 8d

124. Gilbert Adame in Mostawie

Gilbert adame

Followis the loissis of gilbert adame in mostawie

Imprimis the said gilbert adame being deiplie suorne deponit that ther was plunderit from him be the comon enemie at the tymes forsaid of Insicht plenischingis clothis abuilziementis money < *deleted* armor > cornes wictual money houshold provisione and wtheris of that kynd abowewrittin with ane hors pryce – 40 lib' money with ane mair worthe – 20 li' quhilk hors and mair was sufficientlie prowin be Iohne andersone in mostawie and Iohne chayne ther they being deiplie suorne for that effect conforme to the particular compt

Extending the said gilbert adame his loissis abowwrittin to ane hundrethe thrie score 4 lib' 3s 4d

125. Johne Chayne in Mostawie

Iohn chayne

Followis the loissis of Iohne chayne in mostawie

Imprimis the said Iohne chayne being deiplie suorne deponit that ther wes plunderit from him be the comon enemie at the forsaidis tymes of Insicht plenisching cloithis abuilziementis cornes wictual money houshold provisione and wtheris of that kynd abowewrittin with ane cow pryce tuantie markis quhilk cow was sufficientlie prowin be Iohne andersone in mostowie he being deiplie suorne to that effect conforme to the particular compt

Extending the said Iohne chayne his loissis abowwrittin to fyftie sex pund 5s 4d

126. Kathrin Gilbert in Elgin

Followis the loissis of kathrin gilbert in elgin

Imprimis the said kathrin being deiplie suorne deponit that ther was plunderit from hir be the comon enemie at the forsaid tymes of cloithis abuilziementis Insicht plenisching houshold provisione and wtheris of that kynd abow writin conforme to the particular compt

Extending the said kathrin gilbert hir loissis abowewrittin to tuantie nyne pundis 3s 4d

127. Patrik Muirsone, burgess of Elgin

Followis the loissis of patrik meirsone burges of elgin

Imprimis the said Patrik muirsone being deiplie suorne deponit that ther was plunderit and takin avay from him be the comone enemie at the forsaidis tymes of Insicht plenisching cloithis abuilziementis armor money merchand wares wictual houshold provisione and wtheris of that kynd abowewrittin conforme to the particular compt with ane paiced hors worthe – 10 lib' 3s 4d quhilk naige was sufficientlie prowin be Mr gavine douglas and Mr Iames Annand burges of elgin they being deiplie suorne for that effect conforme to the particular compt

Extending the said patrik muirsone his loissis abowe writin to thrie hundrethe tuentie fywe pund 8s

128. William Sutherland, burgess of Elgin

Followis the loissis of william sutherland burges of elgin

Imprimis the said william sutherland being suorne deponit that ther was plunderit from him be the comon enemie at the forsaidis tymes of Insicht plenisching cloithis abuilziementis armor money wictuall houshold provisione and wtheris of that kynd abowe writtin conforme to the particular compt

Extending the said william sutherland his loissis abowe writtin to fywe hundrethe twentie fywe lib' 6s 8d

129. Walter Gilzeane, saddler, burgess of Elgin

Followis the loissis of walter gilzeane saidler burges of elgin

Imprimis the said walter gilzeane being deiplie suorne deponit that ther was plunderit from him be the comon enemie at the forsaidis tymes of Insicht plenisching cloithis abuilziementis Saidle saidle graythe brydlies armor money houshold provisione and wtheris of that kynd abowwrittin conforme to the particular compt

extending the said walter gilzeane his loissis abowwrittin to ij^c thrie score tuell pundis

130. Alexander Murdoche, skinner, burgess of Elgin

Followis the loissis of alexander murdoche skinner burges of elgin

Imprimis the said alexander murdoche being deiplie suorne deponit that ther was plunderit from him be the comon enemie at the forsaidis tymes of Insicht plensiching cloithis abuilziementis money armor wictual gliffis woll almit ledder houshold provisione and wtheris of that kynd abowwrittin with ane hors wurth fyftein dolloris quhilk hors was sufficientlie prowin be Thomas davidsone and michaell andersone induelleris in elgin they being deiplie suorne for that effect conforme to the particular compt

Extending the said alexander murdoche his loissis abowwritin to thrie hundrethe threttie thrie lib' 14s

131. Thomas Warrand, merchant burgess of Elgin

Followis the loissis of Thomas warrande merchand burges of elgin

Imprimis the said Thomas warrand being deiplie suorne deponit that ther was plunderit from him be the comon enemie at the forsaidis tymes of Insicht plenisching cloithis abuilziementis money armor wictual merchand wares houshold provisione and wtheris of that kynd abowwritin with ane hors pryce – 22 lib' quhilk hors was sufficientlie provin be Iames milne in elgin he being deiplie suorne for that effect conforme to the particular compt

Extending the said Thomas warrand his loissis abowwrittin to sevin hundrethe fyftein pundis 7s money

The Elgin Depositions: Document A

132. Androw Innes, burgess of Elgin

Followis the loissis of Androw Innes burges of elgin

Imprimis the said Androw Innes being Deiplie suorne Deponit that ther wes plunderit from him be the Comone Enemie the tymes forsaid of insicht plenissing cloithes abuilziementis armor money merchand wares houshold provisione & wtheris of that kynd abouwritin conforme to the particular compt

Extending the said andro his loissis abouwritin to – ij^{c}ix lib' xiij s iiij d

133. Alexander Hay, skinner, burgess of Elgin

followis the loissis of alexander hay skinner burges of Elgin

Imprimis the said alexander being Deiplie suorne Deponit that ther was plunderit from him be the commone Enemie the tyme forsaid of insicht plenissing cloithes abuilziementis money wictual almit ledder houshold provisione & wtheris of that kynd abouwritin conforme to the particular compt

Extending the said alexander hay his loissis abouwritin to – iij^{c}xlj lib'

134. John Rage, merchant, burgess of Elgin

Followis the loissis of Iohn Rage merchand Burges of elgin

Imprimis the said Iohn rage being Deiplie suorne Deponit that ther was plunderit from him be the commone Enemie at the tymes forsaid of insicht plenissing cloithes abuilziementis money wictual merchand wares houshold provisione & wtheris of that kynd abouwritin conforme to the particular compt

Extending the said Iohn rage his loissis abouw[ri]tin to – v^{c}xj lib'

135. William Warden, burgess of Elgin

followis the loissis of william warden burges of elgin

Imprimis the said william being deiplie suorne Deponit that ther was plunderit from him be the commone Enemie at the tymes forsaid of insicht < *deleted* provisione > plenissing cloithes abuilziementis money armor wictual houshold provisione & wtheris of that kynd abowwrittin with ane hors pryce – 40 lib' quhilk hors was instantlie provin be francis dunbar & robert dunbar burgessis of elgin they being deiplie suorne to that effect conforme to the particular compt

Extending the said william warden his loissis abouwritin to – ij^{c}xlij lib' xiiij s iiii d

136. Walter Myln

followis the loissis of walter myln

Imprimis the said walter being Deiplie suorne Deponit that ther wes plunderit from him be the Comone Enemie at the tymes forsaid of insicht plenissing cloithes abuilziementis cornes wictual money armor merchand wares houshold provisione & wtheris of that kynd abouwritin with ane hors pryce fourscoir markis quhilk hors was instantlie provin be alexander pettrie & thomas patersone burgessis of elgin They being suorne to that effect conforme to the particular compt

Extending the said walter myln his loissis abouwritin to – < *deleted* xj^{c}xx > i^{c}xxix lib' vi s viij d

137. Alexander Stephane, burgess of Elgin

followis the loissis of alexander Stephane burges of elgin

Imprimis the said alexander being Deiplie suorne Deponit that ther wes plunderit from him be the commone Enemie at the tymes forsaid of cloithes abuilziementis insicht plenissing money wictual merchand wares houshold provisione & wtheris of that kynd conforme to the particular compt

Extending the said alexander his loissis abouwritin to – iiij^{c}iij^{xx}xviij lib' vj s viij d

138. William Innes, skinner, burgess of Elgin

Followis the loissis of william Innes skinner burges of elgin

Imprimis the said william Innes being Deiplie suorne Deponit that ther wes plunderit from him be the commone Enemie at the tyme forsaid of insicht plenissing cloithes abuilziementis gliffis almit ledder merchand wares & < *deleted* wtheris > houshold provisione & wtheris of that kynd abouwritin conforme to the particular compt

Extending the said william Innes his loissis abouwritin to – ij^{c}iij^{xx}iiij lib' xiij s iiij d

139. George Baxter, dyer, burgess of Elgin

followes the loissis of george baxter litster burges of elgin

Imprimis the said george baxter being Deiplie suorne deponit that ther was plunderit from him be the commone Enemie at the tyme forsaid of insicht plenissing cloithes abuilziementis wictual armor litster wares houshold provisione & wtheris of the kynd abouwritin with ane hors pryce – 53 lib' 6s 8d quhilk hor was instantlie provin be mr gawin Douglas of murrestonne & Iohn chalmer burges of elgin they being Deiplie suorne to that effect conforme to the particular compt

Extending the said george baxter his loissis abouwritin to – v^{c}xxxvj lib' i7s 4d

Mosstowie tenants

followes the loissis of the Tennentis of mostowie being tennentis to the burghe of elgin

140. Thomas Spens

Thomas Spens

Imprimis the said Thomas Spens being Deiplie suorne Deponit that ther was plunderit from him be the commone Enemie at the tymes forsaid of insicht plenissing cloithes abuilziementis money armor cornes wictual houshold provisione & wtheris of that kynd < *deleted* conforme to the > abouwritin with ane meir pryce – 27 lib' with fourtie head of sheipe at 40s the piece Inde iiij^{xx} lib' with tuo suyne pryce – 46s 8d with ane wther meir worth tuentie dolloris quhilk meiris sheip & suyne was instantlie provin be Iohn gordon in mostowie Iames rage ther & alexander lie ther they being Deiplie suorne to that effect conforme to the compt

Extending the said thomas Spens his loissis to – v^{c}18 lib' 2s 8d

141. Johne Gordone in Mostowie

Followes the loissis of Iohn gordone in mostowie

Imprimis the said Iohn being Deiplie suorne Deponit that ther was Plunderit from him be the commone Enemie at the tymes forsaid of insicht plenissing cloithes abuilziementis money armor cornes wictual houshold provisione & wtheris of that kynd abouwritin with

The Elgin Depositions: Document A

four scoir aucht head of sheip at – 40s the peice Inde – j^{c}iij^{xx}xvj lib' with ane meir pryce – 30 lib' with wther tuo meiris at – 20 lib' the peice Inde – 40 lib' with aucht head of < *deleted* sheipe > goodis at – 13 lib' 6s 8d the peice Inde – j^{c}iij^{xx} lib' 13s 4d quhilk sheip meiris & goodis abouwritin was instantlie provin be thomas Spens in mostowie alexander lie Iames rage ther conforme to the particular compt

 Extending the said < *deleted* thomas spens > Iohn gordon his loissis abouwritin to – viij^{c}xij lib' viij d

142. Donold Johnstone in Mostowie

 followes the loissis of Donold Iohnstone in mostowie

 Imprimis the said Donold Iohnstone being Deiplie suorn Deponit that ther was plunderit from him be the commone Enemie at the tyme forsaid of insicht plenissing cloithes abuilziementis money wictual houshold provisione & wtheris of that kynd abouwritin conforme to the particular compt

 Extending the said Donold Iohnstone his loissis abouwritin to – xl lib'

143. Alexander Lie in Mostowie

 followes the loissis of alexander lie in mostowie

 Imprimis the said alexander lie being Deiplie suorne Deponit that ther was plunderit from him be the commone Enemie at the tymes forsaid of insicht plenissing cloithes abuilziementis money wictual houshold provisione & wtheris of that kynd abouwritin with tuo peice of hors at – 20 lib' the peice Inde – 40 lib' with fourtein head of sheip at – 40s the peice Inde – 20 lib' with an wther hors worth – 16 lib' quhilkis hors and sheip was instantlie provin be Iohn gordone in mostowie & thomas Spens ther they being suorne to that effect conforme to the particular compt

 Extending the said alexander lie his loissis abouwritin to j^{c}ij lib'

144. James Man in Mostowie

 Iames man

 followes the loissis of Iames man in mostowie

 Imprimis the said Iames man being Deiplie suorne Deponit that ther was plunderit from him be the commone Enemie < *deleted* of > at the tyme forsaid of insicht plenissing cloithes abuilziementis money wictual houshold provisione & wtheris of that kynd abouwritin conforme to the particular compt

 Extending the said Iames man his loissis abouwritin to xxxxvj lib' iij s iiij d

145. James Rage in Mostowie

 Iames rage

 followes the loissis of Iames Rage in mostowie

 Imprimis the said Iames Rage being Deiplie suorne Deponit that ther was plunderit from him < *word deleted* > be the commone Enemie the tymes forsaid of insicht plenissing cloithes abuilziementis cornes wictual money houshold provisione & wtheris of that kynd abouwritin with tuo hors pryce – 40 lib' with tuo kye with calff pryce – 26 lib' 13s 4d with aucht head of sheip pryce 16 lib' quhilk hors kye & sheip was instantlie provin be Iohn Gordone in mostowie & Thomas Spens ther They being Deiplie suorne to that effect conforme to the particular compt

 Extending the said Iames his loissis abouwritin to j^{c}liij lib' ij s x d

146. William Rage in Mostowie

William Rage

followes the loissis of william Rage in mostowie

Imprimis the said william Rage being Deiplie suorne Deponit that ther wes plunderit from him be the commone Enemie at the tymes forsaid of insicht plenissing cloithes abuilziementis money cornes wictual houshold provisione & wtheris of that kynd abouwritin with ane < *word deleted* > hors pryce – 16 lib' with ane hors worth – 8 lib' quhilkis horssis was instantly provin be Iames williamsone in mostowie & Iames Rage ther they being Deiplie suorne to that effect conforme to the particular compt givin theranent

Extending the said william Rage his loissis abouwritin to – lij lib' xiij s

147. Patrik Grant in Mostowie

followes the loissis of patrik Grant in mostowie

Imprimis the said Patrik grant being Deiplie suorne Deponit that ther wes plunderit from him be the commone Enemie at the tymes for said of insicht plenissing cloithes abuilziementis money wictual houshold provisione & wtheris of that kynd abouwritin with ane young staige worth – 14 lib' 13s 4d with ane Cow worth – 12 lib' q[uhi]lk staige & cow was instantlie provin be Iames williamsone in mostowie & Iames Rage ther They being Deiplie suorne to that effect conforme to the particular compt

Extending < *deleted* followes > the loissis of the said patrik grant to – xxx lib' xiij s iiij d

148. Olipher Young in Mostowie

followes the loissis of Olipher Zoung in mostowie

Imprimis the said Olipher Zoung being Deiplie suorne Deponit that ther was plunderit from him be the commone Enemie the tyme forsaid of cloithes abuilziementis insicht plenissing cornes wictual money houshold provisione & wtheris of that kynd abouwritin with ane meir pryce – 13 lib' 6s 8d Item ane wther young meir pryce – 4 lib' 6s 8d Quhilkis meiris was instantlie provin be Iohn gordone in mostowie & Thomas Spens ther They being Deiplie suorne to that effect conforme to the particular compt

Extending the said Olipher Zoung his loissis abouwritin to – xlvj lib' xiij s iij d

149. Christane Clerk, liferentrix in Elgin

Followis the loissis of Christane clerk lyiverentrix of ane hous in elgin

Imprimis the said Christane duelling in landuard the provest and bailzies in hir absence being deiplie suorne deponit that ther was ane Ludging of thrie hous height withe the Inner Land therof brunt to hir be montrois armie in maij 1645 the lois quherof with hir timber plenisching

Extending to the soume of aucht hundrethe pundis money

150. Walter Smythe, messenger, burgess of Elgin

Followis the loissis of walter smythe messenger burges of elgin

Imprimis the said walter being deiplie suorne did depone that ther was ane fair Luidging of thrie houshight with wtterland and Inner Land brunt to him be montrois armie in maij 1645 becaus his sone wes capitanne of spynie being weill plenischit with wanscott plenissing with his haill Insicht plenisching therin the loissis wherof

Extending to tua thousand thrie hundrethe threttie thrie pund 6s 8d

endorsement
This endorsement, inscribed in a hand similar to that used for the main text, was written on the dorse of claims 177 – 181 (Janet Maver – Issobell Sutherland).
20 Iuly 1646 walter smith deponit that his brunt ludging of thrie hous hi<ght> and remenent houses therof being sufficientlie plenisched with plenissing the loiss far extending thrie thousand and fyve hundreth markis money The said being brunt for his sones cause being at the tyme Capitane of the garisone of Spynie
endorsement ends

151. Hew Sutherland, indweller in Elgin
Followis the loissis of hew sutherland indueller ther ane minor
Imprimis the saidis provest and bailzies being suorne deponit that ther was ane pairt of ane hous of his brunt in elgin be montrois armie in maij 1645 with ane great pairt of his plenisching the loissis wherof
Extending to ane hundreth thrie score pundis

152. William Gadderar in Mostowie
Followes the loisis of william Gadderar in mostowie
Imprimis the said william gadderar being Deiplie suorne Deponit that ther was plunderit from him be the commone Enemie at the forsaid tymes of Insicht plenissing cloithes houshold provisione & wtheris of that kynd abouwritin with ane meir pryce – 12 lib' with ane steir worth – 3 lib' 6s 8d with fyve head of sheip pryce – 6 lib' 13s 4d quhilkis meir steir & sheip was instantlie prowin be Iohn gordone & Iames williamsone in mostowie They being deiplie suorne for that effect conforme to the particular compt
Extending the said william gadderar his loissis abouwritin to Threttie sex pund 13s 8d

153. James Williamsone in Mostowie
Followes the < *deleted* said > loissis of Iames williamsone in mostowie
Imprimis the said Iames williamsone being Deiplie suorne Deponit that ther was plunderit from him < *deleted* at > Be the commone Enemie at the forsaid tymes of insicht plenissing cloithes houshold provisione & wtheris of that kynd abouwritin with ane meir & ane cow pryce of boith – 26 lib' with thrie head of sheip pryce – 4 lib' quhilkis meir cow & sheip was instantlie prowin be Iohn gordone & Thomas Spens in mostowie They being Deiplie suorne for that effect conforme to the particular compt
Extending the said Iames williamsone his loissis abouwritin to fyiftie fyve pundis

154. Margaret Duncane in Old Mylnes
Followis the loissis of margaret Duncane in old mylnes
Imprimis the said margaret Duncane being Deiplie suorne Deponit That ther was plunderit from hir be the commone Enemie at the tymes forsaid of insicht plenissing cloithes abuilziementis wictuall money houshold provisione & wtheris of that kynd Abouwritin conforme to the particular compt
Extending the said margaret Duncane hir loissis abouwritin to thriescoir fyftein lib' 3s

155. George Smyth, merchant, burgess of Elgin
Followes the loissis of george Smyth merchand burges of Elgin
Imprimis the said george Smyth being Deiplie suorne Deponit that ther wes plunderit

from him be the commone Enemie at the tymes forsaid of insicht plenissing cloithes abuilziementis money wictuall armor merchand wares houshold provisione & wtheris of that kynd abouwritin conforme to the Particular compt givin in theranent

Extending the said george Smyth his loissis abouwritin to Tuo hundreth fourscoir pund

156. David Dunbar, skinner, burgess of Elgin

Followis the loissis of David Dunbar Skinner burges of elgin

Imprimis the said David Dunbar being Deiplie suorne & examinat be the saidis comissioneris That thair was plunderit & avay takin from him be the Comone Enemie in the monethis of februarij and maij 1645 & sensyne of insicht plenissing cloithes abuilziementis money armor gliffis almit ledder merchand wares houshold provisione & wtheris of that kynd abouwritin conforme to the particular compt givin in to the saidis Comissioneris

Extending the said David Dunbar his loisis abouwritin to Nyn Hundreth four scoir fourtein pundis auchtein shillinges money

endorsement
This note is written in a 17th-century hand unlike those used for the main text.
26 throughe
doubtit
endorsement ends

157. Kathrein Annand, relict of Alexander Russell, merchant, burgess of Elgin

Followes the loissis of kathrein Annand relict of wmquhill alexander russell merchand burges of elgin who was Pittifullie murderit be < *deleted* montrois > Iames graham his armie goeing to Spynie in maij 1645

Imprimis thee said Kethrein Annand being Deiplie suorne & examinat be the saidis Comissioneris Did Depone & Declair that ther was plunderit & avay takin from hir be the Comonne Enemie in the moneth of < *deleted* maij > februarij & maij 1645 & at Diverse tymes thereftir of insicht plenissing < *deleted* ho > Cloithes abuilziementis cornes wictuall money armor merchand wares breaking of Dores windowes & makeing of them wnvsefull houshold plenissing & wtheris of that kynd abouwritin conforme to the particular Compt givin in to the saidis Comissioneris with Sevin horsis pryce – 200 lib' < *inserted* provin be thomas dauidsone & Iohn dunbar induelleris in elgin q[uhe]rwpon they wer Deiplie suorne >

Extending the said Kathrein Annand hir loissis abouwritin to – The Soume of Ane Thousand Sex hundreth thrie scoir sevin pundis

158. Johne Andersone, skinner, burgess of Elgin

Followis the loissis of Iohne andersone skinner burges of elgin

Imprimis the said Iohne andersone being solemnelie suorne & examinat be the saidis comissioner<is> did depon & declair be his owne certane informatione and be sure informatione from his wyffe and servantis that ther was plunderit and avay takin from him be the comone enemie in <feb>ruarij and maij 1645 & at diverse tymes therefter of insicht plenissing merchand wares wictual armor houshold provisione and vtheris of that nature conforme to the particular compt givin in to the saidis comissioneris

Extending the said Iohne andersone his loissis abouwritin to the soume of sevine hundreth pundis sex shilingis

159. James Chalmer, skinner, burgess of Elgin

Followis the loissis sustenit be Iames chalmer skinner burges of elgin

Imprimis the said Iames chalmer being solemnelie suorne & examinat be the saidis comissioneris did declair that thair wes plunderit and avay takin from him be the comon enemie in the monethis of februarij & maij 1645 & diverse tymes therefter of insicht plenissing merchand wares almit ledder woll cloithis abuilziementis wictual armor money houshold provisione & vtheris of that kynd conforme to the particular compt givin in to the saidis comissioneris

Extending the said Iames his loissis to ane thowsand thrie scoir tua merkis

160. Alexander Dunbar younger, merchant, burgess of Elgin

Followis the loissis of alexander dunbar zounger merchand burges of elgin

Imprimis the said alexander dunbar being Solemnelie suorne and examinat be the saidis comissioneris did declair that ther wes plunderit and avay takin from him in februarij 1645 and Sensyne of insicht plenissing cloithes abuilziementis wictual armor siluer wark wictual money houshold plenissing & vtheris of that kynd conforme to the particular compt givin in to the saidis comissioneris

extending the said alexander dunbar his loissis to ane hundreth sextein pundis thrie shillingis

161. Christane Kar, relict of Mr Dauid Philpe, minister at Elgin

Followis the loissis of christane kar relict of wmquhill mr dauid philpe minister at elgin

Imprimis the said christane kar being deiplie suorne & examinat be the saidis comissioneris did declair that ther was plunderit & avay takin from hir be the comonne enemie in the monethis of februarij & maij 1645 & sensyne of insicht plenissing cloithes abuilziementis silver wark money lining wictual houshold provisione & vtheris of that kynd with tuo key worth 18 lib' with ten sheip with 20 lib' conforme to the particular compt givin in to the saidis comissioneris Quhilk key & sheip wes instantlie provin be androw Spens in Birney & Iohn douglas burges of elgin being deiplie Suorne to that effect

extending the said christen ker hir loissis abouwritin to sevin hundreth fyiftie sevin lib' nyne shillingis 8d

162. Johne Chalmer elder, skinner, burgess of Elgin

Followis the loissis of Iohne chalmer elder skinner burges of elgin

Imprimis the said Iohne chalmer being deiplie suorne & examinat be the saidis comissioneris did declair that ther was plunderit and takin avay from him in the monethis of februarij & maij 1645 & sensyne be the comonne enemie of insicht plenissing < *deleted* merchand wares > cloithes abuilziementis wictual almit ledder money armor houshold < *deleted* plenissing > provisione merchand wares & wtheris of that kynd conforme to the particular < *word deleted* > compt givin in to the saidis comissioneris

extending the said Iohn chalmer his loissis abouwritin to ane hundreth four scoir 3 lib' 13s 4d

163. William Wier, merchant, burgess of Elgin

Followis the loiss[is] of william wier merchand burges of elgin

Imprimis the said willliam wier being deiplie suorne & examinat be the saidis comissioneris did depon that ther was plunderit and avay takin from him be the comonne enemie in februarij & maij 1645 & sensyne of insicht plenissing merchand wares cloithes abuilziementis money armor houshold provisione & vtheris of that kynd conforme to the particular compt givin in to the saidis comissioneris

 extending the said william his loissis abouwritin to fywe hundreth fourscoir sex pundis viij s

164. Margrat Chalmer, relict of Alexander Tullak, merchant, burgess of Elgin

 Followis the loissis of margrat chalmer relict of wmquhill alexander tullak merchand bur<ges> of elgin

 Imprimis the said margret chalmer being deiplie Suorne & examinat be the saidis comissioneris did depon that ther was plunderit & avay takin from hir be the comonne Enemie in februarij & maij 1645 & sensyne of insicht plenissing cloithes abuilziementis merchand wares money wictual houshold provisione & vtheris of that kynd conforme to the particularis givin in to the saidis comissioneris

 extending the said margret chalmer hir loissis to iij^{c}36 lib' 9s iij d

165. George Carmichall, burgess of Elgin

 Followis the loissis of george carmichall burges of elgin

 Imprimis the said George carmichall being deiplie suorne & examinat be the saidis comissioneris did depon that ther was plunderit and avay takin from him be the comonne enemie in februarij & maij 1645 & sensyne of insicht plenissing bear malt houshold plenissing cloithes & vtheris of that kynd with ten wedderis pryce tuentie pundis money conforme to the particularis givin in to the saidis comissioneris quhilkis wadderis was instantlie provin be Iames hui in Langmorne & hui his sone being deiplie Suorne to that effect

 Extending the said George carmichall his loissis abouwritin to the soume of iiij^c 4 markis 16s 8d

166. William Torrie, burgess of Elgin

 Followis the loissis william Torrie burges of elgin

 Imprimis the said william Torrie being deiplie Suorne & examinat be the saidis comissioneris did depon that thair was plunderit and avay takin from the william of insicht plenissing cloithes abuilziementis wictual money armor houshold provisione & vtheris of that kynd with fywe piece of horssis pryce – 160 lib' with nyne head of goods pryce – 80 lib' with tuentie head of sheip pryce – 40 lib' conforme to the particularis givin in to the saidis Comissioneris quhilkis horssis and sheip were Instantlie provin be alexander piterkin ther Iohne nauchtie in old milnes and Iames nauchtie his Sone being deiplie Suorne to that effect

 Extending the said william Torrie His loissis abouwritin to viiij^{c}iij^{xx} lib'

167. Andro Key, cordwainer, burgess of Elgin

 Followes the loissis of Andro Key cordoner burges of elgin

 Imprimis the said andro key being Deiplie suorne Deponit that ther was plunderit from him be the commone Enemie at the tymes forsaidis of insicht plenissing cloithes barket leather roche leather maid shoone money armes houshold provisione & wtheris of that kynd abouwritin conforme to Ane particular compt

 Extending the said andro key his loissis to – vj^{c}xxiiij lib' xvij s iiij d

168. William Yeaman, tailor in Elgin

followes the loissis of william zeaman tailzior in elgin

Imprimis the said william zeamane being Deiplie suorne Deponit that ther was plunderit from him be the commone Enemie the tymes forsaid of insicht plenissing cloithes abuilziementis money Armor wictual houshold provisio<ne> & wtheris of that kynd abouwritin conforme to ane particular compt

Extending the said william Zeamane his loissis to v^{c}xlij lib' vj s viij d

169. Alexander Russell younger, merchant, burgess of Elgin

followes the loissis of alexander russell zounger merchand burges of elgin

Imprimis the said alexander russell being Deiplie suorne Deponit that ther was plunderit from him be the commone Enemie at the tymes forsaid of plenissing merchand wares armor & broken dores maid wnvsefull – with ane hors saidle & brydale pryce – 30 lib' conforme to the particular compt

Extending the said alexander russell his loissis to j^{c}xxxiij lib' xj s

170. Jeane Leslie and Androw Watson

followes the loissis of androw watson givin wp be Ieane leslie his spous himselfe being fra home

Imprimis the said Ieane leslie being Deiplie suorne Deponit that ther was plunderit from hir be the commone Enemie at the tymes forsaid of insicht plenissing wictual almit ledder maid skinner wark money armor houshold provisione & wtheris of that kynd conforme to the particular compt

Extending the said androw watson his loissis to ij^{c}xxviij lib' j7s 8d

171. Alexander Russell elder, merchant, burgess of Elgin

followes the loissis of Alexander russell elder merchand burges of elgin

Imprimis the said Alexander russell being Deiplie suorne Deponit that ther was plunderit from him be the commone Enemie in the monethis of februarij & maij 1645 & sensyne of insicht plenissing merchand wares cloithes abuilziementis armor money wictual gold silver cunzeit & wncunziet houshold provisione & wtheris of that kynd ellevin ky & tuo bullis at – 10 lib' the peice Inde – i30 lib' with tuo horse pryce ane hundreth markis with Sevintein head of sheip pryce – xxxv lib' x s with ane Cow with calf – xvj lib' with tuo horse & ane mear pryce – 1^{c}ij lib' conforme to the particular Compt Quhilkis horse guidis & sheip was instantlie provin be Iohn Stronache in elgin Iohn hay in Dollas alexander russell staibler in elgin Iohn robin Iohn Dunbar cairter in elgin walter hay & william robertsone burgessis ther

Extending the said alexander russell his loissis to – j^{m}v^{c}iij^{xx}vij lib' xvj s

172. Alexander Dunbar, messenger, burgess of Elgin

followes the loissis of alexander Dunbar messenger burges of elgin

Imprimis the said alexander Dunbar being Deiplie suorne Deponit that ther was plunderit from him be the commone Enemie at the for saidis tymes of insicht plenissing money armor wictual cloithes abuilziementis houshold provisione & wtheris of that kynd conforme to ane particular compt

Extending the said alexander Dunbar his loissis to ij^c lib'

173. Annabill Chalmer

followes the loissis of annabill chalmer

Imprimis the said Annabill Chalmer being Deiplie suorne Deponit that ther was plunderit from hir be the commone Enemie at the tymes forsaid of insicht plenissing cloithing wictual houshold provisione & wtheris of that kynd abouwritin conforme to ane particular compt

Extending the said Annabill Chalmer hir loissis to – ij^{c}iiij^{xx}iiij lib'

174. Alexander Gibsone, burgess of Elgin

followes the loissis of alexander gibsone burges of elgin

Imprimis the said alexander gibsone being being Deiplie suorne Deponit that ther was plunderit from him be the commone Enemie < deleted of > at the tyme forsaid of insicht plenissing cloithes wictual money houshold provisione & wtheris of that kynd abouwritin conforme to the particular compt

Extending the said alexander gibsone his loissis to – viij^{xx}vj markis

175. William Cobane, merchant, burgess of Elgin

followis the loissis of william Cobane merchand burges of elgin

Imprimis the said william Cobane being Deiplie suorne Deponit that ther wes plunderit from him be the commone Enemie at the tyme forsaid of insicht plenissing cloithes wictual money houshold provisione & wtheris of that kynd conforme to the particular compt

Extending the said william Cobane his loissis to – iij^{c}vij lib' xvij s iiij d

176. William Robertsone, litster, burgess of Elgin

followes the loissis of william robertsone litster burges of elgin

Imprimis the said william robertsone being Deiplie suorne Deponit that ther wes plunderit from him be the commone Enem<ie> at the tymes forsaid insicht plenissing wictual cloithes litster wark zairne stuffis claythis litster ware money armor houshold provisione & wther of that kynd abouwritin with thrie horse – 80 lib' with fyve head of guidis – liiij lib' conforme to the particular compt Quhilkis horse & guidis wes instantlie provin be Iames fentone & alexander Fimester burgessis of elgin

Extending the said william robertsone his loissis to – iiij^{c}iij^{xx}xi lib' vj s iij d

177. Janet Maver, relict of James Mylne, maltman, burgess of Elgin

followes the loissis of wmquhill Iames mylne maltman burges of elgin givin wp be Ianet maver his relict

Imprimis the said Ianet mawer being Deiplie suorne & examinat be the saidis comissioneris did depone & declair according to hir owne certane knowledge & by sure informatione of hir wmquhill husband & servantis ther plunderit from hir befor his dec<ease> be the commone Enemie At the tymes forsaid of insicht plenissing cloithes malt beir wictual silver armor houshold provisione & wtheris of that kynd abouwritin with thrie horssis plunderit from him pryce – j00 lib' with ane hors taken be lord lues gordin pryce – 33 lib' 6s 8d conforme to ane particular Compt Quhilkis hors was instantlie provin be thomas cock & Iohn mindziert induelleris in elgin wpon ther aythes deiplie suorne

Extending the said wmquhill Iames myllis loissis to – j^{m}iij^{c}iij^{xx}x lib'

endorsement
see item 150, Walter Smythe

178. Cristen Stewin in Elgin

followis the loissis oissis of cristen Stewin

Imprimis the said cristen being Deiplie suorne Deponit that ther was plunderit from hir be the commone Enemie the tymes forsaid of insicht plenissing cloithes abuilziementis armor money wictual houshold provisione & wtheris of that kynd abouwritin conforme to the compt

Extend the said Cristen hir loissis abouwritin to – ij^c lib' xiij s iiij d

179. Cristen Milne in Elgin

followes the loissis of Cristen milne in elgin

Imprimis the said Cristen being Deiplie suorne Deponit that ther wes plunderit from hir be the common Enemie the tymes forsaid of insicht plenissing Armor money cloithes abuilziementis wictual houshold provisione & wtheris of that kynd abouwritin with tuo hors – 50 lib' tuo ky – 4 markis quhilkis quhilkis was instantlie prowin be Iames & william milnes burgessis of elgin being Deiplie suorne to that effect conforme to the particular compt

Extending the said cristen milne hir loissis abouwritin to iiij^{c}iiij^{xx}x lib'

180. Robert Straquhan, burgess of Elgin

followes the loissis of robert Straquhan burges of elgin

Imprimis the said robert Straquhan being Deiplie suorne Deponit that ther wes plunderit from him be the commone Enemie at the tymes forsaid of insicht cloithes armor money houshold provisione merchand wares & wtheris of that kynd abouwritin conforme to the particular compt

Extending the said robert Straquhan his loissis abouwritin to iiij^{c}iiij^{xx}ix lib'

181. Issobell Sutherland, indweller in Elgin

followes the loissis of Issobell Sutherland induellar in elgin

Imprimis the said Issobell being Deiplie suorne Deponit that ther wes plunderit from hir be the commone Enemie the tymes <forsaid> of insicht plenissing cloithes abuilziementis wictual breaking of Timber plenissing Dores windowes & wtheris of that <kynd> abouwritin conforme to the particular compt

Extending the said Issobell Sutherland hir loissis abouwritin to j^{c}iiij^{xx}xvij lib'

182. William Thom, notary, burgess of Elgin

followes the loissis of william thom notar burges of elgin

Imprimis the said william thom being Deiplie suorne Deponit that ther was plunderit from him be the commone Enemie the ty<mes> tymes forsaid of insicht plenissing cloithes abuilziementis armor wictual houshold provisione & wtheris of that kynd abouwritin conforme To the particular compt Extending the said william Thom his loissis abouwritin to – < *deleted* lix > lix lib' vj s

183. Alexander Andersone, mason

followes the loissis of alexander Andersone measone

Imprimis the said alexander being Deiplie suorne Deponit that ther was plunderit from him < *word deleted* > Be the commone Enemie the tymes forsaid of insicht plenissing wictual measone leimes money armor houshold provisione & great loissis sustenit be him be the Enemie in flying the countrie to eschewe the taking of elgin conforme to ane particular Compt

    Extending the said alexander his loissis to – iij^{c}xxxiiij lib' 2s 8d

184. Thomas Patersone, tailor, burgess of Elgin

    followes the loissis of Thomas Patersone Teilzeor burges of elgin

    Imprimis the said thomas being Deiplie suorne Deponit that ther wes plunderit from him be the commone Enemie at the tymes forsaidis of insicht plenissing wictual money armor houshold provisione & wtheris of that kynd abouwritin with tuo hors – 60 lib' with ane meir – 13 lib' 6s 8d conforme to the particular compt quhilkis horses war provin be Iohn chalmer skinner burges of elgin & richard & Iames wardones ther

    Extending the said thomas his loissis to – iiij^{c}xxj lib'v s iiij d

endorsement

This note, written in a 17th-century hand unlike those used for the 202 surviving entries of the document, appears on the dorse of item 184 (Thomas Patersone). The position of this title-note, with other physical evidence, suggests that the document was originally rolled with the dorse of the final entries on the outside, and that the damaged detached fragment inscribed with items 198-202 (Mariore Winchester – Alexander Petrie) was the final sheet of the roll.

    Toun of Elgynn ther
    loissis in montrose
    tyme

endorsement ends

185. Issobell Forbes

    followes the loissis of Issobell forbes

    Imprimis the said Issobell being Deiplie suorne Deponit that ther was from hir be the commone Enemie the tymes \<forsaid\> of insicht plenissing money cloithes wictual houshold provisione & loissis be the burning of robert gibsones hous conforme to the

    Extending the said Issobell forbes hir loissis to j^{c}iiij^{xx} lib' j s iiij d

186. John Pedder, cordwainer in Elgin

    followis the loissis of Iohn pedder cordoner in elgin

    Imprimis the said Iohn being Deiplie suorne Deponit that ther wes plunderit from him be the commone Enemie at the forsaidis tymes of insicht plenissing Barkit ledder & roche ledder houshold provisione conforme to the particular compt

    Extending the said Iohn pedder his loissis to ij^{c}xlij lib' money

187. Elspet Chalmer, spouse of John Chalmer younger, skinner, burgess of Elgin

    followes the loissis of Iohn chalmer zounger skinner burges of elgin givin wp be Elspet chalmer his spous himselfe being from home

    Imprimis the said Elspet chalmer being Deiplie suorne Didpone that ther wes plunderit from hir be the common Enemie at the tymes forsaid insicht plenissing cloithes abuilziementis wictuall money Armor merchand wares houshold provisione and wtheris of that kynd conforme to the particular compt giwin in theranent

    Extending the said Iohne chalmer his loissis abowewrittin tua hundreth fyftie pund

188. James Pedder, cordwainer, burgess of Elgin

Followis the loissis of Iames pedder cordoner burges of elgin

Imprimis the said Iames pedder being deiplie suorne that ther was plunderit and avay takin from him be the comon enemie in februarij and maij 1645 of Insicht plenisching cloithis wictual Barket ledder houshold provisione and wtheris of that kynd conforme to the particular compt giwin in theranent

Extending the said Iames pedder his loissis to ane hundrethe fyftie pundis 3s 4d

189. Barbara Dunbar, indweller in Elgin

Followis the loissis of Barbara dunbar indueller in elgin

Imprimis the said Barbara dunbar being deiplie suorne deponit that ther was plunderit from hir be the comon enemie of Insicht plenisching cloithis wictual houshold provisione and wtheris of that nature conforme to the particular compt giwin in theranent

Extending the said barbara his loissis to ane hundrethe thriescoir sex pund xj s 4d

190. Alexander Murray, skinner, burgess of Elgin

Followis the loissis of alexander murray skinner burges of elgin

Imprimis the said alexander murray being deiplie suorne deponit that ther was plunderit from him be the comon ene<mie in the> monethis of februarij and maij 1645 and sincesyne of Insicht plenisching wooll wictual armor houshold provisione and <wtheris of> that kynd cloithis abuilziementis with tuentie head of scheipe at 40s the peice 40 lib' conforme to the particular compt quhilk scheipe wes Instantlie prowin be william edvard burges of elgin and alexander edvard ther being deiplie suorne to that effect

Extending the said alexander murray his loissis to tua hundreth tuell pundis xi s

191. Johne Andersone, merchant, burgess of Elgin

Followis the loissis of Iohne andersone merchand burges of elgin

Imprimis the said Iohne andersone being deiplie suorne deponit that ther vas plunderit from him be the comon enemie in februarij and maij 1645 and sincesyne of merchand wares Insicht plenisching money cold cunziet and wncunziet armor Insicht plenisching wictual houshold provisione and wtheris of that kynd conforme to the particular giwin in theranent

extending the said Iohne andersone his loissis to tua hundrethe thrie scoir sex pund

192. George Gordone, skinner, burgess of Elgin

Followis the loissis of george gordone skinner burges of elgin

Imprimis the said george gordone deiplie suorne deponit that according to his certane knawlege and by sure Informatione of his wyiff and servantis ther vas plunderit and takin avay from him be the comone enemie in februarij and maij 1645 and at diverse tymes therefter of Insicht plensiching wooll almit ledder wictual money cloithis armor houshold provisione and wtheris of that kynd conforme to the particular compt giwin in theranent

extending the said george gordone his loissis to fywe hundrethe four scoir fyftein punds 6s 8d

193. James Fentoune, burgess of Elgin

Followis the loissis of Iames fentoune burges of elgin

Imprimis the said Iames fentoune being deiplie suorne deponit that ther was plunderit from him be the comon enemie in februarij and maij 1645 and sincesyne of Insicht plenisching wictual money clothis armor houshold provisione and wtheris of that kynd conforme to the particular compt

extending the said Iames fentone his loissis to ane hundrethe thriescore threttein pund i6s 8d

194. Alexander Watsone, litster, burgess of Elgin

Followis the loissis of alexander watsone litster burges of eglin

Imprimis the said alexander watsone being deiplie suorne deponit that ther was plunderit from him be the comon enemie in februarij and maij 1645 of Insicht plenisching litster ware woll zairne clothis stuffe clothe wictual money armor houshold provisione and wtheris of that kynd with ane horse fiftie pund 13s 4d conforme to the particular compt giwin in theranent quhilk hors wes provin be patrik chalmer burges of elgin and Iames duncan malman ther

extending the said alexander watson his loissis abow writin to four hundrethe fortie pennies 13s iiij d

195. Johne Mackayne, maltman, burgess of Elgin

Followis the loissis of Iohne mackayne maltman burges of elgin

<Imprimis the> said Iohne being deiplie suorne deponit that ther wes plunderit from him be the comon enemie in the moneth <-----------------> 1645 and sincesyne of Insicht plenisching wictual money armor cloithis houshold provisione and wtheris of <that kynd with ane> hors pryce 40 lib' conforme to the particular compt giwin in theranent quhilk hors wes Instantlie <provin be ------ win>chester and androw Innes merchand burgessis of elgin being deiplie suorne to that effect

extending the said Iohne mackayne his haill loissis to fywe hundrethe tuentie sex pund xj s iiij d

196. Alexander Innes, skinner, burgess of Elgin

followis the loissis of alexander Innes skinner burges of elgin

<imprimis the said> alexander Innes being deiplie suorne deponit that ther ves plunderit from him be the comon enemie <in the monethis of> februarij and maij 1645 of Insicht plenisching woll almit ledder merchand wares wictual clothes money <houshold> provisione and wtheris of that kynd conforme to the particular compt giwin in theranent

extending the said alexander Innes his loissis to ane hundreth four scoir tua pund 6s 8d

197. Johne Chalmer, merchant, burgess of Elgin

Followis the loissis of Iohne chalmer < *deleted* being deiplie suorne deponit that ther was plunderit > merchand burges of elgin

<Imprimis the said> Iohne chalmer being deiplie suorne deponit that ther was plunderit and avay takin from him <be the comon enemie> in februarij and maij 1645 of Insicht plenisching wictual armor houshold provisione demolisch<ing of --------> weir caices brokin and made wnvsefull stanceon[is] of windowes lockis and keyis <------------with ane> naige pryce 36 lib' conforme to that particular compt giwin in theranent quhilk <naige was instantlie prowin be> Iohne hardie merchand burges of elgin and david petrie ther

<extending> the said Iohne chalmer his loissis to ane hundrethe thriscore four pund

198. Mariore Winchester, relict of Iohne Chalmer, merchant, burgess of Elgin

<Followis> the loissis of mariore winchester relict of wmquhill Iohne chalmer merchand burges of <elgin>

<Imprimis the said mariore winch>ester being deiplie suorne deponit that ther was plunderit and avay tak<in be the comon enemie in februarij and> maij 1645 and therefter of moneyis wictuall Insicht plenisching <-------------------> houshold provisione and demolisching of timber <------------> with ane hors <----------------- conforme to the> particular compt giwin in theranent

extending the said mariore hir loissis to thrie hundreth thrie score aucht pund aucht shillingis

199. Jonett Skinner, indweller in Elgin

Followis the loissis of Ionett skinner indueller in elgin

Imprimis the said Ionet skinner being deiplie suorne deponit that ther was plunderit from hir be the comon enem<ie> in februarij and maij 1645 and sincesyne of Insicht plenisching woll cloithis wictual moneyis houshold provisione and wtheris of that kynd demolisching and destroing of timber plenisching and making it wnvsefull conforme to the particular compt giwin in theranent

extending the said Ionet skinner hir loissis to tua hundreth fourtie tua markis money

200. William Winchester, merchant, burgess of Elgin

Followis the loissis of william winchester merchand burges of elgin

Imprimis the said william winchester being deiplie suorne and examinat be the saidis comissioneris deponit that according to his owne certane knowledge and sure Informatione of his wyiffe and servantis that ther vas plunderit and avay takin from him be the comon enemie in februarij and maij 1645 of Insicht plenisching malt maill wictual money merchand wares armor houshold provisione of that kynd with timber plenischin destroyit and brokin with ane hors wes Instantlie prowin be Iohne mackayne and robert Innes burgessis of elgin quha war deiplie suorne ther anent

extending the said william winchester his loissis to nyne hundreth tuentie nyne pund thrie schillingis iiii d

201. Mariore Cuming, indweller in Elgin

Followis the loissis of mariore cuming Indueller in elgin

Imprimis the said mariore cuming being deiplie suorne deponit that ther was plunderit from hir be < *deleted* the comon enemie > montrois armie in februarij 1645 and be burning christane clerkis hous quherin sho duelt in maij therefter quhen they cam from <a>uldearin of Insicht plenisching wictual money airmes cloithes houshold provisione of that kynd conforme to the <particular compt giwin in> theranent

<extend>ing the said mariore cuming hir loissis to sex hundreth tua pund iiij s

202. Alexander Petrie, burgess of Elgin

<followis> the loissis of alexander petrie burges of elgin

<Imprimis the said alexander petrie> being deiplie suorne deponit that ther was plunderit from him be the comone enemie <---> and

merchand wares armor cloithis abuilziementis houshold provisione and <------------------
---------------> lib' conforme to the particular compt quhilk tua ky and steir <was instantlie prowin be ------------------------> and Richard waker ther being deiplie suorne theranent
<extending the said alexander petrie his loissis to ---- hun>drethe sevin pundis ten schillingis

The document ends with a detached and damaged fragment commencing part-way through claim 198 (Mariore Winchester) and ending with a torn edge at the foot of claim 202. The final leaf, if complete, might have contained some four or five further short claims.

The Elgin Depositions

Document B
The Town's Losses

Surviving text begins in mid-sentence, suggesting that one or more preceding sheets have been lost. The initial section of text survives only in two typescript versions.

ordinaris The expensis heirof According to the estaittis
32 throughe to the closure
< *deleted* landwarde threatnes to burne the said burghe and to kill Themselves > And this by and attour the loissis < *deleted* and quartering > Sustenit be them at James Grahame and Mckdonoldis handes in februar & Maij 1645

315 lib'
First my Lord marqueis of Argyll came to Elgin One Saturday at nicht the nynteint day of maij I^{m}vj^c & fourtie four yeiris whois Trayne consisted of ane hundreth men and hors quha resided at Elgin whill wednisday thaireftir the Tuentie thrid day of maij forsaid at four aclocke in the eftirnoone being thrie Dayes and ane halfe wpon frie quarteris By & attour his awne ordinar domestickis & some fewe gentlemen quha payit thair avin ordinance at auchtein schillingis the day extendis to _____
< *inserted* prowin be a ticket wnder the quarter maisteris hand >
Extending to the sowme of Thrie Hundreth and fyiftein pundis money

225 lib'
Mair Sir Patricke Mcgie repaired to Elgin wpon Tuysday the aucht day of October followeing Accumpanied with fyve Troupes Ilk ane consisting of fyiftie men And haid frie quarteris Tuentie four houris at Auchtein schillingis the hors & man Except the said Sir Patricke quha payit his awne quarteris < *deleted* quhilkis > quhilk is notoure to this haill countrie The magistratis also Declaired that they receaved Tickettis in wreitt from the Commanderis of the saidis troupis Testifieing the Samyn Bot the saidis Tickettis and manie guid wreittis & evidentis miscarried & war spoyled by the Enemie the expenssis heirof
Extending to the soume of Tuo hundreth Tuentie fyve pund

324 lib'
Item Capitaine william and Capitaine Harie Bruces of Colonell Campbell & Colonell Buchannanis regimentis entered the burghe of elgin with Tuo hundreth & Tuentie foott

Sojoris wpon the Tuentie aucht Day of October I^{m}vj^c & fourtie four yeiris & merched avay the Sext day of Nowember theireftir being nyne dayes within the said burghe wpon frie quarteris at four schillingis the man prowin be a ticket wnder the capitaines hand
 Extending to the Sowme of Thrie hundreth Tuentie four pund

425 lib'
 Item it is knowen That four Troupis of hors viz' My lord Argyll his lyff gaird Comandit be livetennent Archibald Campbell Wmquhill Colonell Campbell of lawers his Troup Comand be livetennent Iames Ramsey and Root maister Durhame of Omachie his Troup And Colonell Cochromes Troup haid thair residence all that Winter in Murray and ane of the saidis Troupes viz' my lord Argyll his lyiff gaird Did frequentlie lye at elgin wpon frie quarteris consisting of fyiftie hors & abowe viz' in the moneth of November ane haill week Togither Being Sevin Dayes and four seuerall Dayes thaireftir being Ellewin Dayes the expenssis thairof auchtein schillingis the man daylie
 Extending to the Soume of Four hundreth Tuentie fyve pund

800 lib'
 Item wpon the Tuentie fourt day of September I^{m}vj^c & fourtie fyve yeiris Entered the lord of Boynd with tuo hundreth hors and < deleted tuik quarteris at thair pleasor >
< inserted vpon the toune distroying thair cornes in the seddis waisting at thair plesor without any payment > fyue dayes which is wndervalued
 Extending to the Sowme of < deleted Aucht Hundreth Pund > ane thousand pundis

1008 lib'
 Item the marqueis of huntlie with his tua sones & forces rekned to be Thrie hundreth hors & above Sex hundreth foott befoir his hielanderis came to him at lethin of theis Sex scoir hors quha war called the wolunteiris And als monye foot wer allowed be the marqueis of huntlie to Take quarteris at elgin Bot manie mad without ardour or warrand stayed at the said toun & all of them for Sevin dayes < deleted wpon frie quarteris at thair awin makeing > < inserted Spending & waisting at thair pleasor without payment > wnder valued
 Extending to the Soume of Ane Thowsand & aucht pund

20 lib'
 Item when the marqueis removed & went to forres & from thence to lethin the poor Peopill of Rothes and some wther countrey peopill wer compelled to come out to assist the blocking wp of Spynie They remained at elgin ane nicht being Towardis ane hundreth men They Depairted the nixt Day finding cauld intertainment Their expenssis was bot
 Extending to the Soume of Tuentie pundis

480 lib'
 Wpon the secund Day of Januar I^{m}vj^c & fourtie sex yeiris Lodovick gordone returned from his father from befoir lethin with Thrie Troupis of hors Ane hundereth of Clan hamerone of theis four scoir of hors & fourtie wther foottmen < deleted quartered >
< inserted lay > at elgin for the < deleted space of > sevin weekis < inserted committing grievous out rages spending & waisting *illegible word* and distroying plenissing, cornes & hous hold stuff the loissis wherof being wndervalued < deleted thair expenss extendis to being wnder valued >

The Elgin Depositions: Document B   113

Extending to the soume of Four Thousand pund

Then when the marqueis returned He keiped about him within the said toun aboue Aucht scoir hors & tuo hundreth foott for the space of tuo dayes Lyke as all the tyme he ley at Lethin The said toune haid daylie sometymes haill Troupes of hors & haill Companies of foott somtymes fewer Bot always some aither advanceing to his camp or Reteirit fra it committing grievous out rages spending & waisting ryotouslie and distroying plenissing cornes & hous hold stuffe the loissis quhairof being wndervalued quhais expenssis was moir Deiper & mor fascheous then the tuo nichtis he ley at elgin all the lose < *deleted* expenss > wndervalued to

typescript page ends; original manuscript page begins

33 nixt the closure

Extending the Sowme of Four Hundreth and four scoir pund.

1800 lib'
Item < when *corrected to* Efter > the marqueis reteered haime he left be hind him his tuo sones & with them four troupes of hors wherof Tua remayned still at Elgin with fourtie foott the wther tuo with a regiment whilk they called the Straboigye Regiment consisting of Tuo hundreth & abowe with thair officiaris was Imployed about the blocking wp of the hous of Spynie Theise Tuo troupes consisting of a hundreth hors strong with Fourtie foott Remained at Elgin Thrie weikis <*deleted* & > Living at Randome < *inserted* committing greivous outrages againes the magistratis & tounes people setting guairdis about them and threat[n]ing them with Imprissonment the loiss[is] q[uhe]rof being > < *deleted* quhais expenssis > wnder valued
Extending to the <S>oume of Ane Thowsand & aucht hundreth pund

cancelled paragraph

2300 lib'
Item during this tyme Thair was extorted from the magistratis & counsell of the said burghe of moneyes Pretending leavies of hors & foott for the kingis service To pay thair awin & thair Commanderis quarteris And to saiff our selffis from periurie being cruellie assalte<d> To Subscryve a wreitt quhilk in effect was the Renunceing of our covenant
Extending to the Soume of Tuo Thousand thrie hundreth pund

end of cancellation

1000 lib'
Wpon The aucht Day of maij j^{m}vj^c & fourtie Sex zeiris when general major middleton Came to releive the seidge of Innernes of whois forces Thair was quarterit in Elgin Aucht hundreth or theirby for ane nicht And when they returnit againe Four hundreth of his forces quarterit at Elgin Tua Dayes and tua nichtis And the reasone that the quarter maisteris gave not tickettis conforme was the suddaine allarme of aberdein the expenssis heirof
Extending to the Soume of Ane Thousand pund

160 lib'

Wpon the Nyntein Day of februar j^{m}vj^c fourtie fyve zeiris enterit Iames grahame sumtyme Erle of Montroise And when they haid plunderit waistit & maid desolat the said Toune of elgin for the space of Ellewin Dayes the publict registeres & evidentis of the said burghe war Pittifullie spoyled and Scattered Thair Comone seale aboue Four hundreth zeir auld Miscarried Thair silver boullis for the Communione plundered Tuo Brasin Candill stick stickes within the kirk torin & pitifullie brokin The pullpittt robbed of a new grein cloith & manie wther Sacriliges comitted The loissis by & attour the registeres & evidentis ar wndervalued

Extending to the Soume of < *deleted* Ane hundreth thrie scoir pund > tua hundreth pundis

cancelled paragraph

i333 lib' 6s 8d:
Mair when the Enemie haid waisted & plundered all within the toune the said Iames grahame callit for theis of best qualitie within the toune fewe of the magistrates and counsell being at home And chairgit them to ransome the toune at Ten Thowsand markis or else he wold burne the toune & comitt the inhabitantes to the mercie of his sojoris quhilk he haid not faillit to hawe Done wnlese the wmquhill lord gordone advysit them that was at home to Schift Tuo Thowsand markis quhilk they war forcit to Borrowe & pay it to montroise quhilk is zet restand

Extending to the Soume of Ane Thowsand thrie hundreth threttie thrie pund sex schillingis aucht penneyes.

end of cancellation

Summa of the loissis givin wp be the saidis provest & baillies Extending to < *deleted* fourtein Thousand thrie hundreth Fyiftie pund Sex schillingis aucht penneyes > Ten thousand nyne hundreth fiftie sevin pundis

Extending the haill loissis abouwritin To the Soume of Ane hundreth < *deleted* and nyne > fyve Thousand < Tuo > Aucht hundreth fourscoir < *deleted* Sevin > fourtein pund < *deleted* allevin > four schillingis < *deleted* Sex penneyes >

endorsement
    ane pairt of the
    loissis of elgin

Appendix 1

The Elgin Burgh Stent Roll of 1646

Moray Council Heritage Service reference ZBEl C62/646/1
Stented individuals bearing names that appear in The Elgin Depositions, either as witnesses or claimants, are indicated by an asterisk *.

Stent of the maintenance 1646

Primo May 1646

Stentiris Nicolas dunbar* Robert hardie Iohne Milne* William Robertsone* William Torrie* Andrew Kay litster* Alexander Russell elder* & Walter hay*

South east quarter
Relict of Alexander Lay 4s
Iames Boynd* 5s 4d
Alexander Syme 8s 4d
Iames Walker* 3s
Iames hutchen 3s
Iames Tulloch & the land 10s
George Stevinsone 4s
Iohne forsyth cordiner* 3s
William Petrie* & the land 12s
Alexander Edward* 4s
Iohne Colloye 5s
Iames Chalmer* 36s
William Wilsone* 4s
Alexander Sinclare* 3s
Isabell Geddes* 4s
Mariorie Cuming* for the land 8s
francis dunbar* 9s
William Warden* 5s
Iohne Corben* 4s
Iohne Parker* 3s
Iohne Andersone skinner* 36s
Annabell Chalmer* 5s
Walter Gilzeane* 5s
Isabell Sutherland* & the land 7s
Iames Grant 9s
Patrik Krystie 9s
George Smith* 9s
Iames nicoll* 3s
Iohne Adame 4s
Elspet Gibsone* 7s
Alexander Smith merchand* 3s
Isabell Warden* 7s
Alexander Tarres 7s
Iames Sibbald* 3s
Iohne Chalmer merchant* 17s
Agnes Leslie 4s
Alexander Stevin* 17s

William Leslie* 18s
Alexander Innes Cordiner* 10s
Iohne Pitirkin* 3s
david dunbar* 17s
Iames Wilsone* 17s
George Piterkin* 4s
William Sutherland* 20s
Alexander Sutherland* 3s

Summa . . . . xviij lib' v s 8 d

South west quarter
Iohne Eles 3s
Mariorie Mcray 3s
Alexander Gibsone* 6s
Thomas Patersone* 10s
Robert Innes* 9s
Iohne Stronache* 4s
Alexander Russell elder* 13s 4d
William Wer* 10s 8d
Thomas Milne 6s
George Cuming 17s
Iohne andersone oriles* 4s
Alexander Russell stabler* 4s
Alexander duff 4s
Iames Pedder* & the land 30s
Christine Milne* 13s 4d
Iohne Chalmer* 3s
< deleted Thomas Warrand* >
Christine Kar* 9s
< deleted Iames >
Robert Strachane* 9s
Ianet Skinner* 3s
Mr Iohne Hay 20s
Andrew Annand* 13s 4d
George Carmichaell* 4s
Iohne Milne* 36s
Iames Milne* 4s
Iames Geddes* 3s
Christine Clerk* 20s
William Milne* 24s
Iohne Winchester 3s
Ieane fergusone 3s
Andrew Ogiluie 4s
Iames Nauchtie* 3s
Christine Gordone 6s
Andrew Laying* 4s
Margaret Gordine 9s

Lachlane Innes 9s
Alexander Murdoche* 4s
Thomas Gadderar 3s
Andrew Clerk 6s
Patrik Murdoche* 3s
Iohne Mcray webster 3s
Robert Tulloche 3s
Thomas Mckeane 4s
Umquhill Richard sutherland 3s
Alexander Smyth smith* 9s
Iohne Alpine* 7s
Michaell young 3s
Iames stevine & the land 15s
Andrew Wilsone* 4s
William Wilsone* 3s
Alexander fimister* 4s
William Robertson litster* 36s
Thomas Gray 3s
Thomas Shipheard* 3s
William Brand 3s
George Purse* 3s
Iohne henrie 3s
William Edward* 4s
Alexander forsythe* 4s
Iames farrer* 4s
Tenants of duffus 53s 4d
Laird of duffus 36s
Cap. Iohne Sutherland 27s
Grissell Vrvell 30s

Summa . . . . xxix lib' 16s

North east quarter
Robert Smith* 4s
Iohne Thomsone* 14s
Andrew Innes* 13s 4d
Hew Hay* 5s
William Philpe 4s
Thomas Calder* 15s
Ianet Gordine 4s
Robert Tulloche 4s
Iohne Geddes land 4s
Alexander Troupe 9s
Alexander Dunbar messenger* 20s
Iames Gordone tailor* 3s
Alexander Geddes 9s
William Tarres* 36s
Barbara Dunbar* 4s

Appendix 1: The Elgin Burgh Stent Roll of 1646

Iames Petrie 5s 4d
Andrew Dick .20s
Iames Mcray* .3s
Iohne Gilzeane 3s
Iohne Hardie* 4s
George Watsone* 4s
William Cobane* 17s
Iames Duncan* 3s
Robert Hardie 20s
George Baxter* 7s
Alexander Vrquhart* 18s
Patrik Muirsone* 9s
Robert Sutherland 18s
Alexander Watsone* 5s
Patrick Chalmer* 38s
Iohne Pedder* .6s
Leonarde Pedder 4s
Robert Imloche 4s
Iames fullertonn 36s
Laird of Pluscarden 36s
Robert Sinclare* 3s
Alexander Imloche 3s
William Laying* 12s
Ianet McCray & her daughter 5s
Patrik LitleIohne* 5s
George Watt* .5s
Iames Gordone cordiner* 5s
Patrik Muiriesone* 4s
Robert Gibsone* 36s

Summa . . . . 23 lib 9s 4d

North west quarter
Thomas Andersone* 3s
Mr Gavin douglas* . . . . 4 lib' 4s
Thomas Purse 5s
Alexander Wilsone 3s
Patrik duncan 3s
Andrew Ross* 7s
George Gordone* 17s
William Purse* 6s
Alexander davidsone 6s
Iohne davidsone 6s
Iannit fentonn 9s
Thomas Murdoches land* 13s 4d
Grissell hepburne 5s
William Torrie* 18s
Thomas davidsone* 3s

Iohne dunbar* 3s
Mariorie Winchester* 6s
Kathiline annand* 16s
Margaret Geddes* 20s
Alexander Watsone* 3s
William Clerk 6s
Thomas Cok* 3s
William hay* .3s
Marione Miller &the land 7s
Andrew Geddes 3s
Iames Milne* & D. land 27s
Elizabeth Douglas* 45s
Iohne Wood* .3s
Elspet falconer* 20s
Iames Paull* & the land 13s 4d
Margaret Andersone* 4s
Alexander Boynd* 6s
Nicolas dunbar* 40s
Alexander dunbar* 5s
Iohne Mckeane & the land* 10s
Andrew fraser 10s
Andrew Kay litster* 16s
Iohne Rag* 9s
Margaret Young 6s
Andrew Mckeane 6s
Andrew Kay cordiner* 20s
Margaret Innes 9s
George Innes* 7s
ThomasMurdoche tailor* 13s 4d
Ieane bonyman* 30s
Walter Milne* 13s 4d
Alexander Petrie* 15s
Alexander May 10s
Iohne Chalmer simple 9s
Robert Malice* 20s
William Innes* 30s
William falconer* 13s 4d
Walter Hay* .20s
William Robertsone younger* 27s
Andrew Vmphray 4s
William Winchester* 6s

Summa . . . . xxxvj lib' 5s 8d

Appendix 2

The Forres Commission

Moray District Record Office reference ZBFo A332/646/1

Att *Edinburgh the twentie fyft day of August* The zeir of god I^mvi^c fourtie sex zeiris Forsameikill as ye lord[is] and vtheris of the committee of moneyis Considering that the estates of parliament be thair act at St androis Hes Remittit and gewin powar to thame do grant Commissiouners for tryell of the loiss[is] of the subjectis of the kingdome baith be sea and land and of brunt and waist landis or ony that are disabled altogidder To pay rent ather be the enemie or be our owne forces And by lykwayis with powar to thame to receave all reportis be vertew of former commissiounes or be vertwe of quhatsumevir Commissiounes heireftir to be grantit And for the better cleiring of the way of tryell Have fund that the pairtie greived or Complaineing may prove be sufficient witnessis that he had in his possessioun Imediatlie befoir the enemie Came to his hous such gudes & geir as he condiscendis vpon in his Complaint And that the enemie cuming thair Thay were takin away and destroyit be the enemie and neuer sene thaireftir in the said places And for the insicht and houshold plennissing and for quhatsumevir vtheris goodis or geir were in the complenatis houssis That the servandis of the complenaris be examined vpoun thair aithis as witnessis thairanent As ane adminicle of the probatioun And in supplement of all the probatioun The pairties complenaris To give thair aithis That to the best knawledge all the said gudes and geir were takin away and destroyit be the enemie and neuer sene thaireftir in the said places alswell thes on the ground as thes in the houss And that this maner of probatioun be extendit Lykwayis to thes goodis and loissis of shippes takin be sea quhilk salbe enterit be the pairties owneris or vtheris haueing powar to give vp entries of shippes and goodis vseing the maner and way of probatioun befoir prescryvit As accordis And the committie forsaid being informed That the proveist baillies Counsall burgessis Inhabitantis and comounitie of the brugh of forres Lyand within the sherefdomed of Elgin & forres Have Sufferit great and manie loissis by burneing of thair landis and houssis destroying of thair cornes away taking of thair bestiall and vther goodis geir and insicht pleinnissing within thair houssis occasioned be the crueltie of the enemie and the present troubles of the kingdome And the said Committie being petitioned To grant ane Commissioun for tryell thairof The Lordis and vtheris of the committie forsaid do heirby give powar warrand and Commissioun To Patrik dunbar of kilboyak Iames dumbar of dunphail Patrik Campbell of boithe (?Iohne) Southerland of Kinsterie Robert dumbar of eistir bin William brodie of Teairie Iohne Brodie of woodheid and Nicolas dumbar baillie burges of Elgin or ony *three* of thame to be ane quorum They being promiscius To tak and receave the tryell and probatioun of the saidis pairties within the said brugh and sherefdome Thair great and greivous loissis sustained be thame In maner forsaid With Powar to the Commissionairs forsaidis or thair quorum To chuse ane clerk & vther officiaris and memberis of Court neidful And to tak thair aithis de fideli administratione And to direct thair owne preceptis for Citatioun of witnessis and vtheris pairties quha are interest and Concernit in the busines And to ammerciat the absentis being chargit personallie apprehendit in scottis money for ilk dyettis absence And that thai take the aithis of the witnessis and pairties quha salbe present and quhais depositiounes salbe admittit be them And to do euerie vthir thing for tryell of the saidis pairties loissis The caus thairof and the persones be quhom the samyn wes committit Observeing the ordour befoir prescryvit Quhilk maner of tryell Is fund to be allowit in this Caice With reservatioun alwayes of the modificatioun to the judge of quhat sall not be Legallie provin be wreit or witnessis Notwithstanding the pairties committeris of the wrangis are not Caled thairto And this tryell being takin in maner forsaid Ordaines the seuerall pairties forsaidis Thair loissis The causis occasioun and quantities thairof with thair owne cariage and deserveingis To be subscrivit be the saidis Commissionaris or thair quorum And report the samyn to the committie appoyntit for that effect That thai may take such convers thairwith As accordis And caus registrat the samyn in the registeris appoyntit for that effect be the clerk of registeris And to be registrat be Mr andro baird clerk deputt for keeping the samyn registeris be the clerk of registeris Quhairanent thir presentis Salbe ane sufficient warrand

Marischall   Cassillis Tullibridine

Forbess Ja: Steuart

Geo^r Iameson

A Baird Clerk deput   I Campbell

endorsement
Com[m]issioun for trying
ye loiss[is] of ye brugh of
Forres

A short note, written in a 19th-century hand, is attached to the foot of the document. an act of the Estates of Parliament appointing Commissioners to examine the waste lands appertaining to the different burghs which lands were given formerly as a recompense because the inhabitants of the burghs < *deleted* corns > Corns < *deleted* and be > had been burnt and their bestial carryed away by the different clans who were at feud with each other there were a number of Gentlemen besides the bailies of the burghs appointed to see the law was rightly laid down concerning the same and < *deleted* any > every three 3 were allowed to be a quorum

Appendix 3

Biographical Notes

BRODIE, Alexander: born 1617, son of David Brodie of Brodie and Katherine, daughter of Thomas Dunbar of Grange; sent to England 1628; returns in the year of his father's death 1632; attends St Andrews university and King's College, Aberdeen, but does not take a degree 1632-3; marries Elizabeth, relict of John Urquhart of Craigston, a daughter of Sir Robert Innes of Innes 1635 – who dies 1640; served heir to the estate of Brodie 1636; assists Robert, young Laird of Innes, in iconoclastic demolition of Elgin cathedral rood screen 1640; supports covenanters; commissioner to Scottish parliament 1643 and member of war committee for Moray; property burnt by Montrose 1645; listed among lords of counsel, 1646; sent as commissioner by ruling kirk party to negotiate with Charles II at The Hague 1649; appointed senator of the court of justice 1649; joins other state commmissioners in inviting Charles II to return, but insists on further concessions and conditions 1650; retires to his estates during Commonwealth period but accepts local office as justice of the peace; returns to bench 1658; superseded at Restoration; fined £4800 (Scots) 1662; supports nonconforming presbyterian ministers during 1670s; dies 17 April 1680 see *The Diary of Alexander Brodie of Brodie MDCLII.- MDCLXXX. and of his son James Brodie of Brodie MDCLXXX. – MDCLXXXV*. Spalding Club, Aberdeen, 1863

CAMPBELL, Archibald: born 1607, son of Archibald, 7th Earl of Argyll; educated at St Andrews university; privy councillor 1628; succeeds to earldom 1638; signs Covenant 1638; created marquis 1641; discovers a plot by Antrim MacDonalls to seize Kintyre and turns against the King; raises a regiment to fight in Ireland 1642; leads covenanter armies against Alasdair MacColla MacDonald and Montrose 1645-6; instrumental in bringing Charles II to Scotland in 1650, placing the crown on his head at Scone 1651; arrested by Cromwellian authorities and forced to sign an oath to live peaceably; travels to London at the Restoration, is arrested and taken as a prisoner to Edinburgh castle; beheaded 1661

DOUGLAS, Gavin: proprietor of property of Shootingacres and Morriston (Muiriestoun); provost of Elgin 1623-31 and 1643-5; his son, John, was provost 1650-3 and 1655-8

GORDON, George: born 1592, eldest son of George Gordon, 6th Earl and 1st Marquis of Huntly, and Henrietta Stewart, daughter of the Duke of Lennox; brought up as a protestant at the court of James VI who creates him Earl of Enzie; marries Lady Anne Campbell, daughter of Earl of Argyll 1607; resolves his father's territorial disputes over lands in Lochaber involving Lochiel and the Camerons 1612-8; denounced as a rebel during a territorial dispute with the Mackintoshes; commissioned by the King for a mission to France in 1622, where he commands a company of gens d'arms; created Viscount Aboyne

Appendix 3: Biographical Notes 121

1632; succeeds to father's titles 1636; shares Roman Catholic sympathies of his parents but supports episcopalian side during Bishops' Wars 1638-41; collaborates with Charles I and Duke of Hamilton in attempting to crush covenanters in the north; supports the King's Covenant; secretly appointed King's lieutenant in the north 1639; is betrayed by Montrose (then a covenanter), arrested and briefly imprisoned in Edinburgh castle 1639; refuses to sign Covenant; appointed as King's lieutenant in the north (subservient to the King's lieutenant-general, Montrose); rises in support of royalist cause, occupying Aberdeen 1644, but flees to Sutherland as covenanter forces commanded by his brother-in-law, Argyll, advance; occupies Aberdeen (again) September 1645, but shortly withdraws to Strathbogie; harries Moray (besieging Lethen and occupying Elgin) 1645-6; self-interest and hatred of Montrose (now a royalist) prevent Huntly supporting the King's cause with the full force of his military potential; excluded from the general pardon of 1647 and captured after a fight at Dalnabo in Strathdon; held as prisoner in the Gordon house of Blairfindy in Glenlivet then transferred to Edinburgh tolbooth; beheaded 22 March 1649

Huntly had five sons and five daughters: his sons, influenced by Argyll, intially support the covenanters but subsequently join their father in the royalist cause: Lord George Gordon is killed at battle of Alford 1645; James Gordon, Viscount Aboyne, fights for Montrose and dies (of grief) in Paris 1649; Lewis (Ludovick), also a noted warrior in the royalist cause, marries Isabel, daughter of Sir James Grant of Grant, and succeeds as 3rd Marquis

GRAHAM, James: born 1612, son of John, 4th Earl of Montrose and Margaret Ruthven, daughter of William, 1st Earl of Gowrie; educated at St Andrews university; succeeds as 5th Earl of Montrose following his father's death 1626; marries Magdalene Carnegie, daughter of Lord Carnegie 1629; travels in Europe 1633-6; assists in drafting National Covenant 1638; fights for Covenant in the Bishops' Wars 1638-40; commissioned to crush opposition to Covenant in the north, seizes Aberdeen three times in 1639 and captures Earl of Huntly despite a safe conduct; falls from supporting Covenant and signs Cumbernauld bond 1640; comissioned lieutenant-general in Scotland and created marquis by Charles I 1644; raises a royalist army around a core of three Irish regiments supplied by Earl of Antrim; in association with Alasdair MacDonald; defeats covenanters at Tippermuir, Aberdeen, Inverlochy, Auldearn, Alford and Kilsyth 1645; defeated at Philliphaugh 1645; escapes to exile on continent; returns to Scotland folllowing execution of Charles I 1649; defeated at Carbisdale 27 April 1650; captured and hanged at Edinburgh 21 May 1650

HAY, John: Master of Arts; married Elspet Douglas 1615; related to Hays of Mayne and, through his family and marriage, to Douglas of Pittendriech; a leading notary public in Elgin; commisioner to parliament from 1629; moderator of Elgin kirk session; provost of Elgin 1631-43, 1645-50 and 1653-5

INNES, Robert: born *c*.1583, son of Robert Innes of Innes; infeft in family estates 1605; marries Grizzel Stuart, daughter of the 'Bonnie Earl' of Moray; created baronet of Nova Scotia 1625; enthusiastic supporter of presbyterianism and the covenants, but also a fervent royalist; commissioner to parliament 1639; appointed a privy councillor 1641; serves on local committee of war 1644; estates harried by Montrose and Huntly and his property, including the town of Garmouth, burnt 1645-6; raises a regiment for the King's cause 1648; welcomes Charles II who returns to Scotland at Garmouth 1650; rebuilds Innes house 1640 - 1653; dies of cancer 17 November 1658

INNES, Robert: 'the young Laird of Innes'; born *c*.1615 son of Sir Robert Innes; educated at King's college, Aberdeen, matriculating 1635; shares his father's presbyterian faith and is uncompromising supporter of covenants ; joins Brodie of Brodie in supervising demolition of Elgin cathedral rood screen 1640; obtains possession of bishop's palace of Spynie through intervention of his father-in-law, the Earl of Moray, and John Innes of Leuchars, hereditary constable, 1642; fights in covenanter army at battle of Auldearn 1645; fortifies Spynie castle to resist siege by Montrose and Huntly 1645-6; member of parliament after the Restoration and sits on various committees; serves as justice of the peace and commissioner of supply for the county; married to Honorable Jean Ross, daughter of James, Lord Ross; dies 1689; daughters marry lairds of Culloden, Kilravock, Clava, Muirton and Echt; succeeded by his son, James, served heir to his father and grandfather 1697

MACDONALD, Alasdair (MacColla): born *c.*1605, 3rd son of Coll Ciotach MacDonald of Colonsay (hanged for supporting royalists 1647); forfeits his lands by refusing to sign Covenant 1639; removes to Antrim and fights with rebel Irish catholics; commissioned by Randal MacDonnell, Earl of Antrim, to lead an Irish army to Scotland to support royalist cause 1644; joins Montrose's campaign 1645; knighted by Montrose; harries the Campbell territory of Argyll 1645-7; defeated in Kintyre 1647 and escapes to Ireland 1647; captured following defeat by English at Knockannas, County Cork; shot without trial November 1647

MIDDLETON, John: born 1619, son of Robert of Caldhame, Kincardineshire (killed by Montrose's troops in his own house 1645); fights in France as a pikeman *c.*1632- 3; returns to Scotland 1639; marries Grizzel Durham, daughter of Sir James Durham of Pitkerro; serves as captain in the covenanter army under Montrose at Brig of Dee 1639; serves as colonel in English parliamentarian army 1642; promoted major-general of horse 1644; purged under self-denying ordinance; raises a regiment of horse and joins army of the Solemn League and Covenant 1644; promoted colonel and lieutenant-general in covenanter army; second-in-command at battle of Philliphaugh 1645; leads an army into Aberdeenshire and Banffshire in October 1645, then lifts the siege of Spynie; appointed commander-in-chief February 1646; leads 800 foot and 600 horse into the north east and raises Montrose's siege of Inverness April 1646; destroys Montrose's castle at Kincardine and massacres its Irish garrison; campaigns against Gordons; campaigns in Jura, Mull and Moidart 1647; joins royalist cause under the Engagement; commands cavalry in defeat at battle of Preston 1648; captured in Cheshire and imprisoned at Hull and Newcastle; paroled to live in Berwick; escapes and joins Pluscardine's rising for Charles II 1649; joins Charles II on his landing in Scotland 1650; fails in attacks on covenanters at the Gordon castles at Bog of Gight and Huntly; submits to covenanters, is excommunicated but restored after penance 1651; commands western wing of Scottish army at battle of Worcester and is captured 1651; escapes to France 1652; returns to join royalist rising in the highlands under Earl of Glencairn 1653-4; defeated in battle at Dalnaspital and escapes to France; created Earl of Middleton by Charles II 1656 (confirmed 1660); returns to Scotland as royal commissioner to the Scottish parliament at the Restoration; supports restoration of episcopacy; deprived of office 1663; appointed governor of Tangier where he dies as the result of a drunken fall 1674

ROSS, Gilbert: Master of Arts; Minister of Colmonell, Aryshire, 1619; translated and admitted as Minister of Elgin 24 September 1640; assists Brodie and Innes in destruction of cathedral rood screen 28 December 1640; member of Commissions of Assembly 1642 and 1644; married (1) Janet Cathcart (2) Elizabeth Napier; died 13 August 1644 aged about 52; his son Gilbert of Ballaird served heir 6 October 1657

Appendix 4

Glossary

Fuller definitions, with etymologies and histories, of all words used in The Elgin Depositions may be found in The Oxford English Dictionary (OED), Scottish National Dictionary (SND) and Dictionary of the Older Scottish Tongue (DOST).

abuilziementis (habiliments) – clothing
almit ledder – leather manufactured by treatment of skins with alum. The process was usually applied to the skins of calves, sheep, lambs, goats and kids to produce thin soft supple leather for gloves
anent – concerning
armour – military equipment and accoutrements of all kinds. The modern armour most appropriate to a man of burgess rank in the 17th century consisted of defensive armour, including breastplate, backplate and helmet, and offensive armour in the form of weapons including musket, pistol, pike and sword. Some may have preferred the typical (lighter and cheaper) highland armour, comprising sword, targe (shield), dirk, long-handled Lochaber axe, bow-and-arrow
aucht – eight
availl – worth, value, estimation

bailzie (baillie) – a member of the town council appointed to sit as a magistrate
barkit ledder – tanned leather, manufactured by treatment of raw hides with infusions of tannin derived from the bark of oak and other trees
bear – barley
buirdis – (wooden) boards
buith (booth) – a small building, often of lean-to construction, which may be permanent or temporary, used as a shop where goods might be displayed for sale. 'Forebooths' erected on the street in front of burgess's houses were a well-documented feature of the Elgin townscape from the 16th century onwards, the property-owner paying additional feu duty in respect of the encroachment onto the public market-street
burgess – a freeman of a royal burgh, entitled to engage in trade and to participate in burgh political affairs
by and attour – in addition to

caice / keass – a window frame; a casement
cardoner / cordoner – a cordwainer: properly a craftsman working with the fine Spanish goatskin leather from Cordova which (medievally) was fashioned into high-quality shoes. Subsequently an ordinary shoemaker might be described as a cordwainer. Some Elgin cordwainers were entrepreneurs rather than simple craftsmen, concerned in the manufacture and sale of high-quality leather goods including gloves.
chirurgiane (chirurgeon) – a surgeon
coal – charcoal
compt – account
couple – a pair of arched timbers, joined at the top, forming the principal frame of a house and supporting the weight of the roof; also known as a **cruck frame**

cornes – threshed grain, presumably oats or barley

cornzeaird (cornyard) – an enclosed area where unthreshed corn is stored; a stackyard or rickyard

cruik – a hook by which a door is fastened; a latch

cunziet – coined

d – Latin *denarius* – a penny. There were 12d. to 1s.; 240d. in a £1.

deallis – planks of sawn timber, typically of pine or fir

dollor (dollar) – one of several Scottish and foreign coins in everyday use. A silver coin issued under James VI, known a 'ryal' or 'sword dollar', was worth 30s. Spanish coins with a face value of eight reals (*pieza de á ocho*, 'pieces of eight') were sometimes known as Spanish dollars. The Rix dollar (*rijksdaler*) from the Netherlands circulated very widely in Scotland, valued from the 1630s to the 1650s variously at 56s., 54s., 53s. 4d. and 53s. (Scots); and by the end of the century at 60s. (Scots) – 5s. (one crown) sterling

eschewe – avoid, escape

flescher (flesher) – a butcher

glasswright – a craftsman working with glass: a glazier rather than a glass-maker

gliffis – gloves, usually of soft, white or off-white leather manufactured from skins of sheep, goats or calves. An essential element of 17th-century costume, no man or woman could be considered properly dressed without gloves, which might be worn on or carried in the hand or tucked visibly into a belt

goods / guidis – livestock

graythe – accoutrements for a horse; fittings for the harness

hail / hoill – whole

haydis – hides

hoge (hog) – a young sheep before its first shearing

hoysit (hoist) – lifted, stolen

imprimis – Latin *in primis*, 'in the first place'

inde – Latin, 'on that account'

indueller (indweller) – an inhabitant, resident or occupant, but not, perhaps a property-owner

inner land (inland) – the inner portion of a tenement or the portion of a burgh feu lying behind the street-front buildings; also, specifically, an inner part of a block of buildings lying between a front and back wing, typically forming one side of a courtyard

insicht (insight) – goods, especially household furniture. The sense overlaps with **plenisching**.

item – Latin, 'also', 'in like manner'. The word is commonly used to introduce each separate subject in a list

kill – a kiln, presumably for drying grain

key / ky / kye – a cow

landuart (landward) – the area of the parish lying outside the burgh

ledder – leather

leimes – lime used for mortar and other purposes in masonry

lib' – Latin *libra*, 'pound': a unit of monetary account unit worth 20s. Silver 20s. coins were minted during the reign of James VI. The relative values of English (sterling) and Scottish money diverged from the 14th century onwards until, in the 17th century, the Scottish pound was worth one-twelfth of the pound sterling (thus one shilling (Scots) was worth one penny sterling)

lining – linen

litster – a dyer

lyiverentrix (liferentrix) – a woman enjoying the use, for her own lifetime, of another's property, though legally a liferenter's (or liferentrix's) right is rather that of an owner for life

luidgeing (lodging) – a dwelling-house, often a particularly substantial and commodious house comprising numerous apartments on several floors

maill (meal) – oatmeal, a staple of Scottish diet

malt – barley prepared for brewing into ale or distilling into whisky by steeping, germination and kiln-drying

maltman – a maltster, an industrialist engaged in the malting of barley

mark / merk – a unit of monetary account representing two-thirds of one pound or thirteen shillings and four pence (13s. 4d.). Silver coins valued at a quarter-merk (3s. 4s.), a half-merk, known as a 'noble' (6s. 8d.), and two merks, known as a 'thistle-dollar' (£1 6s. 8d.) were minted during the reign of James VI

meason – a mason

messenger (messenger-at-arms) – a legal officer whose function is to execute civil and criminal process of the Court of Session and High Court of Justiciary

missive – a letter; in legal terminology, informal and preliminary writing in connection with the negotiation of a contract

naige (nag) – a small riding horse or pony

nota – Latin 'note'

notar (notary) – a legal practitioner whose most important function was recording (and maintaining secure registers of) documents relating to land ownership, bills of exchange and other legal or commercial business; usually referred to as a notary public. There may have been up to a dozen notaries resident or practising in Elgin in 1645-6. Among the number were leading burgesses such as M[aste]r John Hay.

oriloger – a clockmaker. The word was adopted into Middle English from the French *orloge* 'clock'

ox (plural **oxen**) – castrated bull used for meat or as a draught animal typically in a plough team

paiced horse – a riding-horse whose usual gait is a pace – generally equivalent to an amble

plenisching, plenissing – household furniture. The sense overlaps with **insicht**

probatione – proof

provost – the head of the town council

quhair – where. The spelling perhaps suggests an aspirated Scottish pronunciation

quhilk – which. The spelling perhaps suggests an aspirated Scottish pronunciation. The word also appears in the plural form **quhilkis**

quoat – coat

relict – a widow; literally one who is left behind

reteered – returned

rexive / rextiue / rextive – abbreviated form of respective

roche ledder (rough leather) – tanned but undressed leather used for shoe soles

royal burgh – an incorporation created by royal charter giving jurisdiction to the magistrates within certain bounds and vesting certain privileges in the inhabitants and burgesses. Strictly, the burgh comprised only the community of burgesses; other inhabitants (craftsmen, labourers, women) were excluded. A royal burgh was entitled to send a representative to parliament. The common interests of the community of burgesses in Scotland and the influence of royal burghs were focused and enhanced by cooperation in the Convention of Royal Burghs

schilling – a shilling, usually abbreviated to a single initial **s**. There were twelve pennies (12d.) to the shilling and twenty shillings to the pound. During the 17th century one shilling Scots was worth one penny sterling

schoone, shoin, shone – shoes. This plural form (seen also in still-current standard-English plurals such as *oxen* and *brethren*) continues in everyday use in northern dialects of English.

scoir – a score, twenty; abbreviated for accounting purposes to ^{xx}, for example, iij^{xx}vij lib' = three-score-and-seven pounds = £67

sensyne, sincesyne – since then; from that time

skinner – a worker or dealer in animal skins. A skinner burgess was a prosperous freeman, an entrepreneur trading in skins or involved in the manufacture of leather and leather products.

staige (stag) – a young unbroken horse

stancheon – an upright bar, post or support. The context may suggest the vertical wooden mullion dividing a window opening

steir (steer) – a young ox, usually castrated and reared for meat

stent (extent) – a valuation of property for taxation. The **stent roll** for Elgin lists the names of principal property owners with sums of money

(rising from 3s. to £4 4s.) due for maintenance of the Scottish parliamentary armies
stuff(e) – woven textile for garments, probably a woollen cloth

tailit – made by a tailor, tailored
three house height – three-storeyed
timber plenisching – the wooden fixtures and fittings of a house, for example interior panelling and partitions

umquhill – deceased, literally somewhere

wadder, wedder – a castrated male sheep
warkhaus – a workshop
webster / wobster – a weaver. A weaver burgess might be a prosperous townsman: a textile entrepreneur employing journeyman weavers some of whom lived and worked in their master's house, while others worked on looms set up in their own homes either in Elgin or in the townships of the burgh hinterland
weir – a partition or dividing wall within a house

whilk – which; see also **quhilk**
wictuall (victual) – foodstuffs, usually oats, oatmeal, barley or pease. Rents and other dues were often calculated in bolls (containing six bushels) of victual
wmquhill (umquhile) – sometime, formerly, late; usually describing a person who is deceased
wncunziet – uncoined
wnforisfamiliat – a son not yet emancipated from his father. The legal term **forisfamiliat** describes a son who has been assigned part of his father's heritage by sasine in order to establish his own household or to set up in business on his own account
wreitt (writ) – a formal legal document
wtterland (outerland) – the outer part of a burgh feu

zairne – yarn
zounger – younger: the initial **z** derived from the runic letter *yogh* and suggests a guttural pronunciation of the word persisting on north east lips

Notes to Chapters 1-4

Full details of published works cited by author may be found in the Select Bibliography

Abbreviations
APS: *Acts of the Parliaments of Scotland*
Depositions: The Elgin Depositions of 1646, ZBEl C699/646/1
MDRO: Moray District Record Office, Forres
MCHS: Moray Council Heritage Service, Elgin

Chapter 1: In Montrose Tyme
1. Paterson (1998), p.9-10.
2. *ibid.*, p.15.
3. MCHS, Elgin Town Council minutes, ZBEl A2/7.
4. *ibid.*
5. *ibid.*
6. *ibid.*
7. *APS*: vol. V, p.177, 181, 185.
8. Raymond (1993), p.37.
9. Shagan (1997), p.7.
10. Hickson, Vol. 3, (1884), p.163.
11. Clifton (1999), p.109.
12. Fraser (1891), p. 299.
13. MDRO, Elgin Kirk Session minutes, XSEl A2/7.
14. MCHS, Elgin Town Council minutes, ZBEl A2/7.
15. *ibid.*
16. *ibid.*
17. MCHS, Depositions, Document B.
18. *ibid.*
19. Spalding (1829), p.446.
20. Taylor, vol. 3,(1942-61), p.131.
21. Smout (1969), p.152-3.
22. Wishart (1819), p.115.
23. Gordon (1844), p.105.
24. Wishart (1819), p.116.
25. Spalding (1829), p.472 may exaggerate the extent of damage at Innes where agricultural and service buildings were burnt, but probably not the house, which was then undergoing renovation and reconstruction. *see* McKean, Charles 'The architectural evolution of Innes House, Moray' in *Proceedings of the Society of Antiquaries of Scotland*, vol 133 (2003), p.315-42.
26. Macdonald (1892), p.36.
27. Brodie (1863), p.105.
28. Spalding (1829), p.475.
29. MCHS, Depositions, Document B.
30. Gordon (1844), p.110.
31. Maxwell, Alexander, *The History of Old Dundee* (1884), p.490.
32. Spalding (1829), p.476.
33. Fraser (1891), p.300.
34. Barrett (2004), p.140.
35. Brodie (1863), p.110.
36. MDRO Elgin Kirk Session minutes, XSEl A2/7.
37. Spalding (1829), p.473.
38. *ibid.*
39. Gordon (1844), p.126.
40. *ibid.*
41. Barrett (2004), p.136.
42. Wishart (1819), p.139.
43. *National Archives of Scotland*, letter from Earl of Seaforth, 23 September 1645, RH15/77/39.
44. MCHS, Depositions, Document B.
45. *APS*, vol. VI, part ii, p.457-8.
46. MCHS, Depositions, Document B.
47. MDRO, Elgin Kirk Session minutes, XSEl A2/7.
48. MCHS, Depositions, Document B.

Chapter 2: The Said Toune of Elgin
1. Fox (1973), p.76.
2. MCHS, Depositions, Document B.
3. MCHS, Elgin burgh stent roll, (1646), ZBEl C62/646/1.
4. *APS*, vol. VI, part ii, p.491.
5. *APS*, vol. VI, part i, p.51.
6. *APS*, vol. VI, part i, p.55.
7. MCHS, Depositions, Document B.
8. *ibid.*
9. MCHS, Elgin Town Council minutes, ZBEl A2/7.
10. *ibid.*
11. *APS*, volume VI, part i, p.454.

12. Taylor, vol. 2 (1942-61), p.380.
13. MDRO, Stoneyfornoon estate muniments, ZVSt.
14. MDRO, Elgin Kirk Session minutes, XSEl A2/7.
15. Cowan (1977), p.194.
16. Macdonald (1892), p.16.
17. Spalding (1829), p.48.
18. Macdonald (1892), p.19.
19. MCHS, Elgin Town Council minutes, ZBEl A2/7.
20. *The Acts of the General Assemblies of the Church of Scotland* (1691), p.37-8.
21. *The Acts of the General Assemblies of the Church of Scotland* (1691), p.92-3.
22. MDRO, Elgin Presbytery minutes, XPEl A2/3
23. Spalding (1829), p.223.
24. MCHS, Depositions, Document B.
25. MDRO, Elgin Kirk Session minutes, XSEl A2/7.
26. *APS*, vol. VI, part ii, p.457.
27. MCHS, Depositions, Document B.
28. *ibid*.
29. MDRO, Elgin Kirk Session minutes, XSEl A2/8.
30. *ibid*.

Chapter 3: Waisted and Plundered All Within
1. Spalding (1829), p.475.
2. MCHS, Depositions, Document B.
3. Spalding (1829), p.475.
4. MCHS, Depositions, Document B.
5. *ibid*.
6. *ibid*.
7. *ibid*.
8. Braybrooke, Richard (ed.), *Diary and Correspondence of Samuel Pepys*. 3rd edn, vol. 3 (1851), p.275.
9. *ibid*. vol. 4, p.223.
10. MCHS, Depositions, Document B.
11. MCHS, Elgin burgh stent roll (1646), ZBEl C62/646/1.
12. MDRO, Forres commission, ZBFo A332/646/1.
13. Spalding (1829), p.494.
14. MCHS, Elgin Town Council minutes, ZBEL A2/13.
15. Gordon (1844), p.161.
16. Bailey (1972), p.12, 18.
17. *APS*, vol. VI, part ii, p.303.
18. MCHS, Elgin burgh stent roll (1646), ZBEl C62/646/1.
19. *APS*, vol. VI, part i, p.457.
20. *APS*, vol. VI, part i, p.786.
21. MCHS, Depositions, Document B.
22. Fraser (1891), p.302.
23. Angus Archives, M/WK/16(i).
24. *ibid*.
25. Barrett (2004), p.148.
26. Fraser (1891), p.ix.
27. Barrett (2004), p.65.

Chapter 4: Tryell and Probatioun
1. *APS*, vol. VI, part i, p.289-90.
2. *APS*, vol. VI, part i, p.388.
3. *APS*, vol. VI, part i, p.388.
4. *APS*, vol. VI, part i, p.572-3.
5. *APS*, vol. VI, part i, p.803-4.
6. *APS*, vol. VI, part ii, p.78.
7. *APS*, vol. VI, part i, p.572-3.
8. National Archives of Scotland, RH1/2/466.
9. MDRO, Forres commission, ZBFo A332/646/1.
10. Aberdeen City Archives, in-letter, 26 November 1646.
11. Taylor, vol. 3 (1942-61), p.117-24.
12. *APS*, vol. VI, part i, p.632.
13. *APS*, vol. VI, part i, p.203.
14. *APS*, vol. VI, part ii, p.78.
15. *APS*, vol. VI, part i, p.457.
16. *APS*, vol. VI, part i, p.750.
17. *APS*, vol. VI, part i, p.797.
18. *APS*, vol. VI, part i, p.785-6.
19. *APS*, vol. VI, part ii, p.277-8.
20. Taylor, vol. 3 (1942-61), p.227-30.
21. MDRO, ZBFo C632/649 (uncatalogued vouchers).
22. Taylor, vol. 3 (1942-61), p. 3.
23. *APS*, vol. VI, part i, p. 845-6; vol. VI, part ii, p.297.
24. *APS*, vol. 6, part ii, p.303-4.
25. *ibid*.
26. *APS*, vol. VI, part i, p.789.
27. *APS*, vol. VI, part i, p.721.
28. *APS*, vol. VI, part i, p.826.
29. *APS*, vol. VI, part i, p.783.
30. *APS*, vol. VI, part ii, p.457-8.
31. MDRO, Forres commission, ZBFo A332/6646/1.
32. Iredale and Barrett (1999), p.50-1.
33. Spalding (1829), p.494.

Select Bibliography

The Acts of the General Assemblies of the Church of Scotland from the year 1638 to the year 1649 and the Acts of the General Assembly 1690 (1691)
Bailey, S.D., *Prohibitions and Restraints in War* (1972)
Bain, George, *History of Nairnshire* (1893)
Barrett, John, et al., *A Celebration of Forres, 500 Years a Royal Burgh* (1996)
Barrett, John R., *Mr James Allan: the journey of a lifetime* (2004)
Barrett, John and Iredale, David, 'Building royal burghs', *The Scots Magazine*, number 1, vol.142 (1995)
Barrett, John and Mitchell, Alastair, 'Elgin's love-gift: civil war and the burgh community', *Scottish Local History*, issue 68 (2006)
Bingham, Caroline, *Beyond the Highland Line: highland history and culture* (1991)
Blackmore, David J. (ed.), *The Renaissance Drill Book of Jacob de Gheyn* (1986)
Brodie, Alexander, of Brodie, *The Diary of Alexander Brodie of Brodie, MDCLII – MDCLXXX and of his son James Brodie of Brodie, MDCLXXX – MDCLXXXV* (1863)
Buchan, John, *Montrose* (1928)
Burleigh, J.H.S. *A Church History of Scotland* (1973)
Carlton, Charles, *Going to the Wars: the experience of the English Civil Wars, 1638-1651* (1992)
Cavers, Keith, *A Vision of Scotland: the nation observed by John Slezer 1671-1717* (1993)
Clifton, Robin, 'Fear of popery', *The Origins of the English Civil War* (1973)
Clifton, Robin, 'An Indiscriminate blackness? Massacre, counter-massacre and ethnic cleansing in Ireland 1640-1660', *The Massacre in History* (1999)
Cowan, Edward J., *Montrose for Covenant and King* (1977)
Cramond, William (ed.), *The Records of Elgin, 1234-1800* (1903, 1908)
Craven, J.B., *History of the Episcopal Church in the Diocese of Moray* (1889)
Cunningham, Ian C., *The Nation Survey'd: Timothy Pont's maps of Scotland* (2001)
Davies, Godfrey, *The Early Stuarts 1603-1660* (1937)
Donagan, Barbara, 'Codes and conduct in the English civil war', *Past and Present*, no. 118 (1988)
Donagan, Barbara, 'Atrocity, war crime and treason in the English civil war', *The American Historical Review*, vol. 99, no. 4 (1994)
Donaldson, Gordon, *Scotland: the making of the kingdom James V – James VII* (1965)
Donaldson, Gordon, *Scotland: church and nation through sixteen centuries* (1972)
Douglas, J.D., *Light in the North: the story of the Scottish covenanters* (1964)
Douglas, Robert, *The Lord Provosts of Elgin* (1926)
Dwyer, John, et al., *New Perspectives on the Politics and Culture of Early Modern Scotland* (1982)
Fawcett, Richard, *Elgin Cathedral* (1991)
Foster, W.R., *The Church before the Covenants: the Church of Scotland 1596-1638* (1975)
Fox, H.S.A., 'Going to town in thirteenth-century England', *Man Made the Land* (1973)

Fraser, James, *Memoirs of the Rev. James Fraser of Brea* (1891)
Furgol, Edward M., *A Regimental History of the Covenanting Armies 1639-1651* (1990)
Furgol, Edward M., 'George Mackenzie, second earl of Seaforth', *Oxford Dictionary of National Biography* (2004-5)
Furgol, Edward M., 'John Middleton, first earl of Middleton', *Oxford Dictionary of National Biography* (2004-5)
Furgol, Edward M., 'Sir John Hurry', *Oxford Dictionary of National Biography* (2004-5)
Furgol, Edward M., 'William Baillie', *Oxford Dictionary of National Biography* (2004-5)
Furgol, William, 'The Military and ministers as agents of presbyterian imperialism in England and Ireland, 1640-1648', *New Perspectives on the Politics and Culture of Early Modern Scotland* (1982)
Gordon, Patrick, of Ruthven, *A Short Abridgement of Britain's Distemper, 1639-1649* (1844)
Grant, J., et al., *Survey of the Province of Moray* (1798)
Henderson, G.D., *Religious Life in Seventeenth-Century Scotland* (1937)
Hickson, Mary (ed.), *Ireland in the Seventeenth Century or the Irish Massacres of 1641-2* (1884)
Innes, C. and Thomson, T., *The Acts of the Parliaments of Scotland* (1814-75)
Innes-Smith, Robert, *The House of Innes* (1990)
Inverness Field Club, *The 17th Century in the Highlands* (1986)
Iredale, David and Barrett, John, *Discovering Local History* (1999)
Iredale, David and Barrett, John, *Discovering Your Old House* (2002)
Keay, John and Keay, Julia (eds), *Collins Encyclopaedia of Scotland* (1994)
Keith, Alexander, *A Thousand Years of Aberdeen* (1972)
Lewis, John and Pringle, Denys, *Spynie Palace and the Bishops of Moray* (2002)
Lynch, Michael (ed.), *The Early Modern Town in Scotland* (1987)
Macdonald, M., *The Covenanters in Moray and Ross* (1892)
Macinnes, Allan I., *Clan, Commerce and the House of Stuart 1603-1788* (1996)
Macinnes, Allan I., *The British Revolution 1629-1660* (2005)
McKean, Charles, *The District of Moray: an illustrated architectural guide* (1987)
Mackenzie, William, *The Scottish Burghs* (1949)
Mackintosh, H.B., *Elgin Past and Present* (1914)
Mackintosh, H.B., *Pilgrimages in Moray* (1924)
Mackintosh, L., *Elgin, Past and Present* (1891)
MacLeod, Ruairidh H., 'The Battle of Auldearn', *The Seventeenth Century in the Highlands* (1986)
Mair, Craig, *Mercat Cross and Tolbooth: understanding Scotland's old burghs* (1988)
Mitchell, Alastair, 'Waisted and Plundered All Within: Elgin, Montrose and the Scottish Civil War 1645-1646', unpublished M. Litt. dissertation, Aberdeen University (2005)
Mitchison, Rosalind, *Lordship to Patronage: Scotland 1603-1745* (1990)
Moody, David, *Scottish Towns: a guide for local historians* (1992)
Muir, Alison G., 'Alexander Brodie of Brodie', *Oxford Dictionary of National Biography* (2004-5)
Napier, Mark, *Montrose and the Covenanters; their character and and conduct* (1838)
Napier, Mark, *Memoirs of the Marquis of Montrose* (1856)
Paterson, Raymond Campbell, *A Land Afflicted: Scotland and the covenanter wars 1638-1690* (1998)
Rampini, Charles, *A History of Moray and Nairn* (1897)
Raymond, Joad, *Making the News: an anthology of the newsbooks of revolutionary England 1641-1660* (1993)
Reid, Stuart, *The Campaign of Montrose: a military history of the civil war in Scotland 1639 to 1646* (1990)

Reid, Stuart, *Auldearn 1645: the Marquis of Montrose's Scottish campaign* (2003)
Rhind, William, *Sketches of the Past and Present State of Moray* (1839)
Ritchie, J.B., *The Pageant of Morayland* (1953)
Rogers, H.C.B., *Battles and Generals of the Civil Wars 1642-1651* (1968)
Royle, Trevor, *British Civil War: the wars of the three kingdoms 1638-1660* (2004)
Sanderson, Margaret H.B., *Scottish Rural Society in the Sixteenth Century* (1982)
Shagan, Ethan, 'Constructing discord: ideology, propaganda and English responses to the Irish rebellion of 1641', *Journal of British Studies*, no. 1, vol. 36 (1997)
Sharpe, Kevin, *The Personal Rule of Charles I* (1992)
Shaw, Lauchlan, *The History of the Province of Moray*, 2nd edn (1882)
Simpson, A.T. and Stevenson, S., *Historic Elgin: the archaeological implications of Development* (1982)
Slezer, John, *Theatrum Scotiae* (1693)
Smout, T.C., *A History of the Scottish People 1560-1830* (1969)
Spalding, John, *History of the Troubles and Memorable Transactions in Scotland in the Reign of Charles I* (1829)
Stevenson, David, 'Montrose and Dundee', *The Seventeenth Century in the Highlands* (1986)
Stevenson, David, *Highland Warrior: Alasdair MacColla and the Civil Wars* (1994)
Stevenson, David, *Revolution and Counter-Revolution in Scotland 1644-1651* (2003)
Stevenson, David, *The Scottish Revolution 1641-1644: the triumph of the covenanters* (2003)
Stevenson, David, 'Alexander Leslie, first earl of Leven', *Oxford Dictionary of National Biography* (2004-5)
Stevenson, David, 'Archibald Campbell, marquess of Argyll', *Oxford Dictionary of National Biography* (2004-5)
Stevenson, David, 'George Gordon, second marquess of Huntly', *Oxford Dictionary of National Biography* (2004-5)
Stevenson, David, 'James Graham, first marquis of Montrose', *Oxford Dictionary of National Biography* (2004-5)
Stone, Jeffrey C., *The Pont Manuscript Maps of Scotland: sixteenth century origins of a Blaeu atlas* (1989)
Stone, Jeffrey C., *Illustrated Maps of Scotland from Blaeu's Atlas Novus of the Seventeenth Century* (1991)
Taylor, Louise B., *Aberdeen Council Letters* (1942-1961)
Thomas, Jane, 'The Burgh of Elgin in Early Modern Times', unpublished thesis, Aberdeen University, Th1990Tho (1990)
Thomas, Jane, 'Elgin notaries in burgh society and government 1540-1660', *Northern Scotland*, vol.13 (1993)
Thomas, Jane, 'Craftsmen of Elgin 1540-1660', *Freedom and Authority: Scotland c.1050-c.1650* (2000)
Tranter, Nigel, *The Fortified House in Scotland* (1977)
Walsh, Maurice, *And No Quarter: being the chronicles of the wars of Montrose* (1937)
Wedgwood, C.V., *The King's Peace 1637-1641* (1955)
Wedgwood, C.V., *The King's War 1641-1647* (1958)
Whyte, Ian, *Agriculture and Society in Seventeenth-Century Scotland* (1979)
Wishart, George, *Memoirs of the Most Renowned James Graham, Marquis of Montrose* (1819)
Young, Robert, *Annals of the Parish and Burgh of Elgin from the Twelfth Century to 1876* (1879)

Index

Abercrombie: Alexander elder of Birkinboige, 50; Thomas of Skeath, 50
Aberdeen: x, 1, 2, 3, 9-10, 11, 12, 13, 14, 16, 19, 23, 25, 26, 29, 33, 37, 39, 42, 43, 50, 51, 52, 121; university, x, 2
Aboyne, viscount, *see* Gordon, James
Abuilziementis, 13, 24, 34, 37, 40, 41, 64 (Document A) *passim*
Adame, Gilbert, 93, **claim 124**
Adame, Johne, 115
Adie / Aidie, James, 4, 6
Advocate, 10
Agriculture, 17, 20, 27
Ale, 26, 28
Alexander III, 18
Alford, battle, 14, 121
Allan, Mr James, 13, 23, 45, 46, 53-4
Alpein, John, 36, 86-7, **claim 89**, 116
Alves, Alexander, 4
Andersone: Alexander, 11, 28, 105-6, **183**; John(e), 28, 35, **claim 62**, 72, 82, 93, 100, 107, 115, 116, **claim 158**, **claim 191**; Margarat / Margaret, 86, **claim 88**, 117; Michaell, **claim 70**, 83, 94; Thomas, 60, 88, 89, 92, 117, **claim 118**
Annand, Andrew, 4, 63, 94, 116; Kathrein / Kathline, 39, 100, 117, **claim 157**
Anstruther, 19
Antrim, earl, *see* McDonnell, Randall
Anworth, 1
Apothecary, 13
Argyll, marquis, *see* Campbell, Archibald
Armagh, 7
Arms and armour, 3-4, 6, 13, 24, 26, 28, 35, 36, 37, 40, 41, 64 (Document A) *passim*
Atrocity, 6-8, 9-10, 13, 39, 43
Auldearn, 17, 18; battle, 13, 70, 109, 121
Avon river, 23

Baillie, William, 3
Ballindalloch, 12, 52; laird, *see* Grant, John
Balvenie battle, 52
Banff, 12, 17, 42, 51
Barclay, John, x
Barley (bear), 102, 104
Barn, 69
Baxter: 28; George, 68, 96, 117, **claim 139**
Birnie, 101
Blackmarket, 28
Blaeu, Jan, 17
Blandry, _____, 7
Boath / Both / Boithe, laird, *see* Campbell, Patrick *and* Dunbar, Alexander
Bog of Gight, *see* Gordon Castle

Bonnetmaker, 28
Bonyman, Jeane, **claim 5**, 25, 65, 117
Book of Common Order, 1
Bowar, Alexander, 11
Boynd: Alexander, **claim 52**, 80, 117; James, **claim 58**, 81, 115
Bracton, Henry de, 17
Brand, William, 116
Brea laird, *see* Fraser, James
Brechin: 42, 51; bishop, *see* Whitford, Walter; cathedral, 2
Brewer, 28
Brig o' Dee battle, 3, 122
Bruce: captain Harie, 9, 111; captain William, 9, 111
Brodie: 11, 12, 22; Alexander of Brodie, 12, 22, 29-30, 31, 45, 48, 50, 52, 120; Alexander of Lethen, 12, 14, 29, 40, 52; James of Brodie, 120; John(e) of Woodhead, 50, 118; laird, *see* Brodie, Alexander *and* Brodie, James; William of Tearie, 50, 118
Buchanan, George, regiment, 9, 111-12
Bull, 27, 103

Calder family: 26; Thomas, 70, 116
Calf, 35, 66, 69, 97, 103
Cameron clan, 112
Campbell: Archibald, Marquis of Argyll, 3, 9, 10, 31, 34, 47, 65, 111, 112, 120, 121; of Lawers's regiment, 111-12; Lieutenant Archibald, 112; Patrick of Boath, 50, 118; clan, 3, 10
Candlemaker, 28
Cant, Andrew, 29
Cantray, laird, *see* Dolles, William
Carbisdale, battle, 16, 121
Carmichaell, Thomas, **claim 19**, 72
Carmichall / Carmichaell: George, 60, 102, **claim 165**, 116
Carter, 1, 22, 27, 28, 103
Cattle (bovine), 24, 27, 35, 37, 40, 42, 52, 63, 64, 65, 66, 67, 69, 76, 88, 89, 93, 97, 98, 99, 101, 103, 104, 105, 110; *see also* Bull, Calf, Cow, Oxen, Steer
Cellar, 69
Chalmer: Agnes, **claim 63**, 82; Annabell, 104, 115, **claim 173**; Elspet, 40, 106, **claim 187**; Chalmer, Iissobell, **claim 84**, 86; James, 101, 115, **claim 159**, (younger) 4; John(e), 4, 96, 108, 109, 115, 116, 117, **claim 197**, **claim 198**, (elder) 101, **claim 162**, (younger) 40, 106, **claim 187**; Margrat, 102, **claim 164**; Patrick, **claim 11**, 69, 70, 108, 117
Charcoal, 78
Charles I, 1, 2, 3, 6, 8, 28, 31, 33, 41, 48, 49, 121
Charles II, 16, 31, 53, 121, 122
Chayne, Johne, 93, **claim 125**
Cheese, 35

Christmas, 29
Clanranald, captain, *see* Macdonald, Sir John of Moidart
Clava, laird, *see* Rosse, William
Clerical method, 57-8
Clerk: Andrew, 116; Christane, 38, 40, 41, 98, 109, 116, **claim 149**; Thomas, 69; William, 117
Clifton, Robin, 7
Clockmaker, 28, 82, 116
Cloth, 67, 101, 104
Clothing, 1, 8, 13, 14, 24, 27-8, 34, 37, 40, 41, 64 (Document A) *passim*
Cobane, William, 104, 117, **claim 175**
Cochrome, colonel _____, 112
Cok / Cock, Thomas, **claim 42**, 77-8, 104, 117
Cok, Johne, 88, **claim 98**
Col Ciotach, *see* MacDonald, Col MacGillespick *and* MacDonald, Alastair
Collie, Agnes, 87, **claim 92**
Colloye, Johne, 115
Colonsay, 3
Commonwealth, 31-2, 53, 120
Convention of Royal Burghs, 26, 44
Cook, 10
Cooper, 10, 28, 86
Corbane / Corben, Johne, 90, **claim 108**, 115
Cordwainer, 21-2, 77, 78, 91, 102, 106, 107, 115, 116, 117
Corn: 13, 26, 34-5, 40, 42, 52, 64, 65, 67, 68, 69, 70, 71, 75, 76, 78, 79, 80, 83, 84, 85, 87, 88, 89, 91, 92, 93, 95, 96, 97, 98, 100, 112; yard, 69
Cow, 24, 27, 35, 37, 52, 66, 69, 76, 88, 89, 93, 97, 98, 99, 101, 103, 105, 110
Cromwell, Oliver, 32, 51
Culbin: 11; laird, *see* Kinnaird, Walter
Cullen, 12, 17, 19, 37, 42, 51
Culloden, laird, *see* Forbes, Duncan
Cuming, Mariore, 41, 109, 115, **claim 201**; George, 116
Cuthbert, James of Draikes, 50
Cutler, 28

Dallas, 21, 103
David I, 17
Davidsone: Alexander, 117; Johne, 117; Thomas, **claim 59**, 81, 94, 100, 117
Dee River, 9
Dick, Andrew, 117
Dingwall, 17
Distiller, 28
Divine right, 1, 2
Doe, John, 4
Dolles, William of Cantray, 50
Donaldson, George, 55
Donaldsone, William, 21, 91, **claim 111**
Dornoch, 17, 42, 51
Douglas: Alexander, 38, 55; Elizabeth,

claim 7, 66-7, 117; Mr Gavin of Morriston & Shootingacres, 55, 56, 94, 96, 117; James, 4; John of Morriston, 38, 55; John, 101
Dow, John, 4
Dowglas, Dr Alexander, 50
Draikes, laird, *see* Cuthbert, James
Drug, 13, 70
Duff, Alexander, 21, 116
Duffus: laird, *see* Sutherland, Alexander; tenants, 116
Dumbar: James of Dunphail, 50, 118; Robert of Easter Bin, 50, 118
Dunbar / Dumbar, Nicholas, 50, 70, 115, 117, 118
Dunbar: 19; Alexander, 28, 64, 70, 103, **claim 172**, 116, 117, (younger) 101, **claim 160**; Alexander of Boath, 50; Alexander of Westfield, 50; Barbara, 58, 107, 116, **claim 189**; battle, 31; David, 100, 116, **claim 156**; Frances, **claim 24**, 73, 95, 115; James, **claim 16**, 71; John(e), 100, 103, 117; younger, 89, **claim 104**; Ninian of Grangehill, 11, 50; Patrick of Kilbuiack, 50, 118; Robert, **claim 10**, 26, 34-5, 68, 69, 95, (elder) **claim 54**, 80-1, Thomas, 4; William, 53
Duncan: Margaret, 8, 41, 99, **claim 154**; Patrick, 117; Thomas, 92, **claim 117**
Duncan(e), James, 24, **claim 37**, 76, 108, 117
Dundee, 11, 23, 43
Dunkirk pirates, 50
Dunphail, laird, *see* Dunbar, James
Durham, routemaster Mr William of Omachie, 112
Dyer, *see* Litster
Dysart, 19

Easter Bin, laird, *see* Dunbar, Robert
Echt, lady, *see* Innes, Elizabeth
Ecles, Johne, 116
Edinburgh: 3, 19, 26; bishop, *see* Lindsay, David; Greyfriars; 2; St Giles, 1-2
Edvard, Alexander, 91, 107, **claim 114**
Edvard / Edward, William, 91, 107, **claim 115**, 115, 116
Elchies: 9; laird, *see* Grant, Robert
Elgin: 3, 9, 10, 11, 17; arms, 18; Bow Brig, 22, 25; castle, 19, 25, 43; cathedral, x, 19, 29-30, 32, 43, 120, 122; college, 64, 65, 66, 69, 87; friaries, 25, 43-4; Kirk Session, 7-8, 12, 14, 25, 26, 28, 31-2, 39, 121; population, 19; Presbytery, 29; St Giles church, 14, 18, 21, 30, 114; ports, 19, 25; tolbooth, 21; town plan, 20-1, 22-3
Elgin Town Council: 3-4, 5, 11, 14, 28-9, 33, 111, 113, 114; muniments, 18, 21-2, 51-2, 54-5, 57,114; seal, 18, 114

Elizabeth I, 1
Engagement, 31
Ewe, 92

Fairrer / Fayrer, James, 63, **claim 97**, 88, 116
Falconer: Elspet, **claim 15**, 71, 117; William, **claim 3**, 64, 117
Farquharson, Donald, 13
Feldonne, James, **claim 18**, 71
Fento(u)ne, James, 104, 107-8, **claim 193**
Fentonn, Jannit, 117
Fergusone, Jeane, 116
Fimester, Alexander, 104, 116
Findlay, James, 4
Firearms, 3-4, 28, 36, 77
Fish, 26
Fisherman, 10
Flesher, 27, 67, 74, 79, 85
Forbes: Andrew, 4; Duncan of Culloden, 50; Issobell, 14, 106, **claim 185**; John, x
Fordyce, 25
Forebooth, 21, 25, 40, 64, 65, 67, 69
Forfar, 19
Forres, 10, 17, 18, 19, 24, 42, 45, 50, 51, 52, 112, 118-9
Forsyith / Forsyth, John(e): 63, 115, (younger) **claim 31**, 75
Forsyth, George, 41, 89, **claim 101**
Forsythe: Agnes, 88, **claim 96**; Alexander, 21, 25, 28, **claim 34**, 75, 116; David, 88
Fortrose, 17
Frachir, lieutenant colonel ____, 52
Fraser: Andrew, 117; James of Brea, 7, 44, 46; John(e), 3, 91, **claim 112**
Freuchie, laird, see Grant, Sir James of Grant
Fuller, 28
Fullerton: ____, 7; James, 117
Furniture, 24, 37, 65, 66

Gaddarar, William, 99, **claim 152**
Gadderer, Thomas, 116
Gardner, 10, 28
Garmouth, 12, 25, 28, 31, 121
Geddes: Alexander, 116; Andrew, 117; Issobell / Isabell, 90, **claim 109**, 115; James, **claim 83**, 85, 116; Jenny, 2; Johne, 116; Margaret, **claim 77**, 84, 117
General Assembly, 26, 29, 53
German, Mr ____, 7
Gibsone: Alexander, 104, 116, **claim 174**; Elspet, 40-1, 90, **claim 105**, 115; James, 66; Robert of Linkwood, **claim 6**, 14, 26, 40, 65-6, 69, 106, 117; William, 84, **claim 94**
Gilbert, Kathrin, 93, **claim 126**
Gilzeane: Johne, 117; Walter, 94, 115, **claim 129**
Glas, James, 22
Glasgow, 19, 29
Glass, 25, 28, 64, 67, 75, 100, 105, 108
Glasswright, 25, 28, 75
Glencairn's regiment, 52
Gloves, 27, 76, 83, 87, 94, 96, 100
Goat, 40, 52
Gold, 1, 35-6, 64, 65, 67, 70, 71, 103, 107
Goldsmith, 28
Goods, see Cattle
Gordine: Janet, 116; Margaret, 116
Gordon: castle, 10, 122; clan & territory, 1, 2, 3, 6, 10, 20, 34; George, Marquis of Huntly, 3, 10, 12, 14, 19, 34, 43, 47, 52-3, 64, 67, 112, 113, 120-1; Lord George, 12, 14, 33-4, 67, 114, 121; James, **claim 25**, 73, 90, **claim 107**, 117; James of Rhynie, 13, 34, 38, 42, 55; James of Rothiemay, 2; James Viscount

Aboyne, 3, 14, 112, 113, 121; Lord Ludovick (Lewis), 12, 14, 40, 67, 68, 70-1, 104, 112, 113, 121; Patrick, 10, 33, 39, 43; Robert of Straloch, 17; Sir Robert of Gordonstoun, 11; soldiers, 1, 10, 12, 14, 23, 34, 36, 39, 41, 42, 43, 44, 48, 49, 69, 112-13
Gordon(e), John, 39-40, 58, 96-7, 98, 99, **claim 141**
Gordone: Christine, 116; George, 107, 117, **claim 192**; captain Johne, 70
Gordonstoun, laird, see Gordon, Sir Robert
Gordoun, James, 21
Graham, James, Marquis of Montrose, 1, 3, 8-10, 11, 13, 16, 25, 28, 33-4, 35, 41, 43, 44, 47, 56-7, 66, 68, 70, 98, 99, 100, 106, 111, 121
Grangehill:10; laird, see Dunbar, Ninian
Grant: James, 115; John of Ballindalloch, 11, 12, 14, 26, 50, 52-3, 69; John of Moyness, 50; laird, see Grant, Sir James; Patrick, 24, 39, **claim 147**; Robert of Elchies, 9; Thomas, 22, **claim 30**, 70-1, 74; Sir James of Grant (Freuchie), 11, 29, 50, 121
Gray, Thomas, 116
Gregor, Patrick, 21
Grigor: Robert, 4; Walter, 4
Guidis, Jonet, 4
Gunsmith, 28, 36, 77
Gustavus Adolphus, King of Sweden, 3, 37
Guthrie, John, Bishop of Moray, 6

Hamilton, Frederick, regiment, 9
Hanna, John, 1-2
Hardie: Issobell, 41, 89, **claim 101**; John(e), 26, **claim 60**, 82, 108, 117; Robert, 115, 117
Harivood, Johne, 89, **claim 100**
Hastings, ____, 7
Hay: Alexander, 95, **claim 133**; Francis, 8; Hew, **claim 22**, 24, 72-3, 116; Jean, 8; John of Knockdowie, 50; Mr John, 4, 6, 14, 25, 31, 50, 53, 55, 56, 103, 116, 121; Margaret, 8; Marjorie, 8; Walter, **claim 21**, 64, 72, 103, 115, 117; William, 90, **claim 106**, 117
Hendrie, George, 21
Henrie, Johne, 116
Hepburne, Grissell, 117
Hervie: Alexander, 21; John, 21
Hides, 78, 79
Highland regiments, 1, 10, 12, 39, 41
Hog, 92
Horse, 23, 27, 34, 35, 36, 37, 40, 52, 63, 64, 65, 66, 67, 68, 69, 70, 72, 76, 88, 92, 93, 94, 95, 96, 97, 98, 99, 100, 102, 103, 104, 105, 106, 108, 109
Household provision, 13, 14, 23, 24, 26, 28, 35, 37, 40, 41, 64 (Document A) passim
Housing, 21, 22-5, 38, 98
Hui, James, 102
Huntly: castle, 6, 122; marquis, see Gordon, George
Hurry, Sir John, 3, 13
Hutchen, James, 115

Iain Mor clan, 3, 9
Iconoclasm, 29-30
Imloche: Alexander, 117; Robert, 117
Indweller, 38, 41, 63, 67, 73, 76, 77, 79, 80, 81, 83, 84, 86, 88, 89, 91, 94, 99, 100, 104, 105, 107, 109
Innes: 11, 12, 52, 121; Alexander, 21, **claim 46**, 78-9, 108, 116, **claim 196**; Andrew / Andrew, 95, 108, 116, **claim 132**; Elizabeth, lady Echt, 23;

George, **claim 66**, 82-3, 117; Helen, **claim 27**, 74; James, **claim 67**, 83; John of Leucharis, 6, 122; Lachlane, 116; lady, see Stuart, Grissell; laird, see Innes, Sir Robert; Margaret, 117; Robert, 109, 116; Robert, young laird of Innes, 29-30, 120, 121-2; Sir Robert of Innes, 6, 11, 12, 19, 29, 31, 50, 52, 120, 121; William, 96, 117, **claim 138**
Innkeeper, 28
Insicht, 13, 14, 24, 26, 28, 34, 35, 40, 41, 52, 64 (Document A) passim
Inverlochy battle, 10, 11, 121
Inverness, 9, 10, 14, 17, 19, 25, 26, 36, 42, 51, 65, 113
Ireland: 3, 8; depositions, 6-7; 45; rebellion, 6-8
Irish regiments, 1, 3, 8-9, 11, 12, 20, 23, 27, 31, 33, 36, 39, 42-3
Iron, 78
Irvine, 19

James I, 1, 2, 6
James II, 53
James VI, 1, 2, 6
James VII, 53
Jameson, Agnes, **claim 69**, 83
Johnstone, Donald, 97, **claim 142**
Johnstoun, Arthur, x
Justice Mills battle, 9

Kar, Christane / Christine, 35, 101, 116, **claim 161**
Kay / Key, Andro(w) / Andrew, **claim 8**, 21, 67-8, 102, 115, 117, **claim 167**
Keillachie, laird, see Mackintosh, Williame
Ker, colonel ____, 52
Key, James, **claim 15**, 71
Keyis, James, 4
Keys & locks, 23, 36, 64, 66, 67, 108
Kilbuiack, laird, see Dunbar, Patrick
Kilcumin bond, 10, 11, 12, 31, 34, 113
Kiln, 26, 67
Kilravock:10; laird, see Rose, Hugh
Kilsyth battle, 14, 121
Kinloss, 52
Kinnaird, Walter of Culbin, 11, 29
Kinsteary, laird, see Sutherland, John
Kirkcaldy, 19
Kirkudbright, 19
Kleis, Johne, **claim 45**, 78
Knockdowie, laird, see Hay, John
Knox, John, 1, 10
Krystie, Patrick, 115
Kuningham, Patrick, 52

Lamb, 36, 66, 92; Robert, 67
Langmorne, 102
Law, Thomas, 14
Lay, Alexander, relict, 115
Laying, William(e), 65, 68, 72, 117
Lay(i)ng, Andro(w), 21, **claim 44**, 78, 116
Lead, 28, 75
Leather, 26, 27, 42, 72, 73, 76, 77, 82, 83, 87, 91, 93, 94, 95, 96, 100, 101, 102, 103, 106, 107, 108
Lermont, Grissell, frontispiece, **claim 53**, 80
Leslie: Agnes, 115; Sir David, 3, 26; Jean, 103, **claim 170**; John, Earl of Rothes, 14, 34
Leslie / Lesley, Alexander, **claim 4**, **claim 5**, 25, 65
Lesley, William, **claim 12**, 70, 116
Lethen: 12, 13, 14, 112, 113, 121; laird, see Brodie, Alexander
Leucharis, laird, see Innes, John
Lie, Alexander, 97, **claim 143**
Liferentrix, 98
Lillie, James, 66

Lime, 28, 105
Lindsay, David, 2
Linen, 101
Linkwood / Linkvoodes: 26; laird, see Gibsone, Robert
Litster, 27, 67, 68, 96, 104, 108, 115, 116, 117
Littlejohn, Patrik, **claim 73**, 84, 117
Local War Committee, 11, 13, 20, 26, 50
Lochslin, laird, see Mackenzie, Simon
Lords of Council, 48-50, 120
Lorimer, 28
Lossie river, x, 18, 22, 25, 43, 44
Lundie, Robert, 11

Macbeth, 17
McColla, see MacDonald, Alasdair
McCray, Janet, 117
MacDonald: Alasdair (MacColla), 3, 9, 10, 12, 20, 23, 27, 31, 33, 39, 42, 43, 56-7, 111, 120, 121, 122; Col MacGillespick (Col Ciotach), 3, 9; Sir John, captain of Clanranald, 53
McDonnell, Randall, Earl of Antrim, 3, 8, 122
McGie, Sir Patrick of Largs, 9, 111
McGill, Robert, 22
Mackayne, Johne, 108, 109, **claim 195**
McKeane: Andrew, 117; Johne, 65, 117; Thomas, 116
Mackenzie: George, Earl of Seaforth, 11-12, 43; Murdoche, 14; Simon of Lochslin, 11; Thomas of Pluscarden, 9, 11, 19, 37, 43, 50
Mackintosh, William of Keillachie, 50
McRae / McRay, James, 4, 117; John(e), 37, 116
McRay, Mariorie, 116
Maelrubha, 18
Mailling, David, 28, 36, **claim 39**, 77
Mair, Gilbert, 50
Malice: George, 21; James, **claim 55**, 81; Robert, **claim 49**, 79, 117
Malt: 76, 102, 104, 109; maltman, 10, 28, 65, 71, 76, 104, 108
Man, James, 97, **claim 144**
Mare, 66, 103
Marston Moor battle, 26
Mason, 1, 28, 105
Matineasker, James, 35, **claim 85**, 86
Maver, Janet, 99, 104, **claim 177**
May, Alexander, 117
Menzies, Robert, 25
Merchant:10, 13, 26, 34, 35, 39, 63, 64, 65, 66, 69, 70, 71, 72, 79, 80, 81, 82, 94, 95, 99, 100, 101, 102, 103, 104, 107, 108, 109, 115; wares, 24, 26, 34, 40, 64, 65, 68, 69, 70, 71, 72, 73, 79, 80, 81, 82, 83, 86, 89, 94, 95, 96, 100, 101, 102, 103, 105, 106, 108, 109, 110
Mertein, Robert, **claim 7**, 26, 66-7
Messenger, 25, 28, 38, 64, 98, 103, 116
Michell, Jeane, 93, **claim 123**
Middleton, John, 3, 14, 36-7, 47, 51, 65, 113
Miller: 10; Marione, 117
Milne: Cristen / Christine, 105, 116, **claim 179**; James, **claim 17**, 70, 71, 94, 116, 117; John(e), 38, 115, 116; Thomas, 116; Walter, 117; William, 68, 116, (younger) **claim 14**, 70-1
Mindheart / Mindzeirt, John, 71, 104
Mirrisone, Patrick, **claim 40**, 77
Moluag, 18
Monachtie, 21
Money, 14, 24, 26, 35-6, 40, 41, 64 (Document A) passim
Montrose:19, 44; marquis, see Graham, James
Moray, 5, 6, 10-11, 13, 15, 17-18, 20, 35, 36, 48, 112; bishop, see Guthrie,

John; earl, *see* Stewart, James
Moreis, Martin, 69
Morinsh, 53
Mosset burn, 18
Mosstowie: 24, 39-40, 93; tenants, 96-9
Moyness, laird, *see* Grant, John
Muirone, Johne, **claim 27**, 74
Muirsone / Muiriesone, Patrick, 93-4, **claim 127**, 117
Muirton, 26
Munro, major-general Robert, 6
Murder, 39, 100
Murdoch(e), Thomas, 4, **claim 9**, 65, 68, 117
Murdoche: Alexander, 94, **claim 130**, 116; Patrik, **claim 23**, 73, 116
Murray: Alexander, 107, **claim 190**; James, 87, **claim 91**; Johne, **claim 79**, 85; Marjorie, 88, **claim 98**; Mr William, 8
Murrieston, 38
Myln, Walter, 95, **claim 136**
Myln(e) / Myllis, James, 34, 59, 63, 104, **claim 177**
Myln(e), John, **claim 1**, 4, 34, 63

Nairn:10, 17, 18, 19, 42, 51; river, 10, 18; shire,17, 20
National Covenant, 2, 3, 19, 28-9, 30, 31, 41, 113
Nauchtie: James, 91, 102, **claim 113**, 116; Johne, 102
Ness river, 14
Newsbook, 6
Nicoll: Alexander, 88, 89, **claim 103**; James, 91, 115, **claim 116**; William, 69
North Berwick, 19
Notary public, 6, 28, 31, 105, 121

Oatmeal, 109
Officer, 63, 68
Ogiluie, Andrew, 116
Ogilvie, Alexander of Kincardine, 50
Old Mills, 25, 41, 99, 102
Orilogeris, *see* Clockmaker
Ornaments, 13, 65, 70
Oxen, 27, 36, 40, 52, 64, 66

Pa(r)ker, John(e), **claim 76**, 84, 115
Parliament: Scotland, 2, 8, 12, 25, 42, 47-8, 49, 50-3, 56; Westminster, 2, 8, 51
Patersone, Thomas:106, 116, **claim 184**; William, **claim 74**, 84
Paull, Alexander, **claim 41**, 77, 117; Johne, 90, **claim 110**
Peasantry, 17, 24, 27, 29, 39-40
Peat, 17, 23, 37
Pedder: James, 21, 22, 107, 116, **claim 188**; John(e), 106, 117, **claim 186**; Leonard, 117
Peebles, 19
Pepys, Samuel, 35-6
Perth, 19
Peterkin, Alexander, **claim 50**, 79-80
Petrie: Alexander, 106, 109-10, 117, **claim 202**; David, 108, 117; William, 21, 92-3, 115, **claim 122**
Pettindreiche, Patrick, **claim 65**, 82
Petty, William, 7
Pewterer, 28
Philliphaugh battle, 14, 121
Philp, Alexander, **claim 28**, 74
Philpe: Mr David, 35, 101, **claim 161**; William, 116
Phones, 52-3
Physician, 13

Pig, 23, 36, 37, 96
Piper, 10
Pitchaish, 52-3
Piterkin, Alexander, 102; John(e), **claim 68**, 83, 116
Pit(t)erkin, George, **claim 70**, 83, 116
Plaiding, 78, 79
Plague, 10, 28
Plenishing, 1, 13, 14, 20, 24, 26, 34, 37, 40, 41, 52, 64 (Document A) *passim*
Pluscarden, laird, *see* Mackenzie, Thomas
Pont, Timothy, 17
Population, 19
Poultry, 23, 24, 27, 37
Pringill, Robert, **claim 35**, 76
Printer, x, 26
Property damage, 10, 11, 12, 13-14, 18, 19, 21, 23, 30, 33, 34, 36, 38, 40, 41, 42, 43, 47-8, 52-3, 55, 56, 65-6, 67, 98, 99, 100, 105, 108, 109, 111-14
Purs, Johne younger, 87, **claim 90**
Purse: George, **claim 33**, 75, 116; Thomas, 117; William, 92, 117, **claim 120**

Quartering, 9, 12, 13-16, 32, 33-4, 36-7, 42, 43-4, 51-2, 56, 111-14
Quhitefield, 21

Raban, Edward, 26
Rag(e), Johne, 95, 117, **claim 134**
Rage, James, 96, 97, 98, **claim 145**; William, 98, **claim 146**
Ramsey, lieutenant James, 112
Readhead, George, frontispiece, **claim 61**, 82
Redhall, 11
Rhynie, laird, *see* Gordon, James
Riache, Alexander, 88, 89, **claim 95**
Robertson(e), William, **claim 2**, 64, 103, 104, 115, 116, **claim 176**, (younger) 117
Robertsone, John, 4
Robin, John, 103
Rose, Hugh of Kilravock, 29, 50, 122
Ross: Andrew, 117; Mr Gilbert, 29-30, 122
Rosse: Androw, 92, **claim 121**; William of Clava, 50
Rothes: 34, 112; earl, *see* Leslie, John
Rupert, prince, 26
Russell, Alexander, 39, 41, 89, 100, **claim 102**, 103, 116, **claim 157**, (elder) 64, 103, 115, 116, **claim 171**, (younger) 65, **claim 169**
Rutherford, Samuel, 1

Saddler, 27, 73, 94, 103
St Andrews, 11, 19
Schipheard / Shiperd, Thomas, 22, **claim 64**, 82, 89, 116
Seaforth, earl, *see* Mackenzie, George
Seal, 18, 114
Service Book, 1-2
Sheep, 27, 36, 40, 52, 66, 69, 76, 88, 89, 92, 96, 97, 99, 101, 102, 103, 107; *see also* Ewe, Hog, Lamb, Wedder
Shoes, 8, 73, 78, 87, 88, 91, 93, 102
Sibbald, James **claim 72**, 83-4, 115
Silver, 1, 35-6, 64, 65, 67, 70, 71, 101, 103, 104
Sinclar, George, 64
Sinclar(e), Alexander, 64, 115; Robert, **claim 56**, 81, 117
Skene, Alexander, x
Skinner: 27, 40, 64, 67, 69, 70, 72, 83, 87, 94, 95, 96, 100, 101, 106, 107,

108, 115; Jonett / Janet, 109, **claim 199**, 116
Slezer, John, 24, 25
Smith, 28, 63, 78, 85, 88, 116
Smyth / Smith, George, **claim 155**, 99-100, 115; Walter, 8, 13, 25, 28, 38, 47, 98-9, 104, **claim 150**
Smyth, Johne, 69
Smyth(e), Alexander, **claim 43**, **claim 51**, 78, 80, 115, 116
Smythe, captain George, 8, 13, 38, 98, 99; Robert, **claim 32**, 75, 116
Solemn League & Covenant, 8, 28, 30-1, 42
Spalding, John, 33, 43
Spens: Androw, 101; Thomas, 96, 97, 98, 99, **claim 140**
Spey river, 9, 10, 12, 17, 20, 23, 25, 31, 34, 45
Spynie castle / palace, 6, 11, 13, 14, 33, 34, 38, 39, 42, 44, 52, 98-9, 100, 112, 113, 122
Stabler, 41, 89, 103, 116
Steer, 99, 110
Stent roll: 19, 37, 40, 41, 42, 48, 115-17
Stephane / Stevin, Alexander, 96, 115, **claim 137**
Stevine, James, 116
Stewart, James, earl of Moray, 6, 13, 29
Stewin, Cristen, **claim 178**
Stoneyforenoon, 24
Straquhan / Strachane, Robert, 105, 116, **claim 180**
Strathbogie, 14; regiment, 14, 43, 44, 47, 113
Strathearn, 10
Stratherrick, 10
Stronache: John(e), **claim 48**, 79, 103, 116; Kathrein, **claim 57**, 81
Stuart, Grissell, 31
Student, 10
Surgeon, 13, 70
Sutherland: Alexander, **claim 82**, 85; Alexander of Duffus, 19, 50, 116; George, 55; Hew, 38, 99, **claim 151**; Issobell / Isabell, 99, 105, 115, **claim 181**; John of Kinsteary, 50, 116; captain Johne, 116; Richard, 116; Robert, 117; William, 22, 94, 116, **claim 128**
Suthtoune, James, 22
Syme: Alexander, 115; James, **claim 80**, 85
Symsone, James, 69

Tailor, 10, 27, 65, 68, 73, 74, 78, 90, 91, 103, 106, 116, 117
Tain, 17, 19
Tallow chandler, 28
Tannachie, laird, *see* Tulloch, Thomas
Tarres: Alexander, 4, 115; William, **claim 20**, 72, 116
Tavernkeeper, 28
Taxation, 17, 19, 42, 48, 49, 52, 115-17
Tearie, laird, *see* Brodie, William
Textile, 27-8, 42, 78, 87, 108
Thayne, Issobell, **claim 9**, 68
Thom, William, 28, 59, 105, **claim 182**
Thomsone, Johne, **claim 29**, 74, 116
Tickets, 14, 42, 51-2, 111-12, 113
Tinker, 28
Tippermuir battle, 9, 121
Torrie, William, 102, 115, 117, **claim 166**
Town's soldiers, 3-4, 6, 8, 11, 21
Towrie, Williame, 86, **claim 87**
Troupe: Alexander, 116; Margarat, 88, **claim 99**

Tullack, Alexander, 102, **claim 164**
Tulloch, Thomas of Tannachie, 50
Tulloch(e), James, 22, 115
Tulloche, Robert, 116
Tuloch, Thomas, 4
Turner, 28
Tweed river, 3

Ulster, 3
Urquhart / Vrquhart / Wrquhart, Alexander, 13, **claim 13**, 70, 117

Victual, 13, 14, 24, 26, 27, 35, 40, 41, 64 (Document A) *passim*
Vmphray, Andrew, 117
Vrvell, Grissell, 116

Wages, 4, 6, 8, 18, 24, 31
Wainscot, 1, 25, 36, 98
Walker: Alexander, 76; James, 22, **claim 36**, 76, 115
Walker / Waker, Richard, 22, 76, 110
Wappenschaw, 6
Warden: Christen, 41, 89, **claim 102**, Issobell / Isabell, **claim 75**, 84, 115; James, **claim 38**, 76; Janett, **claim 81**, 85; William, 98, 115, **claim 135**
Warkhous, 67
Warrand, Thomas, 63, 94, 116, **claim 131**
Watson, Androw, 103, **claim 170**
Watsone: Alexander, 67, **claim 78**, 84-5, 108, 117, **claim 194**; George, **claim 47**, 79, 117
Watt, George, 92, 117, **claim 119**
Weaver, 10, 27, 36, 37, 74, 79, 81, 85, 90, 91, 92, 116
Wedder, 66, 92, 102
Wer, William, 116
Westfield, laird, *see* Dunbar, Alexander
Whisky, 26, 28
Whitford, Walter, bishop of Brechin, 2
Whithorn, 19
Wier, William, 101-2, **claim 163**
Wighton, George, 11
William III, 53
Williamsone, James, 98, 99, **claim 153**
Wilsone: Alexander, 117; Androw / Andrew, 86, **claim 86**, 116; James, 69, 116; Robert, 50; William, 21, 87, **claim 93**, 115
Winchester: _____, 108; Marior(i)e, 106, 109, 110, 117, **claim 198**; Patrick, 21; William, 109, 117, **claim 200**
Wine, 13, 26, 34, 35, 69, 70
Wishart, George, 33
Women, 40-1
Wood, Johne, 67, 117
Woodheid, laird, *see* Brodie, John
Wool, 94, 101, 107, 108, 109
Worcester battle, 31
Wright, 10, 28
Wynchester, Johne, **claim 26**, 73-4, 116

Yarn, 27, 67, 104, 108
Young: Henry, 23; John, 24; Margaret, 117; Michaell, 116; Olipher, 98, **claim 148**

Zeaman, William, 103, **claim 168**
Zewnie: Robert, 69; William, 69
Zoung, Alexander, 4